I

Welcome to the first editi
all the pubs within the Ea
Epsom and Leatherhead
branch. It is hoped that th
county. The last guide to
Pub Guide, and a lot has
of life that prices have gone up,
most expensive in the country. On a happier note, it is good to say that the vast majority of the pubs sell real ale, and even better, sell good real ale from regional and (occasionally) microbreweries. In fact it is difficult to find the products from the big national brewers at all. This is very different from thirty years ago when this area was awash with such beer.

The area is one of contrasts. The northern part, roughly around the M25 and above, is urban and almost part of London. The much larger part of East Surrey has been protected by the Green Belt and is remarkably rural, with miles of narrow roads connecting attractive villages. In both parts you will find good pubs. The ones we recommend are easily seen in this guide - they are the ones with a Big Black Dot in front of their name, and we are pleased to say that there are many of them.

Not everything is bright on the horizon, however. Many pubs have closed, and although new ones open, they are exclusively in the towns and suburbs. To show how this has affected East Surrey, all pubs that have closed in the last thirty years are highlighted in this publication.

We hope you find this guide useful.

Roy Golding, Editor

CONTENTS

PRODUCTION TEAM

This guide has been produced jointly by the East & Mid Surrey branch and the Kingston & Leatherhead branch of the Campaign for Real Ale (CAMRA). It is an entirely voluntary production, and no pub has paid for inclusion in it. Those who helped with the production were Martin Bundy, Mary Golding, Roy Golding, Keith Jackson, and John Norman. Particular thanks must also to be given to Clive Taylor for the maps, and to Martin Bundy, Colin Cabral, Richard Dallaway, Bernie Peal and Mike Verrall for much thankless background work. We also extend our appreciation to those brewers who have advertised. Finally, many thanks must be given to all those people who gave up their time to survey the pubs: Martin Bundy, David Bunn, Steve Burt, Colin Cabral, Sandra Cabral, Dan Crimmen, David Davis, Sally Gingell, Mary Golding, Roy Golding, Paul Griffiths, Keith Jackson, Jenny Longhurst, Martin Longhurst, Allan Marshall, John Norman, Dave Oram, Adrian Palmer, Bernie Peal, Kim Rennie, Clive Taylor, Mike Verrall, Alistair Wells and Rob Wells. We would also like to record our gratitude to our printer, Wyndeham Gait - you have been fantastic. (Contact them on 01472 356158).
This guide, as far as we know, is up to date as at the time of publication (August 2005), but things do change in the world of brewing and beer retailing (that's pubs to you and me), and CAMRA cannot be held responsible of any errors or omissions contained herein. The opinions expressed are those of individuals, and not necessarily those of CAMRA as a body. ISBN 1 85249 220 1

WHAT IS REAL ALE?

All beers are basically brewed in the same way. The sugars from the malted barley grains are dissolved in hot water in the mash tun. The resulting sugar solution is then boiled with hops, and finally, once cooled, yeast is pitched into it to start fermentation of the sugars. Once fermentation is complete, the difference between keg beer and real ale comes in. Real ales are racked straight from the fermentation vessel into casks where a secondary fermentation or conditioning takes place (hence the term 'cask conditioned'). Keg beers however undergo a period of conditioning in the brewery before being filtered and pasteurised to kill off any remaining life in the beer. They then have to be injected with gas to restore the condition that occurs naturally in real ale. This gas is usually at a much higher pressure than would naturally occur in the beer and gives keg beer its wind inducing fizz. Real ales need no injection of gas as it is produced as a result of the secondary fermentation.

Beer Styles

Real ales come in a variety of styles such that there is something to suit most palates. **Bitter** is the most common and can vary in strength from just over 3% Alcohol by Volume (ABV) to 6%. The bitterness is contributed to by both malt and hops, weaker beers tending to be hoppier. **Mild** is making a bit of a comeback, although it is regularly sold in only one pub in this area (the Garland at Redhill), however it can be found as a guest beer elsewhere. Usually dark in colour, they tend to be more malty than bitters but just as tasty and worth a try. They tend to be weaker than bitters, although there are some exceptions. **Old Ales** mainly appear in the winter and are dark, malty, fruity and rich. **Stouts and Porters** are not that common as real ales in the East Surrey area, most being keg beers. However, when they are available they tend to be bitter and dark through the combined use of roasted malt and some hops. The less common styles of beer are supported within CAMRA by the Light and Dark Supporters committee, known as LADS. They organise promotions for these styles, including the well supported Mild Month in May.

REAL ALE IN A BOTTLE

Real ale in a bottle is the bottle equivalent of the draught real ale found in the pub. Not all bottled beers are real, even though they bear the name of a beer you recognise from the bar. Real beer in a bottle is unpasteurised and not artificially carbonated. It is a live product that contains yeast to give a secondary fermentation in the bottle, and needs to be poured with care to ensure that the sediment in the bottom of the bottle is not disturbed. So that you can easily recognise one of these live beers, CAMRA has come up with a logo, shown here, stating that "CAMRA says this is real ale" and this is starting to appear on a number of bottle labels. Some breweries use the term "bottle conditioned beer", but both mean the same, it is a fresh natural product. Most off licences and supermarkets these days will sell one or more of these beers. Encouragingly a number of pubs and bars are also doing so, especially ones that are unable to keep real draught ale. This guide shows those pubs we know to stock them. For more information check www.camra.org.uk/raib. Note that some pubs also sell bottle conditioned beers from Europe, particularly from Belgium. These, too, are highly recommended.

THE BREWERIES

A number of breweries supply the pubs of East Surrey, and we are fortunate to have three microbreweries actually sited in the area, with a few others from just outside. A number of other breweries have tied houses in the area, and finally there are other brewers who supply the pub chains and the limited free trade of East Surrey.

The letter (S) after a beer name indicates a seasonal beer and the letter (B) a Real Ale in a Bottle.

A) LOCAL MICROBREWIES

BAYNARDS

The Baynards Brewery was to be found in a back room at the Thurlow Arms pub in Baynards. It was set up by Julian Gibb in February 1996, using brewing equipment previously used at the Cyder House at Shackleford. The distinctive beers were brewed only for the pub, and in batches of 130 gallons at a time. Unfortunately brewing stopped with Julian's untimely death in 2000. Occasionally special brews would appear as well as the standard range listed below.

Station Brew	4.2%	Aromatic hoppy bitter
Old Shunter	4.8%	Ruby-red fruity bitter
Tunnel Vision (S)	6.0%	Dark and full bodied winter brew

LEITH HILL

☎ (0306) 711793

www.ploughinn.com

Brewing commenced in 1996 at the Plough in Coldharbour. Originally only producing nine-gallon brews on homemade equipment, a new two-barrel plant was installed in 2001. The beers are only available at the Plough. Production of a third beer, Tickety-Boo (4.6%), is in the pipeline.

Crooked Furrow	4.0%	A rather bitter beer with malt also evident
Tallywhacker	5.6%	A tasty dark and sweet ale

PILGRIM

☎ (01737) 222651

www.pilgrim.co.uk

Originally based in Woldingham, Dave Roberts set up the Pilgrim brewery in1982. Production was moved to a larger site in Reigate in 1985 where it has remained. As well as brewing, Dave wholesales a number of proper German lagers and French ciders. One pub is owned, the Rising Sun in Epsom. Other seasonal beers may also be available.

Surrey Bitter	3.7%	Very good light session bitter
Porter	4.0%	A good dark beer
Progress	4.0%	A fruity, more malty beer
Autumnal (S)	4.5%	Well flavoured copper coloured bitter
Excalibur (S)	4.5%	A bitter brewed around Easter
Crusader	4.9%	A golden bitter
Talisman (S)	5.0%	A darker winter beer

REIGATE BREWERY

The brewery was situated in a store room at John Landregan's off-licence in Glovers Road, Reigate. Malt extract was used in the brewing, which took place using a two barrel plant, and commenced in November 1983. Brewing stopped in 1987. Two beers were produced, solely for the off trade.

Reigate Bitter	4.2%	Tasty bitter
Ten Fifty Five	5.5%	Stronger beer

SURREY HILLS

☎ (01483) 212812

www.surreyhills.co.uk

The newest brewery in the area, the Surrey Hills Brewery produced its first commercial brew in May 2005. Initially two beers are being produced, but others will follow.

Ranmore Ale	3.8%	Superb light session bitter, full of flavour
Shere Drop	4.2%	Pale, hoppy and fruity
Albury Ruby (S)	4.6%	Dark winter ale
Gilt Complex (S)	4.6%	Golden summer beer

WELTONS

Ray Welton started brewing at Capel in 1995, moving to Dorking from 1997 to 2000. Weltons are still brewing, and are now based in Horsham – see section B) below.

B) OTHER NEARBY MICROBREWERIES

HEPWORTH

☎ (01403) 269696

www.thebeerstation.co.uk

The brewery was set up in Horsham in 2000 and mainly produces bottled beer and contract brews. However a couple of cask beers are brewed and can be found in one or two pubs in East Surrey.

Traditional Sussex Bitter	3.6%	Light bitter
Pullman	4.2%	Crisp bitter
Iron Horse	4.8%	Premium sweet bitter

HOG'S BACK

☎ (01252) 783000

www.hogsback.co.uk

Large brewery based in Tongham, Surrey selling their beers in several pubs in the area. A number of seasonal beers are also brewed, along with a good range of Real Ales in a Bottle.

Hair of the Hog	3.5%	A light session bitter
TEA	4.2%	A traditional best bitter, also bottle conditioned
Hop Garden Gold	4.6%	Golden beer.

KING'S

☎ (01403) 272102

www.kingsfamilybrewers.co.uk

Formerly of King & Barnes, Bill King started brewing his own beers in 2001 in Foundry Lane, Horsham. A number of seasonal beers are also brewed, details of which are shown on the website. King's beers can be found in a number of free houses in the area. A good number of Real Ales in a Bottle are also produced.

Horsham Best Bitter	3.8%	Well balanced best bitter
Red River Ale	4.8%	Very malty premium ale

WELTONS

☎ (01403) 242091

www.weltons.co.uk

Originally based at Rugge Farm in Capel in 1995, the brewery moved to Vincent Works in Dorking in 1997. Further moves to Arundel and Horsham followed, and from 2003 the brewery is to be found at its second site in Horsham, on Foundry Lane. As well as the standard range of beers, a large number of seasonal specials and one-off brews are to be found, mostly with amusing pumpclips. Don't be surprised to find real lagers and smoked beers! Some Real Ales in a Bottle are also to be produced.

Kid 'n' Bard	3.5%	Traditional Sussex bitter
Horsham Bitter	3.8%	Traditional session bitter
Old Cocky	4.3%	Good best bitter
Horsham Old (S)	4.5%	Marvellous dark old ale

WESTERHAM

☎ (01959) 565837

www.westerhambrewery.co.uk

Based just outside Crockham Hill, near Edenbridge, Kent, the Westerham Brewery started brewing in 2004, and is already proving to be successful. A large number of beers are regularly available, supplemented by a range of seasonal beers. It is good to see that a number of these beers are to be found in East Surrey. Other seasonal beers may also be produced.

Grasshopper	3.8%	A malty, nutty session bitter
Black Eagle SPA	3.8%	A light and dry bitter
Summer Perle (S)	3.8%	Dry hopped with Perle hops
British Bulldog	4.3%	A full-bodied hoppy best bitter
General Wolfe (S)	4.5%	Autumnal brew with added maple syrup
God's Wallop (S)	4.5%	Spicy Christmas beer
Puddledock Porter (S)	4.5%	Excellent dark traditional porter
7X	4.8%	A strong well-hopped bitter
1965	5.0%	Strong beer based on an original Westerham Brewery recipe

C) REGIONAL BREWERS WITH TIED HOUSES

BADGER

www.badgerbrewery.com

Badger is the trading name of Hall & Woodhouse. The brewery is based in Blandford Forum in Dorset. Badger have a significant presence in our area through their picking up of pubs, mainly free trade outlets, and their purchase and closure of the King & Barnes Brewery in Horsham in

2000. King & Barnes had a number of tied outlets in the area, and brewed a good choice of real ales, including an excellent range of seasonal beers. These disappeared at a stroke, and now only a limited range of rather uninteresting beers is produced for their 15 tied houses in East Surrey. Flowers beers are brewed under licence for InBev.

K&B Sussex	3.5%	A thin beer, nothing like the King & Barnes beer it replaced
Badger Best	4.0%	A malty best bitter
First Gold	4.0%	A new golden brown bitter
Fursty Ferret (S)	4.4%	A bitter sold in summer
Gobbledy Goose (S)	4.6%	The winter bitter
Tanglefoot	4.9%	Strong beer that is dry hopped in the cask

FULLER'S

www.fullers.co.uk

Fuller's, who are based in Chiswick in West London, have a number of tied houses in the area. Most of these came from Allied Breweries in the early 1990s after the beer orders declared that brewers with more than 2,000 pubs had to release some from the tie. Today Fuller's have six pubs in the area, but London Pride is now one of the most successful real ales in the country, and consequently is available in many free-houses and pubs owned by Pub Companies throughout East Surrey. Other seasonal and one-off beers may also be available.

Chiswick Bitter	3.5%	A fine light bitter
Discovery	3.9%	Golden bitter
London Pride	4.1%	Both malt and hops are apparent in this easy drinking beer
Honey Dew (S)	4.3%	Summer beer, brewed with honey
Jack Frost (S)	4.5%	A deep red winter beer
ESB	5.5%	Extra Special Bitter in every way
1845 (B)	6.3%	Excellent strong sipping beer

GALES

www.gales.co.uk

This family brewer from Horndean in Hampshire has only one tied house in the area, the Bull's Head in Dorking, but its beers can be found in the limited free trade from time to time. A number of additional seasonal beers and Real Ales in a Bottle are also available.

Butser Bitter	3.4%	Mid brown malty beer
Summer Hog (S)	3.8%	Light summer beer
Gales Best Bitter	3.9%	Hoppy golden bitter
Winter Brew (S)	4.2%	The winter offering
HSB	4.8%	Classic strong bitter

GREENE KING

www.greeneking.co.uk

All brewing takes place in Bury St Edmunds, Suffolk. Greene King has a reputation for buying large blocks of pubs from breweries and pub companies, and is now the largest regional brewer in Britain, and has 14 tied houses in East Surrey. The Morland brewery in Abingdon was purchased and closed in 1999, that brewery having previously taken over Ruddles.

IPA	3.6%	An award winning session beer
Ruddles County	4.3%	Full bodied best bitter
Abbot Ale	5.0%	A fine strong rich beer
Old Speckled Hen	5.2%	Full flavoured strong beer
Hen's Tooth (B)	6.5%	Very good strong bottled beer

HARVEYS

www.harveys.org.uk

The Harveys brewery is based in Lewes, East Sussex. Only one tied house is situated in the area (the Garland at Redhill), but a number of pubs stock their superb ale as a guest beer. A good number of seasonal beers are also brewed.

XX Mild Ale	3.0%	A traditional dark mild
Long Man Pale Ale	3.5%	Hoppy light bitter
Sussex Best Bitter	4.0%	A distinctive beer, both malty and hoppy
Old Ale (S)	4.3%	Traditional dark old ale
Armada Ale	4.5%	Beautiful hoppy best bitter
Imperial Russian Stout (B)	9.0%	Fantastic strong very dark stout

SHEPHERD NEAME

www.shepherd-neame.co.uk

Although based in Faversham, Kent, Shepherd Neame had no tied houses in East Surrey until the big brewers started selling off large numbers of them in the 1990s. There are currently six tied houses in the area.

Master Brew Bitter	3.7%	Hoppy, tasty beer
Best Bitter	4.1%	More malty beer
Spitfire	4.5%	Stronger bitter

Early Bird (S)	4.5%	Spring beer
Late Red (S)	4.5%	Autumn Ale
Goldings (S)	4.7%	Summer bitter
Original Porter (S)	4.8%	Strong dark winter beer
Bishops Finger	5.0%	Darker malty beer
1698 (B)	6.5%	Three times hopped strong ale

WOLVERHAMPTON & DUDLEY

www.fullpint.co.uk

The second largest regional brewer in Britain has only one tied house in the area, but its beers are often found in Pub Company houses as a guest beer. The beers sold in Surrey are brewed in the old Marston's brewery in Burton-on-Trent, although the company is based in Wolverhampton in the West Midlands. Other beers may be available. Also brews draught Bass under contract for InBev.

Burton Bitter	3.8%	Light fruity bitter
Pedigree	4.5%	Classic Burton beer

YOUNG'S

www.youngs.co.uk

Young's has had a presence in Surrey for a long time, having bought the Reffell brewery in Gomshall in the 1920s, although all these pubs were later sold. Currently has six tied houses in East Surrey. Other seasonal beers may be available.

Bitter	3.7%	Refreshing light bitter beer
St George's Ale (S)	4.3%	Dry hopped spring ale
Special	4.5%	Malty best bitter
Golden Zest (S)	4.7%	Golden summer ale
Waggle Dance	5.0%	Hoppy beer with sweetness from honey
Winter Warmer (S)	5.0%	Dark winter ale, one of Britain's classic beers
Champion (B)	5.0%	Dry golden bitter
Special London Ale (B)	6.4%	Strong and distinctive

D) OTHER REGIONAL BREWERS

ADNAMS

www.adnams.co.uk

An independent brewery from Southwold in Suffolk, Adnams excellent beers are available in several of the Pub Company houses in the county as well as the free trade.

Bitter	3.7%	Dry and refreshing
Broadside	4.7%	Rich and fruity strong beer

CALEDONIAN

www.caledonian-brewery.co.uk

The Caledonian Brewery is based in Edinburgh, and has strong links with Scottish & Newcastle. A superb range of beers is brewed, one of which is a regular in some East Surrey pubs.

Deuchars IPA	3.8%	Light easy drinking hoppy bitter

RINGWOOD

www.ringwoodbrewery.co.uk

The Ringwood brewery from the town of the same name in Hampshire started brewing in 1978, and was one of the first of the new generation of microbreweries that sprung up in the late 1970s. A number of their beers find their way into local pubs. A range of seasonal beers is also available along with four Real Ales in a Bottle.

Best Bitter	3.8%	A sweet traditional bitter
Fortyniner	4.9%	Fruity best bitter
Old Thumper	5.6%	Powerful strong ale

TAYLOR

www.timothytaylor.co.uk

From Keighley in West Yorkshire, this family brewer supplies Landlord to a number of pubs, both as a regular ale and as a guest beer. It is supposedly one of the singer Madonna's favourite drinks.

Landlord	4.3%	Very distinctive award winning pale ale

WADWORTHS

www.wadworth.co.uk

From Devizes in Wiltshire, Wadworth's beer is often seen as a guest ale in Surrey pubs.

6X	4.3%	Classic distinctive malty beer

WELLS

www.wells.co.uk

This Bedford brewer supplies its beer to several local pubs. Bombardier is marketed as the patron pint of England.

Bombardier	4.3%	Dry and lightly hopped

E) NATIONAL BREWERS

CARLSBERG

www.carlsberg.com

Once upon a time there was a very big brewing concern in England called Tetley's. Tetley's bitter was a highly regarded beer, and was brewed in huge quantities in West Yorkshire. Unfortunately Tetley's joined up with an even bigger concern called Carlsberg who came from Copenhagen in Denmark. They called themselves Carlsberg-Tetley, because Tetley was still a relatively popular beer, especially around West Yorkshire. Nowadays they are called just Carlsberg, and the name Tetley has all but been forgotten (even in West Yorkshire). You have to really search the company website to get any information at all about Tetley, but it is still brewed, mostly as a keg product, although the cask version is still around for those who can't get to West Yorkshire.

Tetley Bitter	3.7%	A fairly bitter beer

ADNAMS. BEER FROM THE COAST.
ADNAMS PLC, SOLE BAY BREWERY,
SOUTHWOLD IP18 6JW.
WWW.ADNAMS.CO.UK
ADNAMS

COORS
www.coors.com
This American company, based in Burton-on-Trent, owns a number of brands in the UK, but fortunately few of them are readily available in Surrey, although occasionally Worthington beers may be found. They are more proud of their lagers, Carling and Grolsch.

Worthington White Shield (B)	5.6%	The classic bottled IPA

INBEV
www.inbev.com
The biggest brewer in the world, this Belgian company bought what were two of the biggest names in British brewing in 2000, Bass and Whitbread, although both these companies were mere shadows of what they had been twenty years earlier. The company was called Interbrew, but now has the hideous sounding moniker of InBev, and is responsible for around 14% of the world's beer volumes. The Belgian brands Hoegaarden and Leffe are both owned by InBev, as are Stella, Beck's and Staropramen. Real ale appears to be a minor part of their British portfolio, although their one main brand, draught Bass, was at one time perhaps the best-known beer in Britain. The Flowers beers are now brewed by Badger, and Bass by Wolverhampton & Dudley in Burton-on-Trent.

Flowers IPA	3.6%	Light bitter
Flowers Original	4.3%	A best bitter

Bass	4.4%	A hint of sulphur is apparent in this malty beer.

SCOTTISH & NEWCASTLE

www.scottish-newcastle.com

In this area we know their beers as Courage, and as national beers went, they were OK. Thirty years ago these beers were brewed in London (or, for one or two pubs, in Reading), which wasn't too far away. It was then moved to Bristol, which was also not too far away (by modern standards). All these real ale breweries have gone, and the cask beer now comes from Tadcaster in Yorkshire, which is a long way away. Other beers may be available, for example John Smith's and Webster's brands. The company also owns Bulmers cider.

Courage Best Bitter	4.0%	Hoppy beer with a bitter aftertaste
Courage Directors	4.8%	A fruity well-bodied ale

PUB COMPANIES

Twenty years ago pub companies hardly existed. Following the Beer Orders which resulted from the Monopolies and Mergers Committee report into the supply of beer, brewers had to sell or free from tie half the pubs they owned over the figure of 2,000 by November 1992. This led to the establishment of pub companies, who did not brew, and therefore were not covered by this legislation. However, these were not run as free houses, but negotiated contracts with the big brewers for cheap beer. The large brewers (Allied Domecq ["fondly" remembered as Friary Meux in this area], Bass, Courage, Watney and Whitbread) who owned over 2,000 pubs suddenly realised there was more money to be made out of retailing than brewing. Amalgamations of breweries occurred, and eventually huge pub companies rose up, far, far larger than the old brewery estates had been. Listed below are the main ones in Surrey, but in most cases you would never know you were in one of their pubs as, for some reason, many of these companies are shy of advertising the fact that they own them. Many other pub companies own pubs in the area (for example Admiral Taverns, Barracuda, Regent Inns, Yates's), but in most cases you couldn't tell the difference.

J T DAVIES

www.jtdavies.co.uk

This Croydon based wine merchant has around 50 pubs in the south-east. All are tied to beer from the national breweries, with Harvey's and Fuller's also sometimes available.

ENTERPRISE

www.enterpriseinns.com

Based in Solihull, West Midlands, Enterprise Inns was formed in 1991 with 368 pubs, purchased from Bass. 2002 saw the company acquire the Whitbread tenanted estate (Laurel Inns), and it later bought the Unique Pub Company. In effect this was the old Courage tenanted estate in Surrey, which had become part of the Inntrepreneur pub company in 1991. Several other smaller pub companies have also fallen to Enterprise, which is now the largest operator of leased and tenanted pubs in Britain, with nearly 9,000 pubs. These sell mainly national and large regional products, but pubs do have access to a large number of microbrewery products as well.

Hogs Back
Surreys' Favourite
Brewery
Hogs Back Brewery
Tongham · Surrey
Hair of the Hog
Independent Brewers
Session Bitter
Hogs Back Brewery
Tongham · Surrey
T.E.A
O.G. 1044 A.B.V. 4·2%
Independent Brewers
Traditional English Ale
Hogs Back Brewery
Tongham · Surrey
Hop Garden Gold
O.G. 1048 A.B.V. 4·6%
Independent Brewers
Special Ale
Ales available at a Pub near you,
or direct from our Brewery Shop.
Hogs Back Brewery Ltd
Manor Farm, The Street,
Tongham, Surrey GU10 1DE
01252 783000 www.hogsback.co.uk

LONDON & EDINBURGH

www.londonandedinburghinns.co.uk

This Maidstone based company is one of the more anonymous pub companies. It operates over 100 managed houses and over 600 tenancies nationwide, and this includes a few in East Surrey. A number of these pubs came from Punch.

MASSIVE

www.massivepub.com

The Massive Pub Company was formed in 1993, and currently owns around 40 pubs in the London area. Many are unbranded but it does include the small Tup chain. The company is based in Hampton Hill in West London, and currently has two pubs in East Surrey (the Whyte Harte in Bletchingley, and the Wiremill at Newchapel).

MITCHELLS & BUTLERS

www.mbplc.com

Mitchells & Butlers don't brew, but they have taken the name of a famous midlands brewer. Based in Birmingham, around 2,000 pubs are operated. Some of the brands they operate are All Bar One, Vintage Inns, Toby Carvery, Ember Inns, O'Neill's and Harvester. The company developed out of Bass Taverns in 1989 and in 1995 purchased the Harvester chain from Forte (who had themselves acquired it from Courage). Later, in 1999, Bass acquired 550 pubs from Allied Domecq. In 2001, 988 pubs were sold to Nomura, leaving Bass Taverns with a number of large town centre and suburban outlets. When Bass moved out of brewing in 2000, the company gave themselves the rather odd name of Six Continents. Mitchells & Butlers were formed in October 2002 when Six Continents decided to split the hotel and retail divisions.

PUNCH

www.punchtaverns.com

Punch Taverns is based in Burton-on-Trent, and was formed in 1997 when a number of pubs were acquired from Bass. In 1999 the company purchased the Inn Business Group and the Vanguard estate from Allied Domecq (these were the old Friary Meux tenancies in this area). In 2002 the managed houses became the Spirit Group, and Punch became solely an owner of tenanted and leased pubs. By the middle of 2003 over 4,500 pubs were owned. The next large purchase was Pubmaster in November 2003. This brought a further 3,115 pubs to the group. The Innspired Group was Punch's next major acquisition, in September 2004 – a further 1,064 pubs for the empire. Following the disposal of over 500 pubs that were "non-core to Punch's long term strategy", 7,800 pubs remain. These pubs are mostly tied to beers sold by the national brewers and the large regionals, but one or two more interesting beers may be found.

SCOTTISH & NEWCASTLE PUB ENTERPRISES

www.scottish-newcastle.com

S&NPE is the leased pub division of Scottish Courage, itself part of Scottish & Newcastle. S&N Pub Enterprises manages pubs on behalf of property owners. In 1999 it was contracted to manage 1,000 pubs for the Royal Bank of Scotland, and in December 2004 an agreement was reached to run 364 pubs on behalf of the Globe Pub Company (these were the managed houses that had belonged the Spirit Group).

SPIRIT

www.thespiritgroup.com

The Spirit Group started off as the new owners of Punch's managed houses in 2002, and are also based in Burton-on-Trent. They also took over Scottish & Newcastle Retail's managed houses, and now have over 2,000 pubs nationwide. Several are run as branded concepts, and these include Two For One, Chef & Brewer, Wacky Warehouse, John Barras, and Mr Q's, not all of which may appeal to lovers of traditional beers and traditional pubs. In December 2004 Spirit sold 364 pubs to the Globe Company. Spirit run around 20 pubs in East Surrey.

WETHERSPOONS

www.jdwetherspoon.co.uk

Wetherspoon's own around 700 pubs throughout Britain. Most are huge, they open all day, all offer a choice of real ale, all have no music, and all will be no smoking by May 2006. Two beer festivals are run throughout the estate during the year when an even greater variety of beer is available. Wetherspoon's are to be applauded in their commitment to real ale in their pubs, especially in their support of the microbrewers. Four Wetherspoon's are to be found in East Surrey, at Epsom, Leatherhead, Oxted and Redhill.

WHITBREAD

www.whitbread.co.uk

Whitbread used to be a major British brewer, with its foundations dating from 1742. Now it describes itself as the UK's leading hospitality company. The brands most seen in East Surrey are Premier Travel Inns, Brewers Fayre and Beefeater.

CIDER

By Gillian Williams, Chair of CAMRA's Cider & Perry Committee

For over twenty years CAMRA has campaigned for real cider and perry alongside beer. We have worked away, monitoring the industry, and mapping changes in outlets and producers through guides like this. Today there is a wide choice of real cider and perry available but knowing where to go to find them is a very different matter. This guide will help you find some locally.

Traditionally cider was produced in specific areas which include the West Country, Wales, the South East and East Anglia. These areas have changed slightly over time but they remain the heartland and are thriving today. In the West Country, cider is almost always made using specialist cider apples which can have strange names such as Hoary Morning or Slack my Girdle. The fruit can vary in size, acidity; sweetness and tannin. In Kent, Suffolk and Norfolk cider is more usually made using a mixture of culinary and dessert apples. The cidermaker works with the fruit from late summer to December. First apples are harvested and washed, then the chosen fruit is processed to produce juice by being milled/scratted into a pulp and then pressed. The juice ferments slowly over winter and by early spring, the new pressing is ready to be broached and (wassail!) tested and perhaps blended.

Perry is to pears as cider is to apples. Perry pears tend to be small and hard and again have weird names such as Hendre Huffcap or Nailer. The pears are processed to produce juice in the same way as apples. Perry is however made later in the year as the winter frosts reputedly help "blow" the cells and causes the generally inedible perry pear to produce more juice. The trees tend to be even older than apple trees as they continue to crop for up to 300 years. Although there have been some perry tree plantings over the last decade, it will be a long time before the benefit to the perry drinker will be seen. Perry trees will normally take thirty years at the very least to reach maturity.

CAMRA as a consumer campaigning organisation has recently refreshed our definition of real cider and perry. The main point of the definition is that real cider and perry is simply "the juice, the whole juice and nothing but the juice!" The wild yeasts from the skins of the fruit do the rest. With Guides like this bringing to notice pubs which are selling real cider and perry the future is rosy for both cider apples and perry pears.

The following pubs in East Surrey sell real cider:

Caterham	Clifton Arms
Coldharbour	Plough Inn
Crowhurst	Brickmakers Arms
Friday Street	Stephan Langton
Marsh Green	Wheatsheaf
Merstham	Feathers
Mugswell	Well House Inn
Newdigate	Surrey Oaks
South Nutfield	Station Hotel
Staffhurst Wood	Royal Oak
Westcott	Crown Inn

PUBLIC TRANSPORT IN EAST SURREY

The larger towns in this Guide are well served by trains although services can be infrequent in the late evening to some stations. Recommended pubs in this guide that are close to a station have this indicated in the facilities list. The station is named if it is not the main one in the district. Details of these services can be obtained from National Rail Enquiries on 08457 484950 or on-line at www.nationalrail.co.uk. Real Time Train Information for all stations in this Guide is available on this site. Timetable books and leaflets are usually also available at stations. Unfortunately, bus services are now very sporadic and after 18:00 often non-existent in many rural areas. Transport for London Bus Pass and Travelcards are valid on Transport for London Buses that travel on to destinations in this part of Surrey including Banstead, Caterham, Dorking, Epsom, Redhill and Warlingham.

Surrey County Council issue a comprehensive set of free Bus & Train Guides. These Guides are available from Libraries, Council Offices and Bus Enquiry Offices. The Bus & Train Guides covering this guide are: 7 – Guildford & Cranleigh, 8 - Dorking, 9 - Leatherhead, Epsom & Banstead and 10 – Redhill, Horley & East Surrey. Information is available from traveline on 0870 608 2608 daily from 7 in the morning to 10 at night or on the Internet at www.traveline.org.uk The Surrey County Council Website is also recommended and has Suretime Surrey's Real Time Bus running information service for some areas: www.surreycc.gov.uk/passenger_transport

If you need to travel to the pub of your choice, please use the facilities described above and **Don't Drink and Drive**.

CAMRA BEER FESTIVALS

As well as national beer festivals a number of branches organise their own festivals. The majority of the beer festivals admit card carrying CAMRA members free of charge or offer discounts, so if you are a member remember to bring your card if you go to one. They are organised and staffed by volunteers so, if you are a member and fancy being involved, contact your local festival and offer your services.

There is only one CAMRA beer festival which takes place in the area covered by this guide, which is the Redhill Beer Festival. The first one is taking place in Merstham village hall, a small hall 100 yards from Merstham station, between Thursday 27th October and Saturday 29th October 2005. See the Surrey website (camrasurrey.org.uk) for more details.

There are two other festivals which are organised by Surrey branches. Kingston beer festival is held in the Surrey County Staff Club, in Kingston-upon-Thames (next to Surrey County Hall), at the end of June, and Woking beer festival held in Woking Leisure Centre at the beginning of November (11th and 12th in 2005). Again see the Surrey website for more details.

Nearby there are several festivals held in London, Sussex and Kent. Details of all CAMRA beer festivals can be found on the National Website (www.camra.org.uk) in the Beer Festivals section, which has details of all national festivals and a calendar of local festivals.

DRINKING AROUND GATWICK

Gatwick airport is the world's busiest single runway airport, and sixth busiest international airport with over 30 million passengers per year. It is in a country which has an enormous choice and variety of real ales, yet you will struggle to find a pint of anything decent or exciting to drink within the airport boundaries. There are two terminals and at least eight different bars, but very little good beer and, lets face it, a soulless airport bar is a soulless airport bar, pretty much wherever you are. So what do you do if you have dutifully checked in three hours or more before your flight, or have an even longer connection time, and you fancy a decent pint in a decent pub? Do not despair. Depending on how much time you have available, there are a number of options available within a short train or taxi ride. All trains leave Gatwick airport from the South terminal. If you are at North terminal, South terminal is three minutes away by free dedicated transit train departing every 3-6 minutes.

The closest town is Horley, about two miles away and five minutes in a taxi. It is also served by train. The pub to head for is the Gatwick in the town centre. Another option is the historic Six Bells on Church Road, which is in an idyllic setting by the River Mole. This pub majors on food, although the beer range is less inspiring. Once again a taxi is the best bet. Nearby to Horley is the village of Hookwood where the Black Horse also majors on food but has a few of the Badger range of beers available. This is also a good stopping off point on the way to Gatwick as it is on the A217 between junction 8 on the M25 and the airport. If you have slightly more time, Redhill is the most sensible option with about five trains an hour, and journey times of 7 to 10 minutes. Once alighted at Redhill there are several options. Closest is the Home Cottage, a Young's pub behind the station. Head towards platform three, turn left at the top of the stairs and exit a little further along the platform. The best pub in Redhill is the Garland, which serves the full range of Harveys beer. This is an easy 5 to 10 minute stroll from the station. The final walkable option in Redhill is the Sun, albeit a Wetherspoon's pub, but liable to have a much better choice of beer than that at the airport.

One stop further on the train line to Reading is Reigate, with the Prince of Wales offering Shepherd Neame beers. There is one direct train an hour direct from Gatwick, although during the evening rush hour there is a shuttle service between Redhill and Reigate. At Reigate, go through the underpass and turn right, you can't miss it. Another option, closer to the airport, but a five mile taxi ride away is the Three Horseshoes at Sidlow Bridge, selling Fuller's, Harveys and Young's beers, but be aware it is closed in the afternoons. Saving the best for last, if there is a group of you to share a taxi, try the Surrey Oaks at Newdigate, which is about 7 miles away. Winner of repeated branch pub of the year awards the "Soaks" has a constantly changing selection of guest ales as well as good regular beers. Once again it is closed in the afternoons.

If you take a taxi to one of these pubs it is always best to book the return journey before you intend to leave the pub. Remember, if you have a delayed flight, the delay is not always as long as they say it will be. One last word of warning, the queues at immigration can be quite lengthy at peak times. Finally, enjoy yourself, if you manage to get away from the airport you will find some great beer and pubs. The difficulty will be dragging yourself away.

WALKING IN EAST SURREY

There are several pleasant walks to be had in the area, with a good network of footpaths linking towns and villages. Below is one easy walk which has the advantage of having both the start and finish accessible by public transport. This article was written by Bernie Peal.

...doing the "Greensand Walk"

There are many lovely walks through East Surrey and I have chosen this route along a good stretch of the Greensand Way. You will be starting and finishing at railway stations, so your day can be planned in advance by consulting the National Rail timetables and referring to the opening times of the pubs listed in this guide. You will experience both hills and level ground and in most places the going will be relatively firm. Remember though, paths can get a bit muddy depending on the weather and time of year - also beware of high nettles - so dress appropriately! Please ensure you drink plenty of water en route, as copious quantities of real ale, contrary to what you may think, will actually dehydrate you! I strongly recommend the use of the Explorer Series, Ordnance Survey Map, Sheet 146 for this walk (scale 1:25000). **Please note, all distances in this article are approximate and cumulative.**

We start at Hurst Green station (trains from Oxted, East Croydon and Central London). Leave the station via the London bound platform, turning right into Greenhurst Lane and continue on to a crossroads. Turn right on to Hurst Green Road and then left into Tanhouse Lane. Your first port of call is the **Haycutter** at **Broadham Green**. (1 mile). Moving on, continue along Tanhouse lane and veer left at the grassy open space of Broadham Green itself. You are now actually on the Greensand Way. When you reach the road ahead, look carefully for the entrance to the public footpath between the houses on Broadham Green Road (it is signed). Follow the path for another mile until you descend into the village of **Tandridge** and your next stop, the **Barley Mow** (2½ miles).

On departure, turn right up Tandridge Lane and after 100 yards turn left back onto the footpath. This is a very attractive part of the walk with some great views. Taking great care when crossing the A22, continue on the other side through Castlehill Wood, where a deep pool will be observed on your left. You will cross a ford and pass Leigh Mill. This brings you to the Eastbourne Road, B.2236. Turn left and follow the road for 200 yards or so until you see the 2nd footpath sign on your right. Take this path and you will now skirt to the south of Hopgarden Wood and follow the contours of Brakey Hill until you arrive at Tilburstow Hill Road. Here you take a slight detour south (left), away from the Greensand Way to the **Fox & Hounds**, **South Godstone** (4¾ miles). Suitably refreshed, retrace your steps to where you joined the road and then pick up the path on your left. You are now at the southernmost part of the Tilburstow Hill plantation and on your left you will have great views over the Weald.

You are now working off the beer - it's a fair walk to the next refreshment stop! Continue along the path until you come to the narrow South Park Lane. Turn left and take the 2nd footpath to your right, which is the Greensand Way. Follow this path and continue through Coldharbour Farm, all the time keeping an eye out for Greensand Way signs. Turn right past some disused workings, veer left and keep on until you reach

Outwood Lane. Turn right and continue a short distance up the road until you arrive in the centre of **Bletchingley**, and the **Prince Albert**, (7¼ miles). You now have the choice of visiting some of the other pubs in the village. If you have time, the **William IV** is only a short walk down Little Common Lane (turn right just beyond the Red Lion). If you do all these pubs add another 1 mile to the trip (8¼ miles). If you have had enough walking, buses can be caught from here to Redhill and Oxted.

Return to the Greensand Way via the High Street on the south side opposite Stychens Lane. Walk down Castle Square, past Castle Close and pick up the footpath sign for the Greensand Way. This is another lovely part of the walk and the views are magnificent. You descend steeply through land belonging to Castle Hill Farm and the noise of the M23 will now become more apparent. You can't miss it as it's on your right! The Greensand Way takes a sharp right at a crossroads of footpaths after about a mile since starting your descent. Go under the M23 via a subway and emerge to farm buildings on your left. Continue and turn right into Cooper's Hill Road, past the Cricket Ground and turn left into a footpath again just after Lyttel Hall. Follow the path on its winding descent into **South Nutfield** and turn left into Mid Street, carry on under the Railway Bridge and turn right into the Avenue. You will arrive at the **Station Hotel** (11 miles). If you want to call it a day, you can catch trains from Nutfield Station to Redhill or Tonbridge.

If there is still life in you, leave the pub and continue walking down the Avenue to Kings Cross Lane and then turn right. Carry on for roughly 400 yards and turn left into Kings Mill Lane. After about another 400 yards, look for the footpath to your right and take this - you are now back on the Greensand Way and into open countryside. You will soon see the former Royal Earlswood Hospital - now transformed into an upmarket residential development. Continue until you see Redhill Brook to your right. The footpath now diverges and you now take the right fork (leaving the Greensand Way) and after 300 yards you will emerge into Brambletye Park Road. Turn left and follow the signs for Earlswood Station. Cross under the railway tracks and on your left is the **Old Chestnut** (13½ miles).

From this point on the choice is yours. You can throw in the towel and catch a train from Earlswood to Redhill, Horley, East Croydon, or Central London, or you can carry on to **Redhill** on foot along the A23 passing several pubs on the way: the **Joshua Tree**, **Flying Scud**, **Greyhound**, ending at the **Garland** (14½ miles*). The short walk to Redhill station from the Garland will take the total distance to approximately 15 miles. How long it takes - is entirely up to you!

NEWS AND ALE

A quarterly magazine, "News and Ale" is published by the Surrey Hants Borders branch of CAMRA giving up to date information on pubs throughout the county. This can be found in several of the featured pubs in this guide. As well as pub features, it will let you know about local breweries, beer festivals, pub crawls, and much more.

For more information please contact newsandale@camrasurrey.org.uk

PUB HERITAGE

Pubs have been a vital element of British community life for many hundreds of years. Pubs have been in existence since at least the eleventh century when almost every other household welcomed passers-by to drop in and refresh themselves with a tankard of the local brew.

Like the church, pubs were central to the life of a community. Indeed many early public houses came into being because of the need to provide church builders with a place of relaxation. As time moved on, the responsibility of innkeeping passed to local lords of the manor. This partly explains why many inn signs and names reflect important local or national aristocratic names or heraldic symbols. 'The Red Lion' remains the most common pub name, and many of these date back to the sixteenth century. Coaching inns, many of which still exist on key routes, dropped in importance in the nineteenth century when the railways became the most prominent form of transport. In the Victorian era, large extravagant pubs became the norm and thousands of examples of these fine buildings still exist on the street corners of most towns and cities.

The industrial revolution also marked the creation of large regional brewers which bought up pubs in their area and began to supply them with their own beer. Publicans became tenants, paying low levels of rent to brewer landlords and agreeing, in return, to exclusively sell their beer. The pub 'tie' was born and this remains an important aspect of the pub scene today. But not all was rosy for the future of the pub. During the end of the nineteenth century and throughout the First World War, drinking alcohol became a major social and moral issue and this led to the creation of controls and licensing laws to protect the British public from the evils of alcohol abuse. Many of these laws are still in existence today. During the inter-war period methods of transport continued to influence the type and style of new pubs. As the motor car grew in importance, so too did the popularity of roadside inns reflecting the art-deco design preference of the time. In the late 1960s and early 1970s 'merger fever' led to the creation of six huge national companies which spelled the end of many regional and family brewers. Companies like Bass and Whitbread began to merge with and buy out other brewers and their pub estates in a quest for market power.

Throughout the 1980s the majority of pubs were in the control of a handful of companies. Many of the traditional names and regional pub identities began to disappear as companies tried to segment the market. The themed or concept pub was born and establishing corporate identity on a national scale changed the face of the pub scene forever. Pubs no longer existed only to serve local communities, but became 'destination pubs' offering a uniform experience to an increasingly sophisticated customer. At the end of the 1980s the extent of the market power of the big brewers led to a government investigation which aimed to restrict this power. But the resulting legislation was a watered down version of the recommendations of the Monopolies and Mergers Commission report. Restricting the number of pubs big brewers could own and tie meant that many thousands of pubs were put up for sale in the early 1990s. This led to the creation of several large non-brewing pub-companies which invariably signed supply deals with the selling brewers. It did not lead to more choice for consumers as initially intended and served only to accelerate the move towards managed concept pubs.

A pub can never serve to meet the needs of all people. But modern investment trends have led to our high streets becoming saturated with large themed pubs which are often aimed at the high-spending under 25 year old group. Lack of investment in local community pubs continues to threaten their survival, as owning companies plough millions into the development of short-term concepts to please a fickle group of customers who will soon move onto the next popular theme.

YOUR PUB IS UNDER THREAT

CAMRA is committed to the British pub. CAMRA believes that pubs are a unique and precious part of British heritage and way of life. Like many of our best traditions they face an uncertain future. Whether threatened by closure or by 'improvement', our public houses deserve the serious attention of all with a commitment to conservation.

The Threat

Modern retail philosophy is threatening the traditional British pub. The majority of pub companies and developers are obsessed with developing and establishing recognisable brands. Our town centres are becoming saturated with large themed pubs chasing short-term profits. This 'McDonaldisation' of the pub industry puts the traditional community pub at risk. The huge majority of investment in the market is concentrated on themed and concept outlets while smaller community locals struggle to compete without long-term investment and support. It's not just the pub as an institution which is at risk. The fabric of some of our greatest pubs is also under threat from unsympathetic development. Short-term commercial considerations have already brought the loss and ruin of many valuable pubs. CAMRA deplores the fact that historically important pub buildings and interiors remain exposed to such forces.

What is CAMRA doing?

CAMRA's Pubs Group campaigns at a national level to promote and defend the British pub. Local groups campaign for specific pubs and are available to help and advise communities whose local is threatened with unwanted change or closure. Pubs Group campaigned for pub interiors to be considered for listing in the same way as exteriors. We now work in close partnership with English Heritage to ensure important pub interiors are listed. CAMRA publishes a National Inventory of pubs with interiors of outstanding importance. Each year we hold *the Pub Design Awards,* a competition to reward innovative and sensitive pub design and refurbishment. We also host the *Pub of the Year* competition at local, regional and national levels. CAMRA supports and encourages part-time and dual-use pubs. Several pubs have been saved from closure through these methods.

CAMRA's Three Main Aims for Pub preservation

- to conserve our stock of pubs, helping to maintain a healthy and varied choice of pubs as a social asset to serve the needs of different communities
- to preserve and promote the pub as an institution helping to ensure the survival of the essential character of the British pub as a place for responsible social drinking. CAMRA believes that pubs with a choice of rooms and a competent resident publican are best positioned to achieve this.
- To conserve outstanding pub buildings with important internal and external features.

GOLD PLATED,
COPPER BOTTOMED,
UTTERLY RIVETING.
Summer Lightning
AWARD WINNING ALE
ODYSSEY
BEST BITTER
CAST IRON
GUARANTEED!

VARIETY WITHOUT MEDIOCRITY

This article is by Ross Hunter from the Surrey Hills Brewery

Much has been said about pub companies currently dominating the beer market. There is a great deal of excellent lobbying and campaigning taking place to try and improve the situation.

Stepping back twenty years or so to when I first started regularly frequenting pubs in this part of the world, apart from the odd diamond of a free house the only question when choosing a pub was "Courage or Friary?" The current pub environment gives the consumer far more choice than was previously available, with a number of pubs in most towns owned by regional breweries, others owned by pub companies and still the odd diamond of a free house.

Despite the increased choice of beer, problems remain. Pubs local to a brewery are usually very keen to stock that brewery's beers, but are not permitted to as they are tied into agreements with the owning pub companies that ensure they purchase all their beer centrally through the pub company. A small brewery cannot throw all their eggs into one basket and supply a large amount of beer to a pub company as the brewery would then have a high risk of bankruptcy should the pub company suddenly decide to no longer purchase beer from them.

Ultimately, the outcome of the current situation rests with the consumer. As long as consumers are kept accurately informed of current issues, they will vote with their mouths where they can.

It is great to see so many new breweries starting up. Every brewer has new or different ideas about the styles of beer they want to produce and the methods used to produce them. This healthy situation has led to many great beers coming to the market in recent years. There are also a lot of mediocre beers appearing.

People like to try new beers, so pubs like to stock new beers, and this is generally a good thing, but I wonder if things have gone a little too far. Breweries appear to be creating more and more different brands, and not spending the time getting these beers just right. This approach has probably led to some breweries stumbling upon a winning formula for a beer, but meanwhile there are many drab beers appearing in our pubs.

Variety and innovation are welcome traits in the real ale arena, but not if quality is sacrificed. Many of the very successful breweries have a handful of great beers that have been honed to perfection and occasionally introduce a new beer when they know they have got it right.

The number of smaller beer festivals has increased dramatically recently. Many pubs are giving it a go, and the events are well attended. The popularity of these events provides a welcome platform for smaller breweries to showcase their beers to a larger number of people.

In an environment of reducing UK cask ale sales overall, many of the national cask ale brands are suffering. There is substantial growth in output and consumption of beer from the smaller breweries however. I believe there is room for optimism in the future for our ever-increasing variety of exceptional cask conditioned ales.

WHY START A BREWERY

Robert Wicks from the newly established Westerham Brewery was asked why would anyone want to start a brewery. This is his response:

From Broking to Brewing…

Within a year of getting married and after just two years of working in the City, Liz and I moved to Tokyo with the stockbroking firm James Capel & Co. Here I sold Japanese equities to foreign fund managers and enjoyed the ex-pat lifestyle, travelling around Japan and thriving on the challenges of the job and life overseas. Over four years later, with our first child just three months old, my job took me to New York, where a further three years were spent as a broker of Japanese equities.

During the years in the USA I began to feel restless in my job and started to consider my options. One possibility was to take a degree in viticulture in the United States, with a view to buying a vineyard. I was offered a place at Davis University in California, but Liz was not convinced! So, back to England and back to the City. I was still restless. No longer satisfied by the 6.21am train to Cannon Street, the long day in front of a computer, the grey office and the sense of being detached from 'real life', I wanted to be closer to home, see more of my family and be more involved with the local community. Liz agreed wholeheartedly and encouraged me to take the risk and step out onto a completely different path.

When choosing a degree course and university years earlier, fermentation technology had been one of my choices, although I finally chose to read biochemistry at Trinity College, Oxford. Brewing had been on my mind for a quite a while! The seeds were sown by my godfather, who introduced me to the delights of a good pint at the tender age of eight. His home-brewed beer was always exceptional and the inspiration for my venture.

After several years of dreaming and two years of active and at times intensive planning and asking the Lord for guidance, I established the Westerham Brewery Company (WBC) in January 2004. With brewer Anthony Richardson, we rolled up our sleeves and spent five months preparing an old dairy building for brewing. The first beer flowed from the brewery in May of that year. Brewing methods are traditional and use locally grown hops wherever possible. WBC is tied to the 250-year brewing tradition in Westerham by the re-culturing of the original yeast used by The Black Eagle Brewery in Westerham. Its head brewer, Bill Wickett, no doubt sensing the imminent demise of the brewery, deposited the yeast strains at the National Collection of Yeast Cultures in 1958.

Having reached the anniversary of our first brew, WBC is growing from strength to strength. Life has been turned on its head in the Wicks household, but the whole family are very positive and supportive. I see more of his family, have a six-minute commute along pretty country lanes, and am quite convinced it is the best thing I have ever done.

THE INTERNET

Although we hope books like this will always be around, the internet is increasingly becoming a great way of obtaining information. We hope the two mediums will work in conjunction with each other, and it is for this reason we will be publishing an on-line version of this guide which will be kept up to date. This will be found at the CAMRA Surrey website, www.camrasurrey.org.uk/pubguide.htm

www.camrasurrey.org.uk

This website was first established on 20 April 1996 and was one of the first official Camra websites in Britain. All four of the Surrey branches of Camra are an integral part of this site. The website contains pictures, branch news including newsletters and branch diaries (so you can get to one of our social or branch meetings).

If you have comments about the pubs in this guide, or want more information, you can email us. Also, if you have more up to date information about the pubs, please let us know. Much as we would like to, unfortunately we cannot visit all these pubs on a regular basis. If you find a pub that has been refurbished, is selling particularly good beer, is running a beer festival, has changed hands.....anything really about your visit, please let us know.

One other thing we would love to hear about is the availability of real ale in clubs, and we will try to put this information on the website (as long as we know what the entry restrictions are). The email addresses are:

Pub News	pubnews@camrasurrey.org.uk
Club News	clubnews@camrasurrey.org.uk
East & Mid Surrey Branch	eams@camrasurrey.org.uk
Kingston & Leatherhead Branch	kandl@camrasurrey.org.uk
Comments about the Website	comments@surreyorg.uk

Below are some website addresses you may find useful:

CAMRA Nationally	www.camra.org.uk
Brewery Information	www.quaffale.org.uk
Beer Information	www.beermad.org.uk

The last two named are not CAMRA sites, but are excellent sources of information on all breweries and the beers they brew.

Finally, for those who do not have access to email, if you have any comments please contact us at the postal address shown inside the front cover.

CLOSED PUBS

This guide contains information about 391 outlets. 66 of them, almost 1 in 6, have closed in the period 1975-2005. Each of these was someone's local, and each one different. These closed pubs are clearly shown in this guide - they have a grey background to them. Don't allow this to happen to your pub - use it. See the article in this guide on Pub Heritage for more information on what can be done.

ACCOMMODATION

The following fully recommended pubs offer accommodation. Please check the pub listing for more details. Please note that we have not been able to check out any of these facilities.

Abinger Hammer	Abinger Arms
Albury	Drummond Arms
Beare Green	Duke's Head
Betchworth	Red Lion
Bletchingley	Whyte Harte Inn
Coldharbour	Plough Inn
Copthorne	Copthorne Effingham Park Hotel
Copthorne	Hedgehog Inn
Dorking	Lincoln Arms Hotel
Dorking	Pilgrim
Epsom	Haywain
Gomshall	Compasses
Horley	Coppingham Arms
Lingfield	Star Inn
Lower Kingswood	Fox on the Hill
Mickleham	Running Horses
Newchapel	Blacksmith's Head
Ockley	Inn on the Green
Ockley	King's Arms Inn
Peaslake	Hurtwood Inn
Redhill	Toby Lodge
Salfords	Mill House
Shere	Prince of Wales
Tandridge	Barley Mow

THE LICENSING ACT 2003

This piece of legislation is the first major change to the licensing system for over 100 years and will bring several changes to the pubs as described in this guide. Now licensing comes under the control of the local council, and each will have their own way of dealing with things.

The new license is known as a "Premises Licence" and is required for each place alcohol is sold. This will dictate the hours when alcohol is sold, and once granted, does not need to be renewed. The pub does not have to open for all the hours it is licensed for and so most pubs are applying for far longer hours than they actually intend to use.

The person running the pub requires a "Personal Licence". The person holding this licence can then run any other place requiring such a licence. This lasts for ten years. The objectives of these new licences are to help promote public safety and reduce crime, and to protect children from harm. This last named point could prove to be one of the most significant changes. Children are now considered to be anyone under the age of 16, and it will be an offence to allow unaccompanied children into a bar area. Children aged 16 or 17 will be able to drink beer, wine or cider with a meal, but not buy it themselves.

All pubs in this guide were surveyed before this Act comes into effect (7 November 2005), so please bear this in mind when visiting them - things may have changed.

ALPHABETICAL PUB LIST SHOWING LOCATION

Abbot	Redhill
Abergavenny Arms	Copthorne
Abinger Arms	Abinger Hammer
Abinger Hatch	Abinger Common
Admiral Inn	Reigate
Air Balloon	Horley
Albion	Epsom
Amato	Epsom
Anchor	Great Bookham
Angel	Reigate
Arkle Manor	Betchworth
Arty P's	Dorking
Arundel Arms	Dorking
Assembly Rooms	Epsom
Bakery	Tatsfield
Barley Mow	Epsom
Barley Mow	Reigate
Barley Mow	Tandridge
Batchelors	Reigate
Beehive	Reigate
Bell	Dorking
Bell	Fetcham
Bell	Godstone
Bell	Reigate
Bell	Walton-on-the-Hill
Bell Inn	Outwood
Black Horse	Gomshall
Black Horse	Hookwood
Black Horse	Reigate
Blacksmiths Arms	Caterham
Blacksmiths Head	Newchapel
Blenheim Arms	Epsom
Blue Anchor	Blindley Heath
Blue Anchor	Reigate
Blue Anchor	Tadworth
Blue Ball	Walton-on-the-Hill
Boogie Lounge	Epsom
Bookham Grange Hotel	Little Bookham
Botley Hill Farmhouse	Titsey
Boy & Donkey	Cranleigh
Brahm's & Liszt	Leatherhead
Brennan's	Leatherhead
Brewery Inn	Ashtead
Brickmakers	Crowhurst
Bridge House Hotel	Reigate
Bull	Chelsham
Bull	Horley
Bull	Limpsfield
Cheers	Fetcham
Chequers	Walton-on-the-Hill
Cherry Tree	Copthorne
Chicago Rock Café	Epsom
Clifton Arms	Caterham
Cloisters	Caterham
Coach House	Dormans Park
Cock Inn	Headley
Compasses	Gomshall
Coppingham Arms	Horley
Copthorne Effingham Park Hotel	Copthorne
Copthorne Hotel London Gatwick	Copthorne
Cranley Hotel	Cranleigh
Cricketers	Dorking
Cricketers	Epsom
Cricketers	Westcott
Cricketers Arms	Ockley
Crown	Capel
Crown	Oxted
Crown Inn	Nutfield
Crown Inn	Westcott
Derby Arms	Epsom Downs
Diamond	Hurst Green
Dog & Duck	Outwood
Dog & Duck	Redhill
Dolphin	Betchworth
Dorking Halls	Dorking
Dragon	Redhill
Driftbridge	Drift Bridge
Drummond Arms	Albury
Dukes Head	Beare Green
Dukes Head	Brockham
Dukes Head	Copthorne
Dukes Head	Leatherhead
Dukes Head	Tadworth
Eclipse	Epsom
Edmund Tylney	Leatherhead
Eight Bells	Ewell
Elmshades	Redhill
Epsom Playhouse Bar	Epsom
Falkland	Dorking
Farmhouse	Horley
Farola	Dorking
Feathers	Merstham

Flight Tavern	Charlwood
Flying Scud	Redhill
Foresters	Horley
Four Elms	Smithwood Common
Fox & Hounds	South Godstone
Fox & Hounds	Walton-on-the-Hill
Fox on the Hill	Lower Kingswood
Fox Revived	Norwood Hill
Gamecock	Worcester Park
Garibaldi	Redhill
Garland	Redhill
Gatton Manor	Ockley
Gatton Point	Redhill
Gatwick	Horley
Gatwick Moat House	Horley
General Napier	Salfords
George Inn	Oxted
Golden Lion	Caterham
Good Companions	Hamsey Green
Grasshopper Inn	Moorhouse
Green Man	Ewell
Greyhound	Charlwood
Greyhound	Horley
Greyhound	Lingfield
Greyhound	Redhill
Half Moon	Charlwood
Hand in Hand	Boxhill
Hare & Hounds	Godstone
Hare & Hounds	Lingfield
Hare & Hounds	Warlingham
Harlequin Theatre	Redhill
Harrow	Chaldon
Harrow	Farleigh
Harvester	Salfords
Hatch	Redhill
Haxted Mill	Haxted
Haycutter	Broadham Green
Haywain	Epsom
Heathside Hotel	Burgh Heath
Hedgehog	Copthorne
Hobo's	Redhill
Hogsmill Tavern	Worcester Park
Holiday Inn Gatwick Airport	Horley
Holly & Laurel	South Holmwood
Holmesdale	Reigate

Home Cottage	Redhill
Horseshoe	Warlingham
Horton Park Country Club	Ewell
Hoskins Arms	Oxted
Hunters Moon	Copthorne
Hurtwood Inn	Peaslake
Inn on the Green	Ockley
Inn on the Pond	Nutfield Marsh
Iron Horse	Merstham
Jacque's Wine Bar	Banstead
Jarvis Felbridge Hotel	Felbridge
Jim Thompson's Oriental Bar	Ewell
Jolly Brickmakers	Redhill
Jolly Coopers	Epsom
Jolly Farmer	Horne
Jolly Farmers	Buckland
Jolly Waggoners	Ewell
Joshua Tree	Redhill
King & Queen	Caterham
King William IV	Ewell
King William IV	Mickleham
Kingfisher	Ewell
Kings Arms	Dorking
Kings Arms	Epsom
Kings Arms Inn	Ockley
Kings Head	Capel
Kings Head	Holmbury St Mary
Kings Head	Horley
King's Head Coffee House	Dorking
Kingswood Arms	Kingswood
Ladas	Epsom
Leg Of Mutton & Cauliflower	Ashtead
Lime Bar	Epsom
Limes	Merstham
Lincoln Arms	Dorking
Lingfield	Lingfield
Little Park Hatch	Cranleigh
Locomotive	Redhill
Malthouse	Dorking
Market Hotel	Reigate
Marquis of Granby	Epsom
Marquis of Granby	Redhill
Midday Sun	Chipstead
Mill House	Salfords
Mint	Banstead
Mint Arms	Lower Kingswood
Moles Wine Bar	Leatherhead
Monson Arms	Redhill

Nags Head	Redhill	Prince of Wales	Reigate
Natasha's	Cranleigh	Prince of Wales	Shere
New Inn	Redhill	Prince of Wales	Westcott
Noah's Ark	Redhill	Priory	Reigate
Nutley Hall	Reigate	Puccino's	Dorking
Office	Dorking	Puccino's	Reigate
Old Bell	Oxted	Punchbowl	Dorking
Old Cage	Lingfield	Punchbowl	Oakwood Hill
Old Chestnut	Redhill	Queen Adelaide	Ewell
Old Crown	Great Bookham	Queens Head	Dorking
		Queens Head	Epsom
Old House at Home	Dorking	Queens Head	Nutfield
Old House at Home	Dormansland	Railway	South Godstone
Old Leather Bottle	Warlingham		
Old Oak	Redhill	Railway Arms	Leatherhead
Old School House	Ockley	Railway Arms	Merstham
Old Ship	Tatsfield	Railway Guard	Epsom
Old Six Bells	Horley	Railway Hotel	Reigate
Old Surrey Hounds	Caterham	Ramblers Rest	Chipstead
Old Surrey Hounds	Godstone	Ranmore Arms	Ranmore Common
Olde Kings Head	Epsom		
Olde Windsor Castle	Little Bookham	Red Barn	Blindley Heath
		Red Cross Inn	Reigate
Oliver's	Redhill	Red Lion	Betchworth
Omnia	Drift Bridge	Red Lion	Bletchingley
O'Neill's	Redhill	Red Lion	Redhill
Onslow Arms	Cranleigh	Reigate Manor Hotel	Reigate
Oxted Inn	Oxted		
Panther Inn	Reigate	Renaissance London Gatwick Hotel	Horley
Parrot Inn	Forest Green		
Peacock	Newchapel		
Pengelly's Wine Bar	Caterham	Rifleman	Epsom
		Rising Sun	Charlwood
Penny Black	Leatherhead	Rising Sun	Epsom
Pilgrim	Dorking	Rising Sun	Fetcham
Plough	Coldharbour	Rookwood House Hotel	Merstham
Plough	Dormansland		
Plough	Ewell	Royal Oak	Brockham
Plough	Leatherhead	Royal Oak	Caterham
Plough	Leigh	Royal Oak	Dormansland
Plough	Smallfield	Royal Oak	Great Bookham
Plough	Bletchingley		
Plough & Harrow	Epsom	Royal Oak	Holmbury St Mary
Plough at Blackbrook	Blackbrook	Royal Oak	Leatherhead
Plough Inn	Redhill	Royal Oak	Staffhurst Wood
Preston Cross Hotel & Country Club	Great Bookham	Royal Oak	Stonebridge
		Rubbing House	Epsom Downs
Prince Albert	Bletchingley	Running Horse	Leatherhead
Prince Albert	Copthorne	Running Horses	Mickleham
Prince Albert	Redhill	Rusper Golf Club	Newdigate
Prince of Wales	Baldwins Hill	Russ Hill Hotel	Charlwood
Prince of Wales	Dorking	Salthouse	Epsom
Prince of Wales	Leatherhead	Scarlett Arms	Walliswood

Sefton Arms	Epsom
Seven Stars	Leigh
Shepherds Pen	Merstham
Ship Inn	Redhill
Shipley Bridge	Burstow
Six Bells	Newdigate
Skimmington Castle	Reigate Heath
Skylane Hotel	Horley
Smith & Western	Boxhill
Somers Arms	Redhill
South Eastern	Redhill
Sportsman	Mogador
Spotted Cow	Strood Green
Spotted Dog	Dorking
Spread Eagle	Epsom
Spring	Ewell
Stanhill Court Hotel	Charlwood
Star	Ewell
Star	Felbridge
Star	Hooley
Star	Leatherhead Common
Star	Lingfield
Star Inn	Dorking
Station	Horley
Station Hotel	South Nutfield
Stephan Langton	Friday Street
Stepping Stones	Westhumble
Stoneleigh Inn	Stoneleigh
Sultan	Redhill
Sun	Redhill
Surrey Hills Hotel	Capel
Surrey Oaks	Newdigate
Surrey Yeoman	Burgh Heath
Surrey Yeoman	Dorking
Symonds Well	Epsom
Tally Ho	Caterham
Tattenham Corner	Epsom Downs
Thistle London Gatwick	Horley
Three Horseshoes	Cranleigh
Three Horseshoes	Sidlow Bridge
Thurlow Arms	Baynards
Tickled Ivory	Reigate
Toby Carvery	Ewell
Toby Lodge	Redhill
Troggs Wine Bar	Oxted
Tumble Beacon	Tadworth
Valley	Caterham
Valley	Caterham
Venture Inn	Reigate
Vestry	Epsom
Vibe	Epsom
Victoria	Banstead
Village Inn	Gatwick Airport
Volunteer Inn	Sutton Abinger
Watermill	Dorking
Well House Inn	Mugswell
Wellington	Epsom
Wesleyan	Warlingham
Wheatsheaf	Banstead
Wheatsheaf	Ellens Green
Wheatsheaf	Ewell
Wheatsheaf	Marsh Green
Wheatsheaf Inn	Oxted
White Bear	Fickleshole
White Hart	Beare Green
White Hart	Chipstead
White Hart	Cranleigh
White Hart	Dorking
White Hart	Epsom
White Hart	Godstone
White Hart	Reigate
White Horse	Dorking
White Horse	Epsom
White Horse	Shere
White House Hotel	Blindley Heath
White Lion	Redhill
White Lion	Warlingham
White Swan	Godstone
Why Nots	Dorking
Whyte Hart	Bletchingley
Whyteleafe Tavern	Whyteleafe
William IV	Albury Heath
William IV	Bletchingley
Windmill	Dorking
Windmill	Ewhurst
Wiremill Inn	Newchapel
Wonham House	South Godstone
Woodcock	Felbridge
Woodman	Woodmansterne
Woodman	Ashtead
Woolpack	Banstead
Wotton Hatch	Wotton
Yates's Wine Lodge	Epsom
Yew Tree	Reigate

THE COVER

The cover was designed by Martin Bundy, and features pub signs and other decorative features outside pubs that we may not notice. In case you were wondering where they came from, here is the answer, from the Prince of Wales in Reigate to the Onslow Arms in Cranleigh:

All the pubs on the cover

<table>
<tr><td>Prince of Wales Reigate</td><td>Black Horse Hookwood</td><td>Greyhound Redhill</td><td>Plough Bletchingley</td><td>Garibaldi Redhill</td><td>Bell Oxted</td></tr>
<tr><td>Cricketers Dorking</td><td>Blue Anchor Blindley</td><td colspan="2">Little Park Hatch Cranleigh</td><td rowspan="2">Plough Inn Coldharbour</td><td>Blue Bat Walton on the Hill</td></tr>
<tr><td>Parrot Forest Green</td><td colspan="2">Running Horses Mickleham</td><td>Six Bells Horley</td><td>Jolly Farmers Buckland</td></tr>
<tr><td>Coppingham Arms Horley</td><td rowspan="2">Hare & Jounds Lingfield</td><td>Three H/shoes Cranleigh</td><td colspan="2">Crown Nutfield</td><td>Hurtwood Inn Peaslake</td></tr>
<tr><td>Home Cottage Redhill</td><td colspan="2" rowspan="2">Dolphin Betchworth</td><td>Rising Sun Epsom</td><td>Red Lion Bletchingley</td></tr>
<tr><td>Admiral Reigate</td><td>Chequers Walton on the Hill</td><td rowspan="2">Abinger Arms Abinger</td><td>Royal Oak Brockham</td></tr>
<tr><td>Blacksmiths Head Newchapel</td><td colspan="2">Scarlett Arms Walliswood</td><td>Royal Oak Staffhurstwood</td><td>Pilgrim Brewery Reigate</td></tr>
<tr><td>Surrey Oaks Newdigate</td><td rowspan="2">William IV Bletchingley</td><td>Bulls Head Ewhurst</td><td colspan="2">White Horse Dorking</td><td>Compasses Gomshall</td></tr>
<tr><td>White Hart Bletchingley</td><td colspan="2">Joshua Tree Redhill</td><td>Hare & Hounds Godstone</td><td>Crown Inn Westcott</td></tr>
<tr><td>White Horse Shere</td><td>Diamond Hurst Green</td><td>Queens Head Dorking</td><td>Plough Cranleigh</td><td>Haycutter Broadham Green</td><td>Old House at Home Dormansland</td></tr>
<tr><td colspan="2">Barley Mow Reigate</td><td colspan="2">Fox Revived N/wood Hill</td><td colspan="2">Onslow Arms Cranleigh</td></tr>
</table>

ABINGER COMMON (A2)

It is claimed that this is the longest occupied English village, with evidence of Mesolithic pit dwellings and a Norman castle motte. There are stocks in front of the village church, which was bombed by a doodlebug in August 1944. Nearby Abinger Mill, now a private house, has been the site of several mills manufacturing gunpowder, copper plate and also corn. Lutyens designed the war memorial. In 1924 Abinger was chosen for the location of a branch of the Royal Observatory and from 1940 until 1955 the six pips of the Greenwich time signal came from here.

● Abinger Hatch

Abinger Lane, RH5 6HZ
OS: 115460
☎ (01306) 730737
11-11 (12-10:30 Sunday)
Fuller's London Pride
Greene King Old Speckled Hen
Ringwood Best Bitter, Fortyniner
Guest Beers

Ducks from the nearby pond on the village green often waddle into the car park of this very attractive 17th century inn found opposite the church. The pub interior rambles over four levels, all served by a single L-shaped brick built bar. The far part of the uppermost area, to the left of the pub, is festooned with hops. The lowest part of the bar has large flagstones on the floor, with the other areas having bare boards. Throughout there are wooden beams and posts, solid wooden furniture, and walls displaying a large number of interesting sporting photos and prints. Home-cooked food is a feature with a varied menu on offer, although no food is sold Sunday evening. Two guest beers are sold, changing seasonally. The pub was a former Surrey Trust Company house. Outside there are large gardens.

ABINGER HAMMER (A2)

The name Abinger Hammer is a reminder of the iron industry that once existed here. The hammer ponds, which now grow watercress, were used to hold the water needed to drive the waterwheel that powered the hammers beating the iron. The forge on the Tillingbourne probably existed before 1567. The blacksmith, whose motto is "By me you know how fast to go", stands by the clock hanging over the main road, and is an indication of the historical importance of iron working in this village The clock dates from the early 1900s, and Jack the Hammer strikes the hour on his anvil. A Burton-on-Trent company that specialised in carving fairground gallopers carved the figure from teak. The cricket ground is land given as a memorial to the village men killed in the Great War. In nearby Abinger Roughs a stone cross was erected in memory of Bishop Samuel Wilberforce who was killed in a riding accident on his way to dine with Lord Gladstone in July 1873.

● Abinger Arms

Guildford Road, RH5 6RZ
OS: 095475 (A25)
☎ (01306) 730145
11-11 (12-10:30 Sunday)
Adnams Bitter
Marston's Pedigree

Tile hung two bar pub in the village centre, adjacent to the famous clock and close to the tiny cricket ground. Formerly a tannery, the pub was first licenced in 1840. It has two entrances, both approached up a flight of steps. There is a separate restaurant, up a further step, where a good selection of home cooked food is served every day. Bar snacks are also available. Note the impressive ironwork around the bar where the design includes several horseshoes, tools, and the village name. There are games in the public bar including pool and darts, and a big screen TV is put here up for football. Accommodation is available – two rooms.

🛏◁▶✂🐎🚗☸

🚌 (Gomshall)

ALBURY (A2)

One of the most interesting villages in the Tillingbourne Valley, Albury was moved from its original location near the Saxon church to its present location in what was formerly the hamlet of Weston Street. This process was started in 1784 by magisterial orders and was not completed until well into the 19th century. Henry Drummond bought the Albury Estate, which was mentioned in the Domesday Book, in 1819 and had Augustus Pugin, who was known for his work on the Houses of Parliament, rebuild the Saxon parish church, St Peter and St Paul. Pugin's work included remodeling the south chapel as a mortuary chapel for the Drummond family. The church also contains fine 15th century brasses and paintings. Drummond then had the architect William Macintosh Brookes build the gothic Catholic Apostolic church which stands near the junction of the A248 and A25. Henry Drummond also commissioned Pugin to rebuild Albury Park House, complete with 63 differently designed chimneys. His influence is also seen in the other chimneys in the village. A rare Tudor pigeon house stands in the yard of the original manor house. It provided meat in winter and the pigeon droppings were used as fertiliser and in the manufacture of gunpowder in the local mills. Nearby is the Silent Pool, whose clear waters rise from a natural spring, and which features in Martin Tupper's novel "Stephan Langton". Sherbourne Farm, next to the Silent Pool, is a working farm that is open to the public at weekends.

● Drummond Arms

The Street, GU5 9DG
OS: 049478 (A248)
☎ (01483) 202039
11-11 (12-10:30 Sunday)
Courage Best Bitter
Gales HSB
Greene King Old Speckled Hen
Guest Beer

This 19th century pub used to be owned by the Duke of Northumberland, and until 1910 had its own brewery when it was taken over by the Surrey Trust Company. Today it comprises one beamed bar with a separate food counter, and a restaurant. There are two fireplaces, one of which has only recently been opened up, and this is put to good use in winter. Around the walls can be found a number of plates. Good quality home-cooked food is available each lunchtime from 12-2:30 (3 Sunday) and from 6:30-9:30 Monday to Saturday, and a number of daily specials are always available. Of particular note are the homemade sweets. Accommodation consists of 11 en-suite rooms, four of which are in a separate annexe. Families are welcome in the non-smoking conservatory at all times. The guest beer will tend to come from one of the larger independent breweries.

🛏◁▶✕🚗☸⊗

ALBURY HEATH (A2)

A rural collection of houses between the railway and Albury Park.

● William IV

Dark Lane, Little London, GU5 9DG OS: 066467
☎ (01483) 202685
11-3, 5:30-11 (12-3, 7-10:30 Sunday)
Flowers IPA
Hogs Back TEA, Hop Garden Gold
Surrey Hills Ranmore Ale, Shere Drop

The building has its origins in the 16th century and boasts beams, flagstones and a large fireplace where a welcoming wood fire burns brightly in winter. Set on a quiet lane adjoining extensive woodland, the area is popular with walkers. There are two traditional bars with a dining room up a few steps and a function room upstairs from this. Excellent home-made meals are served, though not on Sunday evenings, nor Monday evenings in winter. Shove halfpenny can be played.

◁▶✕🚗☸🚲

ASHTEAD (B1)

During the Roman period, roof and hypocaust tiles were made at a tile works attached to a villa. Pottery and coins found at the site show that it was occupied between the 1st and 3rd centuries. St Giles church, in Ashtead Park, dates from the 12th century, and Ashtead Woods and Commons, with their ancient oaks, are popular for walking and riding. Until the 1930s, Ashtead was an agricultural village, but is now a popular commuter location, still trying to distance itself from Epsom and Leatherhead.

Brewery Inn

15 The Street, KT21 2AD
OS: 185581 (A24)
☎ (01372) 271218
Greene King IPA, Old Speckled Hen
Fuller's London Pride
Shepherd Neame Spitfire

Large Ember Inns pub, which was the former site of George Sayer's Ashtead Brewery in the 19th century. The cellar still includes the brewing well which extends 100 metres under the road, although the brewery closed in 1910. Open all day.

● Leg Of Mutton & Cauliflower

48 The Street, KT21 1AZ
OS: 186581 (A24)
www.thelomac.co.uk
☎ (01372) 277200
11-11 (12-10:30 Sunday)
Fuller's London Pride
Taylor Landlord
Occasional **Guest Beer**

Former 18th century coaching inn which now caters mainly for the younger generation, but not to the exclusion of others. The pub sign says LOMAC, but the proper pub name is displayed on the front of the building. Decorated in modern

style with bare wood floors, and includes works of art on the wall that are for sale. There is a restaurant area to the rear reached through a no smoking area, which features comfy chairs. Good fresh food using local ingredients is served each day from 12-3 and 6-10, with new menus printed daily. Outside is a patio at the front and a garden to the rear. Families are welcome until 9:30 in the top bar area.

● **Woodman**

238 Barnett Wood Lane, KT21 2DA OS: 180587
☎ (01372) 274524
12-11 (12-10:30 Sunday)
Fuller's London Pride
Shepherd Neame Spitfire
Young's Bitter

A large pub, overlooking Ashtead Common, which is decorated in typical Ember Inns style with painted walls and dividing partitions. Several of these partitions include open gas fires as a feature. There is a patio at the front and a fenced garden to the rear. Quizzes are held on Tuesday and Sunday evenings. Food is served all day until 8pm. Only children over 14 are allowed, and they must be dining. Another beer may replace the Spitfire in due course.

BALDWINS HILL (D3)

Today just an extension of East Grinstead.

Prince of Wales

Lingfield Road, RH19 2EQ
OS: 386395
☎ (01342) 325703
Courage Best Bitter, Directors
Fuller's London Pride
This is a two bar pub with pool and darts in the public and an open fire in the saloon. It is mainly a drinkers' pub, although children are welcome until 9pm and the garden has a play area with slides.

BANSTEAD (C1)

Although it styles itself as a village, Banstead has grown into a small town. There is an ancient flint church dating from 1170, and at the junction of Sutton Lane and Woodmansterne Lane is an old wellhead. This listed building dates from the 19th century and covers a medieval well that goes down around 300 feet (90 metres). The high street is modern, however. Banstead was famous for its wholesome air, which led to a number of mental asylums springing up in the 19th century to treat the sick people of London. Peppermint was grown in the area and the oil sent to sweet factories in Mitcham, and the mint name is still to be found in the name of several local buildings.

Jacque's Wine Bar

49 High Street OS: 256598
Keg Sam Smith's was the best that the bar could offer. It closed in the 1990s and is now an Italian restaurant, Caffe Italia.

● Mint

Park Road, SM7 3DS OS: 262592
☎ (01737) 371851
11:30-11 (12-10:30 Sunday)
Bass
Fuller's London Pride

Next to the charming weather-boarded Mint Cottages and opposite Place Farm, this pub was once in the heart of the mint growing district some distance to the south of Banstead village centre. It became a beerhouse in 1871 and was purchased by Page and Overton's Croydon brewery at auction in 1899. It is now part of M&B's Vintage Inns chain and is decorated very much in their house style. Food is available all day. There is one bar but many nooks and crannies to sit in. Most of the pub is non-smoking with only a small area set aside for smokers. There are real log fires in the winter and a pleasant garden for use in the warmer months.

Victoria

1 High Street, SM7 2LY
OS: 252596

This was a large Courage pub at the beginning of the High Street at the junction of Bolters Lane. A good pint was to be had here, and, indeed, the Victoria was a Good Beer Guide regular between 1976 and 1987. At the front of this Victorian pub was a fairly small public bar. This led to a large lounge area that had much wood paneling in evidence. The pub, which used to be extremely busy, was converted into Zizzi's pizza restaurant in 2004.

Wheatsheaf Inn

Brighton Road, SM7 1AT
OS: 247593 (A217)
☎ (01737) 373337
Tetley Bitter

From the outside this is a most attractive example of an inter-war Brewer's Tudor roadhouse in cottage-style of red brick, steeply pitched tile roof incorporating a dormer and splendid original Crittall windows. Sadly, that's where all interest ends as the interior has had a severe attack of the Mr Q's treatment. The open plan interior is a riot of pool tables (4), television screens (6), video juke box (1), and electronic games machines (too many to list). Darts is also played. A very close inspection will reveal remnants of an original fireplace and some wood paneling - but that's it. Food is served from 12-6 every day. A local pub for local people.

Woolpack

186 High Street, SM7 2NZ
OS: 258598
☎ (01737) 354560
Courage Best Bitter, Directors

The only remaining pub in the town centre since the conversion of the Victoria at the other end of the High St to a pizza restaurant, the Woolpack is a fairly uninspiring brick and tile building with a clutter of large umbrellas at the front, masking the main entrance. Inside it is a pub of two halves (sic). To the left is a lounge area with a non-smoking section for diners at the rear and to the right is a very basic public type area with the pool table dominating the floor space and live sport shown on TVs. The trouble is that there is only one bar serving both and the pub seems to lack any identity. It may have been quite a nice place when you could choose which bar you wanted to drink in. Labelled as a John Barras establishment (a long defunct Gateshead brewery with absolutely no connection with the stockbroker belt!), it is actually a part of the Spirit Group, who recently inherited the chain from Scottish and Newcastle. It was formerly a Barclay Perkins house and latterly Courage for many years. Open all day with children welcome until 9pm.

BAYNARDS (A3)

The hamlet of Baynards is near the West Sussex border. The historic Tudor country house of Baynards was once the home of Margaret Roper, daughter of Sir Thomas More. She allegedly brought his head back to Baynards after his execution, leading to the legend of the Baynards ghost which meets the Loseley ghost for dinner annually, alternating between the two historic sites. Cranes were bred here in Tudor times for royal consumption. Reverend Thurlow owned the park in 1865 when he agreed to the railway running through the grounds, as long as a station was built there. Fuller's earth used to be sent by rail from here, but the line closed in 1965. The former railway is now part of the Downs Link long distance footpath.

● Thurlow Arms

Off Baynards Lane, RH12 3AD
OS: 076351
☎ (01403) 822459
12-3, 6-11 (11-3, 6-11 Saturday, 12-3, 7-10:30 Sunday, and open 12-10:30 on Sunday during British Summer Time)
Badger Best, Tanglefoot
Ringwood Best Bitter, Fortyniner
A Victorian building, it was built as a railway hotel for the adjoining Baynards station which last saw a train in 1965. This remote country pub is split into a lounge bar, with a restaurant off it, and an area containing a pool table where children are permitted. Darts is also played. There is a large collection of memorabilia, including railway collectibles, and reputedly four friendly ghosts have been seen in the pub or the area immediately outside. It is beside the Downs link path and cycle way, which largely follows the old railway line, and walkers and dogs are welcome. The food is home cooked. The Baynards brewery was set up at the pub in February 1996 but this sadly closed in 2000. Today three beers are sold with only one of either Tanglefoot or Fortyniner available at one time. The pub's long-term future is unknown as it was up for sale at the time this guide was produced.

◁▶✂ ⚘ 🚗 ❁

BEARE GREEN (B3)

The village has been divided by the main A24. Busy roads are probably the most interesting thing about the place, as Beare Green is the start of the A29 route to Bognor Regis.

● Duke's Head

Horsham Road, RH5 4QP
OS: 178431 (A24)
www.the-dukes-head-hotel.co.uk
☎ (01306) 711778
10:30-11 (12-10:30 Sunday)
Fuller's London Pride
Shepherd Neame Spitfire
Dating from 1701, the Dukes Head is on the southbound carriageway of the A24. A small tiled entrance hall (containing a cash machine) leads to doors for a bar and a restaurant. The bar has darts and pool, the latter in a separate room, and quizzes are held on Wednesdays. The main feature of the bar is a large inglenook fireplace. On the beam above this are hundreds of metal regimental cap badges. The separate restaurant is non-smoking and has disabled access. The food is of a high standard, and everything is home-cooked. A number of daily specials, including

vegetarian meals, are always available. Food is served all day from 7:30am to 9pm Monday to Wednesday (10pm Thursday and Friday) and from 8am to 10pm at weekends. Accommodation consists of 9 en-suite rooms, varying from singles to family rooms. Two of these are in a separate building and are suitable for the disabled. Families are welcome in the pub and there is children's play equipment in the garden.

White Hart
Old Horsham Road, RH5 4QY
OS: 177436
This huge Friary Meux pub was a popular stopping off point for motor coaches going to and from the coast. Inside there were several rooms, and pool and darts were popular. However, being by-passed meant that the traffic using it diminished and the pub finally closed in 1991 and housing was put on the site.

BETCHWORTH (B2)

A scattered village split by the A25, with the station and landfill site to the north, and the old village to the south. St Michael's church is mainly 13th century, but was renovated in Victorian times. It was featured in the film "Four Weddings and a Funeral". The River Mole runs to the south, with a bridge near Betchworth House. There are several attractive buildings dating from the 16th to the 18th centuries in The Street. Betchworth station was once important for the sending out of local lime. There is a pleasant circular walk to and from Brockham.

Arkle Manor
Reigate Road, RH3 7HB
OS: 198504 (A25)
☎ (01737) 842110
Fuller's London Pride
Unusually for a Harvester restaurant, this well proportioned tile-hung building also has a separate drinkers' bar. This is to be found to the left of the pub, and leads to a large garden area. Pool is played in a raised area away from the bar. The pub is open all day, with food served from 12-10, and was originally called the Barley Mow.

● **Dolphin Inn**
The Street, RH3 7DW OS: 211498
☎ (01737) 842288
11-3, 5:30-11 (11-11 Saturday and 12-10:30 Sunday)
Young's Bitter, Special, seasonal beers
Young's Golden Champion, Special London Ale in bottle

The Dolphin is said to be over 400 years old, although the earliest written record dates from 1785. The present building features a flagstone floor and two wood-burning inglenook fireplaces and dates from the 18th century. The pub is known to have brewed its own beer and cider until 1926. It is a busy local but also attracts many drinkers from further afield, especially at weekends. Outside there is a pleasant seating area in front of the pub as well as a separate garden. There are some very good solid tables in the pub, which also benefits from the absence of music or noisy electronic games. Excellent value food is served at all sessions, with specials always available. The Dolphin is well known for selling some of the best pints of Young's for miles around.

◁▶🚗☸🚲

● Red Lion

Old Road, RH3 7DS OS: 214504
www.redlion-betchworth.com
☎ (01737) 843336
12-11 (12-10:30 Sunday)
Adnams Broadside
Fuller's London Pride
Greene King IPA

The Red Lion dates in part from the 16th century, and is a family friendly pub specialising in good homemade food. This is sold 12-3 and 6-9:30 during the week and from 12-9:30 Saturday and 12-9 Sunday. A number of specials are chalked up on a blackboard, and these change at least weekly and will always contain a number of vegetarian options. Also featured are a number of genuine Turkish meals, reflecting the licensees' heritage. The pub is primarily a restaurant, so do not be surprised to find the tables set out for dining. Drinkers are welcome, however. A separate room, built into the cellars, is found down a number of steps, and this can be hired out for parties. The pub is set in 18 acres of land, and has its own cricket pitch. This is leased to the Reigate Pilgrims who play here every summer Sunday, with other teams using the ground on Saturdays. Accommodation comprises six en-suite rooms. These have been built in the former squash courts next to the pub. Note the round wooden barn underneath the pub – this is actually the oldest part of the pub.

🛏◁▶✕🐴🚗☸🚭

BLACKBROOK (B2)

Small hamlet on the edge of Holmwood Common.

● Plough at Blackbrook

Blackbrook Road, RH5 4DS
OS: 181466
☎ (01306) 886603
11-3, 6-11 (12-3, 7-10:30 Sunday)
Badger K&B Sussex, Best, Tanglefoot, seasonal beer

A very well run country pub, the Plough has had the same licensee for nearly 25 years, and serves the best Badger beers anywhere. The pub has a good old- fashioned atmosphere, enhanced by the absence of any noisy machines (and mobile phones are banned). Externally the pub is very attractively covered in hanging baskets. All over the walls of the two small bars are old pictures and photographs. Several of these are of the now demolished King and Barnes brewery from Horsham, to which the pub was tied. The bar on the left, the Holmwood Bar, is completely non-smoking. The split-level Blackbrook Bar is where locals tend to congregate, and well-behaved dogs are welcome. The pub is several hundred years old and was a coaching inn. Although built as the Plough, it was known for a while in the 19th century as the William IV. Excellent fresh homemade food is served in both bars, with number of frequently changing daily specials to be found on the blackboard. Proper children's meals are also sold and families are welcome until 9pm. Food is available every lunchtime from 12-2, and evenings from 7-9 Tuesday to Sunday). The Plough is renowned for its wine list, with 16 available by the glass and a further 20 by the bottle, with monthly specials supplementing this.

◁▶🐴🚗☸🚭

BLETCHINGLEY (C2)

An attractive village, there are tile-hung cottages along the picturesque High Street dating from the late 12th century. There were two hunting parks, a Norman castle demolished in 1264, and a Tudor mansion given by Henry VIII to Anne of Cleves in the village. As a rotten borough, it returned two Members of Parliament from 1285. The church dates from Norman times, although there has been restoration over the centuries, and it has a priest's room above the porch. It also houses a monument to Sir Robert Clayton, a former Lord Mayor of London, and a medieval brass of the Trinity.

● Plough Inn

2 High Street, RH1 4PE
OS: 330507 (A25)
☎ (01883) 743711
11-11 (12-10:30 Sunday)
Courage Best Bitter, Directors

Vast establishment on two levels off the main A25 at the east end of the village. You can tell from the signs outside that owners Spirit Group would rather you call the place Millers and not the Plough so it is not surprising to find that this is more restaurant than pub, and quite successful it is too judging by the numbers of cars in the car park on a Sunday afternoon. Food is served all day from an extensive menu until 9.45 (9:30 Sunday). Unusually, you do not need to go to the bar for drinks if you have ordered food, you can order them from one of several till points. Despite the concentration on food, the beer is remarkably good for what it is. There are several distinct areas, not all of which are obvious at first sight - wander round a corner and there are another half dozen tables, then around another corner and there are more tables. It is mostly carpeted in what could be described as a bold pattern, while the area to the front and side of the bar is laid out in floorboards. Outside, the beer garden is also on a large scale and set out in two sections. The upper area is more of a patio while the lower one is grassed over and provides scintillating views of the extensive car park.

● Prince Albert

1 Outwood Lane, RH1 4LR
OS: 327507 (A25)
☎ (01883) 743257
www.thealbert.com
11-11 (Closed 3-6 Monday and Tuesday; open 12-10:30 Sunday)
Itchen Valley Godfathers, Fagin's
Guest Beer

The Prince Albert has been known as such since 1882, although the building dates back to about 1500. It was originally a three bay medieval timber framed open hall house. Today it is a very welcoming pub which has a central bar serving three rooms. The separate non-smoking restaurant for 30 can be booked for private parties. The culinary highlight each month is a fresh fish night on the last Friday with 18 or more seasonal varieties being available. In the summer the secluded suntrap of a garden, with fishpond, can be a good place enjoy a quiet pint or three. The guest beer changes regularly. Food is available every session, lunchtime from 12-2:30 and evenings from 6:30-9:30 (9 Sunday). Darts is played in one of the three bars. Although the pub does not have its own car park, there is ample parking space in front.

Red Lion

Castle Street, RH1 4NU
OS: 324507 (A25)
☎ (01883) 743342
Greene King IPA, Abbot Ale, guest beer

Dating from 1309 when it was known as the Maid, this is the oldest pub in the area, although the main building is of much later construction. The oldest parts are on the right hand side. It is now a smoky, traditional, L-shaped bar with no gimmicks other than good food, which is available every session except Monday night, and is served in the separate restaurant. Pictures of the pub adorn the walls, showing it in all its liveries since its Mellersh & Neale days, and a wood burning stove supplies the heat. The guest beer is supplied by Greene King.

● Whyte Harte Inn

11/21 High Street, RH1 4PB
OS: 326507 (A25)
☎ (01883) 743231
11-11 (12-10:30 Sunday)
Fuller's London Pride
Wells Bombardier
Guest Beer

A very old grade II listed inn on the widest part of the High Street, the Whyte Harte has reputedly been a hostelry since 1388. It is constructed from ships' timbers that were said to be 400 years old then. There have been several alterations and additions since but a lot of character and attractive features remain within. Note the most unusual inn sign in the forecourt. The main entrance opens on to a fairly modern style (but well beamed) bar, and to the right, the building seems to have had a Brewer's Tudor makeover many years ago. On your left, however, is the most interesting part of the building. There are no less than three impressive fireplaces. The first, known as "chimney corner", is surrounded by comfy leather settees and has a fire-back in the grate dated 1613. Beyond is the restaurant area divided into three sections (all no smoking) and each quite different. There are many exposed beams and rough plasterwork throughout and a variety of flooring materials have been used. In the back room is an old recess next to the fireplace, thought to be an old bread oven, which now houses an illuminated display of various objects. When Bletchingley was a rotten borough, the elections were held in here. It is good to see that the present owners have striven hard and succeeded in raising the standards in this historic inn, which had sadly seen a decline in its fortunes in recent years. Food is served Monday to Thursday from 12-3 and 6- 9; Friday and Saturday 12-10; and Sunday 12-6. There are nine well-appointed letting rooms. For lovers of the grape, twenty different wines are sold by the glass. There are seats outside the pub plus a rear beer garden. Darts competitions are held regularly, and there is a quiz every Thursday. Whilst records show that from the 1930s this was a Mellersh & Neale house and latterly Friary Meux, an old photo in the bar reveals that the Southwark brewers, Barclay Perkins once held the tie, when the pub was just called the White Hart. It is now part of the Massive Pub Co. chain, and the guest beer will be from one of the larger regional brewers.

● William IV

Little Common Lane, RH1 4QF
OS: 322509
☎ (01883) 743278
12-3, 6-11 (12-11 Saturday and 12-10:30 Sunday)
Adnams Bitter
Fuller's London Pride
Greene King Ruddles County
Harveys Sussex Best Bitter

A warm, quiet, low-beamed two-bar Victorian pub, the William IV was originally built as two cottages in the 1850s. The pub is entered via stone steps from a narrow country lane, although a ramp provides easier access at the side of the pub for the less mobile. Seating is available in both of the small bars at the front. The bar to the left of the pub is larger and L-shaped; the other bar is tiny. There is also a separate restaurant lying to the rear. Food is available all day Saturday and Sunday, although in winter this stops at 3:15 on Sunday; otherwise fresh homemade food is available each lunchtime and evening. The restaurant even provides a take-away service. Outside is a pleasant old-fashioned garden

◁▶ ✕ 🚗 ☸

BLINDLEY HEATH (D2)

Village strung out down either side of the main A22. The Tsar of Russia, among others, attended a boxing match here in 1815.

Blue Anchor

Eastbourne Road, RH7 6JL
OS: 363455 (A22)
☎ (01342) 830001
Bass (summer only)
Harveys Sussex Best Bitter
Food orientated pub on the A22, which does food all day, every day. There are three separate areas, with a couple of steps between each, all containing open fires. The main area is non-smoking. There are disabled parking spaces and the second entrance is the one that is for wheelchair use. For a period in the 1990s the pub changed its name to the Farmhouse Table, reverting to its original name a few years later.

Red Barn

Tandridge Lane, RH7 6LL
OS: 370452
☎ (01342) 834272
Greene King Old Speckled Hen
Marston's Pedigree
Family pub-restaurant, the converted old barn is non-smoking and is laid for diners. It has wooden beams and is decorated with farm implements. There is another, smaller, area round the bar and a children's section consisting of three rooms, two of which are play areas, with a table football table in one. There is also a children's play area in the garden and the Brewers Fayre food includes a children's menu. Food is served all day, every day. The disabled toilet has nappy changing facilities and there are disabled spaces in the large car park.

White House Hotel
off Eastbourne Road OS: 368445
This hotel, bar and restaurant was hidden away down a track off the main road. Only keg beers were sold, and the whole place burnt down in the 1980s.

BOXHILL (B2)

Well known beauty spot that is long famous as a destination for day-trippers from London. It comprises an extensive area of woodland and chalk downs with several varieties of box tree growing on its slopes. Owned by the National Trust, there are many beautiful walks, and views to the South Downs, with an Information Centre, shop and snack servery. A fort dates from the 1890s and was

part of London's defences. Below this, Major Peter Labilliere was buried upside down, so that "as the world was turned topsy turvey he might come right at last". The area is associated with several literary figures including Keats and George Meredith. Boxhill village sits at the summit of the hill and comprises scattered houses interspersed with mobile home parks.

Hand In Hand

Boxhill Road, KT20 7PS
OS: 203520
☎ (01737) 843352
Fuller's London Pride
Occasional **Guest Beer**
Two bar brick-built pub on the eastern end of the village. There are darts and pool in the public bar to the side, an eating area in the front lounge bar and a large function room at the back. Food, most of which is home cooked, is served lunchtimes and evenings, Monday till Friday, and till 7pm on Sundays. Fridays is live music night and it is open all day, and till midnight on a Saturday.

Smith & Western

Boxhill Road, KT20 7LB
OS: 187513
☎ (01737) 841666
No real ale
This modern American bar/grill/diner is to be found on the western edge of the village. Most of the space is taken up by the restaurant, which seats 150, but there is also a bar area at the front. Food, which includes a kids' menu and sandwiches as well as steaks, ribs, fajitas etc, is served all day. Previous names of this pub have been Boxers, the Smugglers Inn, La Collina and the Boxhill Tavern.

BROADHAM GREEN (D2)

Small village slowly becoming part of Oxted to the north.

● Haycutter

69 Tanhouse Road, RH8 9PE
OS: 391513
☎ (01883) 712550
11:30-3, 5-11 (11:30-3, 6-11 Saturday and 12-10:30 Sunday)
Fuller's London Pride
Young's Bitter
Freshly prepared restaurant quality food is one of the features of this country pub. This is available every day apart from Sunday evening, although it is sold until 5pm on that day. Two-thirds of the main bar is non-smoking. The pub was built in 1851 and was originally part of the Westerham Ales estate. Today the pub is also notable for its separate skittle alley. This is very popular and must be booked in advance.

◁▶ 🚗 ❄ 🚭

BROCKHAM (B2)

A picture postcard village with a large green surrounded by attractive cottages, a white firestone church dating from 1847 that was designed by Benjamin Ferrey, a pupil of Augustus Pugin, and Box Hill to the north. The green is used for several annual events including a Victorian Fair and a schools fête and flower show. For several years, in October, the Village Club has hosted an excellent three-day beer festival. An Act of Parliament in 1812 allowed only poultry to de-pasture the green, and cattle and horses were impounded in the Pound (still standing) until a fine had been paid to the Lord of the Manor. This Act is thought to have been passed following the goring to death of a Mr Edward Worley by a boar on the green. There were limekilns in use locally until the 1930s. There are many delightful walks starting and finishing on the green passing along bridleways and footpaths along the River Mole and across open countryside. The major event of the year is the Brockham Bonfire, which takes place on the Saturday nearest to the 5th November. Construction of this begins in September. On the day of the bonfire the village is taken over by thousands of visitors who enjoy the spectacle of a torchlight procession with a magnificent Guy, the ceremonial lighting of the bonfire, and a brilliant firework display. Unfortunately the green is no longer used for village cricket, but in days gone by high calibre players such as WG Grace were known to have played there. The name Brockham is usually associated with badgers, but may more simply mean the settlement by the brook. Just to the north of the village is Dorking Rugby Club, and to the west is Betchworth Castle, a mostly ruined 14th century construction.

● **Duke's Head**

Brockham Green, RH3 7JS
OS: 197497
www.dukeshead-surrey.co.uk
☎ (01737) 845101
11-3, 5-11 (11-11 Friday and Saturday, 12-10:30 Sunday)
Adnams Bitter
Fuller's London Pride
Occasional **Guest Beer**

In a pleasant spot in the far corner of the village green, the Dukes Head only dates from around 1900, although there has been a pub on the site since at least 1711. The present building replaced one that burnt down in 1899. The single bar serves a number of different beamed areas including a separate restaurant. Here the walls have been attractively stripped back to the bare bricks, and a real fire is to be found here. The main bar has a wooden floor and some comfortable seats set back into the window. The subdued lighting helps to create a relaxing atmosphere throughout the pub. To the right of the bar is a raised area with four tables and some local pictures on the wall. At the rear of the pub, leading to the garden is a small area containing a couple of electronic games. The food is homemade and most of the produce is locally sourced. The main menu is supplemented by several specials written on the blackboard. Food is available 12-2:30 and 6-9:30 Monday to Saturday, and 12-4 Sunday for roasts. Families are welcome until 9pm. Disabled access is from the car park.

● Royal Oak

Brockham Green, OS: 197496
☎ (01737) 843241
11-3, 5:30-11 (11-11 Friday and Saturday, 12-10:30 Sunday)
Adnams Bitter, Broadside
Fuller's London Pride
Guest Beer

Overlooking the village green to the front and with Box Hill to the rear, the Royal Oak is in a very attractive spot. The single bar serves very distinct public and lounge areas. The former has a wooden floor and darts to one side. A log-burning stove is a welcome addition on cold days. The carpeted lounge is popular with diners. Traditional English food is available each lunchtime and evening Monday to Saturday, and up until 5pm Sunday night. At the bottom part of the lounge is a small non-smoking area. As the pub is situated on the Greensand Way footpath it is a popular stopping off point for walkers. The pub is due to be tastefully extended and refurbished.

◁▶

BUCKLAND (B2)

A small village, with a picturesque pond and green, which straddles the A25. A gruesome legend exists about the Buckland Shag, a monster that lived by a stone by a stream. Nowadays a Morris Side goes by this name. The church has a 15th century timber belfry and 14th century stained glass, but was rebuilt in 1860. Next to the pond is a tithe barn with turret and weather vane.

Jolly Farmers

Reigate Road, RH3 7BG
OS: 229508 (A25)
☎ (01737) 221355
Adnams Bitter

A comfortable and pleasant dining pub, food is available each day from 12-10 (9:30 Sunday). The single bar is well broken up into separate areas, much of it non-smoking, and hops are to be found on many of the internal beams. The area to the front of the bar has a tiled floor and a wood-burning stove, and towards the rear of the pub is another real fire. A couple of dozen wines are available by the glass, and families are welcome in the bar or in the heated patio garden. The pub also has facilities for the disabled.

BURGH HEATH (B1)

A residential area with a large supermarket; the name comes from the de Burgh family. It has now merged with Banstead to the north and Tadworth to the southwest.

Heathside

Brighton Road, KT20 6BW
OS: 243575 (A217)
☎ (01737) 353355
No real ale

Opened in 1998 on the site of the former Heathside Hotel, this large, food orientated, pub is attached to a Premier Lodge which has accommodation. The open plan bar is split into several seating areas, most of which are laid for food, and which is served all day. The Brewers Fayre menu includes a Kids' Menu.

Surrey Yeoman

Reigate Road, KT20 5NT
OS: 242578

This 19th century listed building was one of the very few pubs in

East Surrey that originally took advantage of all day opening when this was introduced in 1988. A former Charrington pub, it was swapped with Greene King who closed it down in the late 1990s, by which time it was rather run down. Housing is now on the site.

BURSTOW (C3)

The birthplace of the 19th century cricketer William Lambert, who was the first to score a century in both innings at Lords. He is buried in the churchyard. The church has a timber tower and shingle spire and the first Astronomer Royal, John Flamsteed, was rector here for 35 years until his death in 1719. While in charge of the Greenwich Observatory, he determined the position of almost 3,000 stars. The winter quarters of Lord John Sanger's circus were at Burstow Lodge Farm from 1900-1941.

● Shipley Bridge Inn

Antland Lane, RH6 9TE
OS: 307404
☎ (01293) 785237
11-11 (12-10:30 Sunday)
Harveys Sussex Best Bitter
Guest Beers

This old world, food orientated pub has been split into several separate areas. There are hop covered wooden beams, real fires and a specials menu, which always includes some fish dishes. Main meals are served all day from 12-10 Monday to Saturday and from 12-9:30 on Sunday with snacks served until 6pm each day. Two-thirds of the pub is non-smoking and the background music tends to be classical or jazz. The two guest beers, from the pub company Spirit's list, change weekly, and are usually from the larger independent breweries.

◁▶ 🚗 ☸ 🚭 ♿

CAPEL (B3)

A quiet village now bypassed by the A24. The village was once a staging post on the old London to Worthing coaching route. A number of old farms and houses in the area date from between the 15th and 17th centuries. The church is 13th century, but was rebuilt in Victorian times. The parish once had a curate who wrote a charm against toothache. A legend exists that if you walk around the yew tree in the churchyard 100 times at midnight, a ghost will appear. A local family brought the Quaker movement to the village, with their home becoming the local Headquarters.

● Crown

98 The Street, RH5 5JY
OS: 175406
☎ (01306) 711130
12-11 (open 11-11 Saturday, 12-10-30 Sunday)
Guest Beers

This attractive 16th century local is set back from the main road and has two separate bars. Set back from the main road, the frontage comprises old bricks and wooden beams. The wooden floored front bar is called the Sportsman's Bar and has a pool table in a raised area, and a television for sport. The small lounge area has many old pennies and other coins stuck onto the beams. This leads to a large single storey extension which is used as a restaurant, part of which has flagstones, where a variety of food is served from 12-2:30 and 6:30-9:30 Monday to Saturday, and from 12-8 Sunday. The menu consists of fresh fish and English and authentic Greek dishes. Two frequently changing beers are sold, often from microbreweries. Cottage is a particular favourite. Outside is a large and pleasant garden. Children are welcome here or in the restaurant.

◁▶✕🚗☸♿🚲

Kings Head
The Street OS: 175409
The King's Head was a large old L-shaped building, with two distinct parts dating from different times. It was a Friary Meux pub that was converted into housing around 1986. The building still stands today.

Surrey Hills Hotel
Horsham Road, RH5 4PG
OS: 177425
☎ (01306) 711522
www.surreyhillshotel.co.uk
No real ale
The bar in this hotel is only open Monday to Saturday evenings. The hotel specialises in functions such as cabaret nights and dinner-dances, which are held in a large function room with its own bar. The hotel is popular for wedding receptions and for corporate events, and the bar may be closed to the public when these are held. Ten en-suite bedrooms are available.

CATERHAM (C2)

Caterham is split into two distinct parts. Remnants of the old downland village can be seen in Caterham-on-the-Hill. The modern town developed after the arrival of the railway in 1856. The Guards Depot, now converted to housing, was built in 1877, as was St Lawrence's hospital.

Blacksmiths Arms (Map 1)
39 High Street, CR3 5UE
OS: 334559 (B2030)
☎ (01883) 347917
Fuller's London Pride
Guest Beer
One basic L-shaped bar with a rear raised area. A tiled side awning at 1st-floor level provides cover for outside tables, whilst the former off-sales department fronting the High Street may yet be restored as a dining area. The side entrance door contains a few vestigial remnants of Charrington leaded glass. Pool and darts are played, and the pub is open all day from 10:00am (12 on Sunday). The illuminated garden contains a water feature. Black Rod is inscribed on the pub sign - ask the landlord for an explanation! The one guest beer tends to come from the larger breweries. Food is available each session apart from Sunday evening.

Caterham Arms (Map 2)
Coulsdon Road, CR3 5NF
OS: 326560
☎ (01883) 341871
No real ale
This large late Victorian/Edwardian building has several later additions to it. Once popular with soldiers from the (now gone) Caterham Barracks, an IRA pub bombing took place here on Sunday 28th September 1975, causing huge damage and injuries, but fortunately no fatalities. Now it is an open plan bar with darts and pool tables galore and is open all day. Sport is shown on large screen TVs.

● Clifton Arms (Map 3)
110 Chaldon Road, CR3 5PH
OS: 328556 (B2031)
☎ (01883) 343525
11-2:30, 4-11 (12-11 Saturday and 12-10:30 Sunday)
Fuller's London Pride
Young's Bitter
Guest Beer

Westons Organic Vintage, Old Rosie, Country Perry

This former Charrington pub is host to a fantastic collection of artefacts relating to both local history and militaria which have to be seen to be believed: photos, uniforms, flags, deactivated firearms, swords, musical instruments, enamel advertisements plus much more cover almost every inch of the walls! The place rivals Caterham's East Surrey Museum! The wooden bar-back is also most impressive and a fine example of the genre. A fine selection of real ciders (and occasionally, perry) is served from containers behind the bar. The back room doubles as a restaurant and on Saturday evenings, a Rock 'n' Roll disco. Armstrong-Siddeley enthusiasts will enjoy this pub. The guest beer changes and is usually from an independent brewery. Games enthusiasts can choose between darts, pool and shove halfpenny. A pub that is really well worth a visit for the beer, food and ambience - once visited it is very hard to leave. No food is available Sunday or Monday evening.

◁▶🚗☸

Cloisters
19a Godstone Road, CR3 6RE
OS: 343553 (B2030)
Closed and converted to an Indian restaurant in 2004. Once K.C.'s wine bar, these former shop premises used to sell three real ales.

Golden Lion (Map 4)

2 Town End, CR3 5UG
OS: 334560 (B2031)
☎ (01883) 349453
Greene King IPA
Wells Bombardier
One bar corner pub, with a few structural divisions giving the impression that this was once a multi-roomed pub. Flat screen televisions in all areas mean there is no escape from this medium. A locals' pub which has a strong sports following, with pool and darts predominating in the area which was probably once the public bar. A large conservatory at the rear is mostly used for functions. There is a small no smoking area, which ceases to be designated as such at 6:30 every night. Food is served 12-4 every day - roast dinners only on Sunday. No evidence remains of its former life as an Ind Coope house. Open all day.

● King & Queen (Map 5)

34 High Street, CR3 5UA
OS: 334558 (B2030)
☎ (01883) 345438
11-11 (12-10:30 Sunday)
Fuller's Chiswick Bitter, Discovery, London Pride, ESB

Wonderful 400-year old red brick and Surrey flint pub, which, in the 1840s, evolved from three former cottages, one of which was a former bakery. It was one of Caterham's early alehouses. It still retains three distinct areas – a front bar facing the main road, a high-ceilinged wooden-beamed middle room, with inglenook fireplace, where darts is played, and a small lower-level rear area leading adjoining a rear patio garden. The name refers to Britain's only joint monarchy, William & Mary. No food is available on Sunday.

◁▶🚗☸

● Old Surrey Hounds (Map 6)

1 The Square, CR3 6QA
OS: 341556 (B2208)
☎ (01883) 343267
11-11 (12-10:30 Sunday)
Greene King Abbot Ale
Shepherd Neame Spitfire
Young's Special
Guest Beer

Busy and popular, a Brewer's Tudor bay-windowed town centre pub handy for Caterham station. Although the usual single bar knock-through has occurred, two side wings of differing length remain, the larger of these playing host to the big screen TV on which sport is shown. Formerly a Barclay Perkins establishment, of which a few old photos can be found, it is now very much reminiscent of the Scottish Courage house style before they abandoned their pubs to PubCos. Guest beers from the Spirit group often make an appearance. Food is available every day from 12-6. Darts played.

◁☸♿🚌🚲

Pengelly's Wine Bar
161 Coulsdon Road, CR3 5NG
OS: 325564
Small wine bar that sold real ale and cider for a while in the mid 1980s. It later became Spirals Wine Bar, selling no real ale, before closing for good.

● Royal Oak (Map 7)

68 High Street, CR3 5UB
OS: 334556 (B2030)
☎ (01883) 343510
11-11 (12-10:30 Sunday)
Fuller's London Pride
Harveys Sussex Best Bitter
Guest Beer

The front L-shaped bar is decorated with period military and naval photos and prints, whilst a separate rear bar (without real ale) is sports-themed and has its own servery. Some delightful art nouveau stained-glass windows survive in the side wall. This former Charrington's pub used to be a bakery, becoming a pub around about 1877. Darts is played, and families are welcome until 8pm. The rotating guest beer tends to come from one of the larger independents. No food is sold on Sunday.

◁🐴☸♿

Tally Ho (Map 8)
200 Coulsdon Road, CR3 5ND
OS: 324565
☎ (01883) ex directory
Greene King IPA
Near the county boundary, the brick and Brewer's Tudor exterior still bears reminders of the pub's previous life under Charrington's. The inside reveals that extreme rarity nowadays - separate saloon and public bars. Note the classic Charrington's wooden bar-back

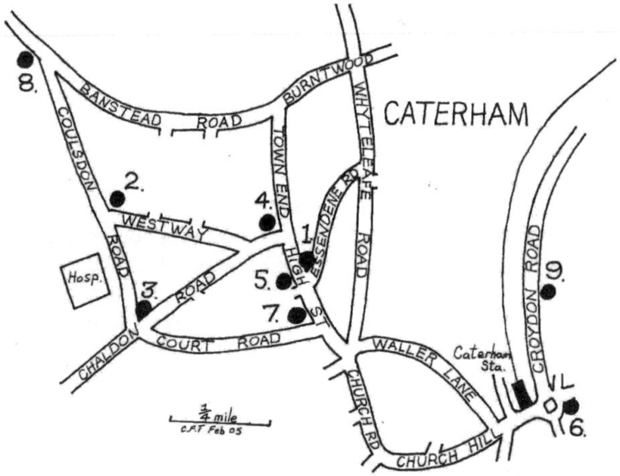

surviving in the former. Darts and pool are both played. Close to the former barracks - now converted to housing and handy for Tesco. The pub is open all day.

● Valley (Map 9)

78 Croydon Road, CR3 6QD
OS: 341557 (B2208)
☎ (01883) 332800
11-11 (12-10:30 Sunday)
Adnams Broadside
Fuller's London Pride
Young's Bitter

Converted from two cottages is 1866 and called the Dominion, it then became the Commonwealth (possibly to reflect the shift away from Empire). It was renamed the Fountain in the early 1990s and is now the Valley, not to be confused with the pub of the same name which stood opposite the station. With so many former names, it's a wonder this pub doesn't suffer from an identity crisis! Its new name may reflect the fact that the old Valley Cinema used to be situated behind it. Originally the pub was a Nalder & Collyer (Croydon) house, latterly Ind Coope and Friary Meux. Note the distinctive scallop shaped entrance portico. Darts played. No food on Sunday evening.

Valley
7 Station Avenue, CR3 6LB
OS: 342554
Unusually for Surrey, the Valley was a Whitbread pub. It even made the Good Beer Guide from 1982 to 1984 when it was enticingly described as an "expensive steakhouse". Originally the pub was the Valley Hotel and was a Trust House with nine bedrooms and an assembly room with a dance floor, which accommodated 100 people. By 1986 part of the pub was converted into a Pizza Hut, and the bar became a noisy place with video screens around the walls. The pub became a full part of the pizza restaurant in the late 1980s.

CHALDON (C2)

The 11th century church of St Peter and St Paul is near the old Pilgrim's Way and contains one of the most outstanding medieval wall paintings still in existence in Britain. The mural covers the entire west wall of the church and is believed to have been painted around 1200, but was covered over during the reformation, and was only uncovered in 1870. Now known as the Chaldon Doom, it depicts gory scenes from the Last Judgement and the Ladder of Salvation.

● Harrow

235 Stanstead Road, CR3 6AJ
OS: 327538
☎ (01883) 343260
12-11 (12-10:30 Sunday)
Greene King Abbot Ale
Marston's Pedigree
Ringwood Best Bitter
Wadworth 6X

Situated a few yards from the Pilgrim's Way on the ridge of the North Downs, this pub claims to be the highest in Surrey (it is actually the second highest). Through the front stable-door, a small low-ceilinged bar leads to a larger room and then to partially-separate restaurant area which was originally converted from a previously freestanding outhouse. Food is served every day from 12-3 and 6-9. All the rear part of the pub is non-smoking. This was an original Westerham Brewery house, which latterly became part of Allied's Friary Meux chain and indeed still described as such on the pub sign. Live music (bands) on Friday nights and a quiz night every Monday. Loyal staff - one has worked here for over 35 years!

◁▶✗ (lunchtime only)
🚗 ❄ ⊘ ♿

CHARLWOOD (B3)

Charlwood prospered in medieval and Tudor times due to the local iron industry, but is now overshadowed by Gatwick Airport, which replaced a racecourse and a small aerodrome in the 1930s. St Nicholas church is grade I listed, and has murals dating from around 1300 which tell the story of St Margaret, and a medieval screen. The non-conformist Providence Chapel is Grade 2* listed and is built in an unusual American colonial style. Lowfield Heath windmill is a post mill which originally stood near the airport, but was moved and re-erected on the outskirts of the village towards Russ Hill. The 1972 Local Government Act, which came into force on 1 April 1974, actually transferred Charlwood (and Horley) to West Sussex, but such was the local outcry over this, the separate "Charlwood and Horley Act 1974" reversed this decision. However, much of the village could be destroyed should Gatwick Airport build a second runway.

Flight Tavern

Charlwood Road, Lowfield Heath
RH11 0QA OS: 261398
☎ (01293) 653951
Fullers London Pride
Greene King IPA

A former club, this attractive bow fronted pub opened in the 1980s. The small serving area serves a large split bar, which includes a cosy snug area housed in an extension to the right. The pub is decorated in rustic style with beams, fireplaces and wooden floors. It is open all day and food is food always available. The pub is in West Sussex, but is in an area that was part of Surrey until 1974. Outside there is a garden which has good views of the many planes flying overhead.

Greyhound

12 The Street, RH6 0BY
OS: 243411
☎ (01293) 862203
Greene King IPA, Abbot Ale

Dishonestly advertising itself as a free house, this Greene King tied pub offers a Hungry Horse menu all day. Originally a Charrington's house, it consists of a large and bright front bar leading to a rear restaurant section. A small no-smoking area can be found to the left of the bar. A small patio garden is beyond the restaurant. The walls of the bar are mainly covered with adverts for food and drink offers. A quiz night is held Tuesday, and children are admitted until 9pm. Disabled facilities are to be found in the ladies toilet only.

● Half Moon

73 The Street, RH 6 0DS
OS: 242411
☎ (01293) 863414
12-11 (12-10:30 Sunday)
Greene King Old Speckled Hen
Young's Bitter
This attractive, partly Horsham tiled, 15th century pub is to be found next to the church. It has been extended several times in its history, and further work is planned which will increase the floor space. A number of separate drinking areas are served from the single bar, each painted a striking red colour. The bar itself has some low beams, and throughout the pub are pieces of polished brassware, including some old guns. A drinking area up from the bar contains an unobtrusive TV and there is a secluded bar near the entrance. The main bar area extends and narrows towards the rear. There are some excellent wooden beams in the central part of the pub. Good food is served, and families are welcome until 5pm. No food Sunday evening. A third beer may well be available.
◁▶🐎❄

Rising Sun

64 The Street, RH6 0DS
OS: 242413
☎ (01293) 863709
Fuller's London Pride
Greene King IPA, Old Speckled Hen
Harveys Sussex Best Bitter
Guest Beer
Very much a workingman's village pub, with colourful language to match, the Rising Sun used to belong to Page & Overtons, and a photo inside shows this. Above the fireplace is a Thompson's of Walmer mirror, a relic of another brewery snapped up by Charrington's. One of the beams in the bar is engraved with the date 1888. Traditional home made food is available at lunchtime, and the pub is open all day for drinking. There is a separate function room / restaurant to the rear.

Russ Hill Hotel

Russ Hill, RH6 0EL
OS: 227402
☎ (01293) 862171
No real ale
Built as a country house in the 1880s, this large hotel serves food each session, but the bar serves nothing but keg and bottled beers.

Stanhill Court Hotel

Stanhill, RH6 0EP
OS: 231423
www.stanhillcourthotel.co.uk
☎ (01293) 862166
No real ale
A 14-bedroom hotel, it was built in 1881 by William Young, a marine underwriter with Lloyds of London, and is set in 35 acres of countryside. The Patio Bar has a glass roof, two stories above floor level, making it surprisingly light. One of the bar walls is adorned with a complete set of champagne bottles of all sizes, including a Nebuchadnezzar, which holds 20 normal sized bottles. The bar also has seven huge barrels perched above it. Food is served each session and there is a wine list comprising 200 bottles. The bar is open all day.

CHELSHAM (D1)

High up on the slopes in north-east Surrey, it is said that from

The Pilgrim Brewery

"Your thirst fought every day"

PILGRIM DRAUGHT BEERS

Regular Favourites

Surrey Bitter 3.7%
Progress Best Bitter 4.0%
Porter 4.0%

Summer/Winter Beers

Crusader Premium Bitter 4.9%
Talisman Winetr Warmer 5.0%

Seasonal Beers

Excalibur 4.5%
Autumnal 4.5%
Pudding 7.3%

Pilgrim Brewery
West Street
Reigate
RH2 9BL
01737 222651
www.pilgrim.co.uk

the 13th century St Leonard's Church one can see Crystal Palace and Greenwich Observatory. Thomas Kelly, the son of a local farmer, who became Lord Mayor of London in 1836, is buried in the churchyard.

● Bull Inn

The Common, CR6 9PB
OS: 372590
☎ (01883) 622970
12-11 (11-11 Saturday and 12-10:30 Sunday)
Fuller's London Pride
Greene King IPA
The Bull is a large detached Victorian former Charrington's pub overlooking the common. It is very much a locals' pub and features live music (Saturday) and a quiz night (Tuesday), which are keenly supported. A television and juke box dominate the bar, where darts is also played. Lunchtime food is sold Tuesday to Sunday from 12-3. A recent addition is the Thai Garden Restaurant, situated in the old lounge to the left of the bar, which is open from 6-10, Monday to Saturday. The Bull is on the 409 and 411 bus routes.

◁▶✕🐎🚗☸

CHIPSTEAD (C1)

Sir Edward Banks, a distinguished public works contractor, built London, Waterloo and Southwark bridges, and is commemorated in the 12th century church of St Margaret. The village is mainly residential, but has open countryside close by.

Midday Sun

Outwood Lane, CR5 3NA
OS: 282590
☎ (01737) 552644
Greene King IPA, Abbot Ale, Old Speckled Hen
Built in 1938 by Watney's and named in honour of the 1937 Derby winner, the first to be owned by a woman, Mrs G B Miller. Ironically, it later was bought by the Magic Pub Company and re-named the Hungry Horse. Fortunately it has reverted back to its proper name but it still carries that epithet which is used by the current owners, Greene King, for their chain of budget, family oriented food outlets. There are two separate bars, the right-hand one being the public and dominated by big screen projector TV and pool table. The entrance to the left takes you into the restaurant but there is also a no-smoking lounge bar area. There is a separate children's play area and a function room at the rear with its own bar. Food is available all day from 12-9.

● Rambler's Rest

Outwood Lane, CR5 3NP
OS: 274575
☎ (01737) 552661
12-11 (12-10:30 Sunday)
Wadworth 6X
Guest Beer
A rambling collection of old buildings once known as Dene Farm, with records dating back to 1301 - although the oldest surviving building dates from the time of Queen Elizabeth I. It ceased to operate as a farm in 1932 when it became a teashop charging 1/3d for cream teas! After the war some of the outbuildings were turned into a large antique shop and in 1966 the whole lot was sold and became a restaurant. In 1993 Whitbread bought it and turned it into a pub. It is still owned by them but trades under the pub chain name of Out & Out. It is unashamedly food oriented and the whole operation is geared up for this, with numbered tables throughout the bar and garden as well as a separate restaurant. Sadly little of the original interior survives, as most of the internal walls have been knocked out for open plan drinking/dining. However there are some exposed beams,

flag-stoned floors and several real fires. The pub section decor is minimalist-contemporary, whilst the restaurant does retain traces of its ancestry and is a lot cosier. Service is most hospitable and the two real ales reasonably well kept. The rotating guest beer tends to be one of the national brands. The shiny stainless steel handpumps are unusual. Food is available every day from
12-10. At present only the restaurant is non-smoking but this is likely to change.

● White Hart
Hazelwood Lane, CR5 3QW
OS: 278570
☎ (01737) 554455
12-11 (12-10:30 Sunday)
Fuller's London Pride
Young's Bitter
Guest Beer

Attractive 19th century Inn at the south end of Chipstead village with good views across the recreation ground to open country. The opening in December 2004 of a no-smoking restaurant at the rear of the pub (happily in-keeping with the existing architectural style) has increased capacity considerably. The old front bar, which also has a non-smoking area, is the bastion of local drinkers and remains traditional in design with some pleasant moulded cornices, original wood paneling and real fires. A former Charrington's house, evidence of the Croydon brewer Page & Overton's original ownership is contained in an old photograph just inside the front entrance along with a potted history of a former tenant from the late 1800s. Diners are well catered for in the new extension known as the "Red Room" for reasons that will be come apparent upon entry! Food is available all day, every day from 12.00 to 10pm. The current lessee has made his mark on the pub and all electronic games and piped music have been consigned to history - the emphasis is entirely on drink and food. The guest beer rotates from a list. Curiously, the only ATM in Chipstead is to be found in the side lobby! The pub has no garden but there is a fair sized outdoor drinking area at the front.

COLDHARBOUR (B3)
Coldharbour clings to the steep escarpment below Leith Hill and is the highest village in Surrey. In the past it was associated with smuggling, as were other villages in the vicinity. The area is popular with walkers. Close by Leith Hill Tower was built in 1765 to bring the height of the hill from 965 feet (294 metres) to 1,000 feet (a mountain!). An Iron Age camp at Anstiebury was used in the Napoleonic Wars to shelter women and children from Dorking while the men fought the French. Ralph Vaughan Williams lived at Leith Hill Place and founded the Leith Hill Festival, held annually in Dorking Halls.

● Plough Inn
Coldharbour Lane, RH5 6HD
OS: 152441
www.ploughinn.com
☎ (01306) 711793
11:30-11 (12-10:30 Sunday)
Leith Hill Crooked Furrow, Tallywhacker
Ringwood Old Thumper

Shepherd Neame Master Brew Bitter, Spitfire
Guest Beer
Biddenden Medium Cider
The Plough is the home of the Leith Hill Brewery, which is situated in an outbuilding at the rear. The pub dates from the 17th century and was originally on one of the coaching routes from London to the south coast. Despite being tucked away in a sleepy village, first-rate meals are served in the restaurant, and six en-suite guest rooms are available. In summer the large garden comes into its own, as does a converted barn, now the Family Room, making it a good stop on a country walk. An additional beer is sold in spring and summer.

COPTHORNE (C3)

The main part of the village is in West Sussex but Copthorne Bank is in Surrey. Edward Wilson, who accompanied Captain Scott on his ill-fated attempt on the South Pole, is remembered in the Copthorne School chapel where he visited his brother-in-law.

Abergavenny Arms
Common Road, RH10 3LB
OS: 327393 (A264)
This 100 year old pub was owned by Tamplins, who were part of the Watney's empire. Situated just over the Sussex county boundary, the Sussex Border footpath ran past the pub. The basic public bar had pool and darts, and there was a real fire in the lounge.

● Cherry Tree

Copthorne Bank, RH10 3JG
OS: 332400
☎ (01342) 712427
11-11 (12-10:30 Sunday)
Badger K&B Sussex, Best, seasonal beer
This gem of a pub on the outskirts of Copthorne village is over 400 years old, and used to be a library. There are two entrances off the main road into what were once two separate bars, plus an entrance from the beer garden in summer. The interior is a wild mixture with floorboards, flagstones and carpet, while the walls are either panelled, papered or bare brick. The walls throughout are adorned with tasteful bric-a-brac and old black and white photographs. A large inglenook fireplace dominates the area to the right of the bar. There are two distinct drinking areas separated by a knocked through doorway, both served by the one central bar. In addition to fairly standard pub food there are also curries which can be ordered to take away as well as eat in. The restaurant area is round the back, and if it is not too busy, they will let you drink there without eating. The large beer garden also has a fenced off children's play area including a swing or two. At the time of survey, the Cherry Tree was about to change from tenancy to management, so things may change.

● Copthorne Effingham Park Hotel

West Park Road, RH10 3EU
OS: 337396 (B2037)
☎ (01342) 714994
11-11 (12-10:30 Sunday)
King Horsham Best
Guest Beer
This large 122-room hotel is built around an old country house and is set in 40 acres of land. It also has its own nine-hole golf course. Forget the uninteresting keg only bar on the ground floor and go to the Sports Bar, down one floor beside the hotel gym instead. It can also be entered via its own entrance at the left hand side of the car park, as well as though the hotel. Although the main function of this

bar is as a member's bar, it is open to the general public as well. The bar itself has a raised area in one corner with a large TV for Sky sports, while a pool table provides alternative entertainment in the main part of the bar. It is a comfortable enough bar without getting the pulse racing, that's what the gym next door is for.

🛏 ◁ ▶ ✕ 🐴 🚗 ❁ ♿

Copthorne Hotel London Gatwick

Copthorne Road, RH10 3PG
OS: 314388 (A264)
☎ (01342) 348800
No real ale

The Copthorne Hotel is built around a 16th century farmhouse, and is just in West Sussex. It contains two separate bars, the Library and the White Swan. At the time of survey neither bar sold real ale, although there were plans to start stocking a proper beer from the Scottish Courage range in the White Swan, which is a genuine pub in its own right. With oak beams and an inglenook fireplace it has far more character than the average chain hotel bar. Food is served all day between 12 and 10 in the White Swan. There is a conservatory off the bar which is non-smoking and where children are allowed. The hotel itself has all the facilities expected from a 4 star hotel.

Duke's Head

Turners Hill Road, Crawley Down
RH10 4HH
OS: 336392 (B2028)
☎ (01342) 712431
Flowers IPA
Fuller's London Pride

Just inside West Sussex, the Dukes Head has a commanding position on the roundabout where Snow Hill meets Turners Hill Road. It is currently the model on which all future Beefeater Inns will be based. As would be expected, over half the pub is dedicated to diners. The car park and roundabout were originally the village pond. Formerly a farmhouse, then a coaching inn, it is now a barn of a place. Open all day, families are welcome until 9pm, and there are facilities for the disabled.

● Hedgehog Inn

Effingham Road, RH10 3HY
OS: 331405 (B2037)
☎ (01342) 716202
11-11 (12-10:30 Sunday)
Harveys Sussex Best Bitter
Wadworth 6X
Guest Beer (summer)

Formerly the Effingham Arms, the pub has one large room with several distinct areas. This includes "the cellar", which it isn't, but is almost a room to itself with several two seater sofas to lounge about in. To the back is the "Garden Room" which leads onto the garden itself where a Mongolian barbecue and outdoor heaters are planned to extend outdoor dining opportunities on colder evenings. The restaurant area itself is to the left of the bar. Food is the main seller here, but there are enough locals, and enough drinking space to make you feel you are still in a pub. The food that is served is all freshly prepared, except for the chips, and is served most of the day between 12 and 10 (8:30 Sunday), although there is usually a break between 4 and 5. If you want something that is not on the menu, just ask, they are always happy to oblige. Given a couple days notice and they can be even more flexible. Nine rooms are also available to let. The guest beer often comes from Harveys. Backgammon, cribbage and chess can be played.

🛏◁▶✕🚗☸♿

Hunters Moon Inn
Copthorne Bank, RH10 3JF
OS: 320397
An old coaching inn which had its own ghost, the Hunters Moon closed in 2004. It was originally called the Builder's Inn, changing its name to the Hunters Moon in 1959. A free house serving a number of beers, its name was the Jamaica Inn for a while in the 1980s. During the 1980s it was run partly as a disco pub, but towards the end of its life it was a hotel catering for the Gatwick trade. At this stage it was advertising itself as a "true English Inn with open log fireplace, comfortable lounges and a walled patio garden". Food was a major part of the pub's trade in these latter years. The building is still standing and is part of a housing development.

Prince Albert
Copthorne Bank, RH10 3QX
OS: 313394
☎ (01342) 712702
Fuller's London Pride
Greene King Abbot Ale
Brash one roomed village centre bar which has been knocked through. A large blue pool table dominates one corner. Mostly laid out with floorboards, but partly carpeted as well. There is a large screen for the main sports events. Pub food is available lunchtimes (not Sunday); however kids' meals are limited and consist of the type of things Jamie Oliver is trying to remove from school meals. Open all day.

CRANLEIGH (A3)

The village expanded rapidly after the railway closed in 1965. It makes claims to be the largest village in England. Charcoal was made in the area from Roman times, and the industry was revived for the manufacture of gasmasks during the Great War. The glass and iron industries were important during the 15th and 16th centuries, and it was a centre for hawking and hunting in the Middle Ages. The Cottage Hospital was founded in a 14th century timbered cottage in 1859, and was the first village hospital in England. Cranleigh School was founded in 1865 by a local rector and doctor for the sons of wealthy farmers. The obelisk commemorates the opening of a turnpike road from Guildford to Horsham in 1794. Vachery Pond to the south was used in the 16th century for the local iron industry and was later developed to feed the summit level of the Wey & Arun Junction canal. The village was originally called Cranley but the name was changed by the Post Office to avoid confusion with Crawley.

Boy & Donkey
Knowle Road, GU6 8JW
OS: 057374
Situated a mile out of Cranleigh, the Boy & Donkey was a fine rural local. It dated from the 16th century and comprised three small rooms, one of which was used as a dining room. Real fires were to be found in each room, with the public bar having an inglenook. In the 1980s the pub was unusual in having a London 5s dartboard as well as a conventional one. Originally a Hodgsons of Kingston pub, it became part of the Courage estate and was sold to Morland of Abingdon in the early 1990s who closed it a few years later. It is now a private house.

INDEPENDENT FAMILY BREWERS

ESTD 1845

GRIFFIN BREWERY

FULLER'S

CHISWICK

If you are looking for great food, traditional surroundings, or a lively atmosphere, there are six great Fuller's pubs in Surrey that will meet your requirements. All serve Fuller's cask ales in excellent condition, including London Pride. Customers will always find a warm welcome whether wanting a place to lunch with family, somewhere to watch the rugby, or a chance to enjoy a quiet pint. All six of the pubs can be found within the pages of this guide.

Caterham-on-the Hill

The King & Queen

Epsom

The Barley Mow

Dorking

The Cricketers Inn

Dorking

The Queen's Head

Westcott

The Prince of Wales

Outwood

The Bell

Cranley Hotel
The Common, GU6 8SQ
OS: 051394 (B2128)
☎ (01483) 272827
Courage Best Bitter
Greene King Old Speckled Hen
Marston's Pedigree
This ivy clad 19th century pub with accommodation was originally built as the Railway Hotel when Cranleigh had a station. The bar is open all day and is split into separate areas, with sofas in the small lower part at the back. Darts and pool are both available. Accommodation consists of seven en-suite rooms. There is a disco some weekends, and a big screen TV for sports.

● **Little Park Hatch**
Bookhurst Road, GU6 7DN
OS: 070397 (B2127)
☎ (01483) 274374
11-11 (12-10:30 Sunday)
Bass
Shepherd Neame Spitfire
Young's Bitter
This friendly one bar pub, was originally an old farmhouse, and was converted to a pub about 30 years ago. Open all day, it is sports orientated, with successful golf and darts teams, and a TV for rugby, golf, cricket etc. There are large flagstones and an inglenook with a proper fire in the bar. Outside, in the summer, a trampoline comes out to add to the other children's garden furniture. Families are also welcome in the bar. Homemade food, including daily specials, is available lunchtimes and evenings, except for Sunday evenings. There are quiz nights on Wednesday and Sunday for general knowledge and Thursday for music. Friday and Saturday nights often feature a DJ or karaoke.

◁▶ 🐴 🚗 ❁

Natasha's
The Old Barn, Ewhurst Road
GU6 7EF OS: 065395 (B2127)
Primarily a wine bar and restaurant, the small bar sold no real ale. It closed in the late 1990s and the building is now used as industrial premises.

Onslow Arms
113-117 High Street, GU6 8AU
OS: 057391 (B2128)
☎ (01483) 272590
No real ale
Sports orientated pub, open all day, with three pool tables, darts and a large screen TV in the public bar. The lounge bar also has a television, and some old photos of Cranleigh. The car park and garden, round the back, are not obvious unless you spot the sign. Food is served all day till 6pm, with snacks available between 8-10pm all week.

● **Three Horseshoes**
4 High Street, GU6 8AE
OS: 059390 (B2128)
☎ (01483) 276978
11-11 (12-10:30 Sunday)
Courage Best Bitter
Greene King IPA
Young's Bitter
This 17th century pub has two bars, darts being played in one. The small lounge bar to the right used to be used by the draymen from the long gone Brufords Brewery which used to stand behind the pub. The brewery tower can be seen in some photos in the lounge. There is also an old bottle from the brewery with a glass marble stopper behind the bar. The main bar features an inglenook, and a notice board gives details of the active golf club, and of the charity events organised by the pub.

🚗 ❁ 🚲

White Hart Hotel
Ewhurst Road, GU6 7AE
OS: 062391 (B2127)
☎ (01483) 268647
Courage Best Bitter, Directors
Old coaching inn just off the High Street. There are darts and pool in the public bar and a real fire in the lounge which has a couple of separate seating areas. There is a strong local trade, as well as people using the pub for bed and breakfast, some passing trade, and it is popular with a mixture of ages. Food is served each lunchtime and evening. The pub is on the Surrey Cycleway.

CROWHURST (D2)

A scattered village with a part-Norman church which contains the only Sussex Iron tombstone in Surrey. There are several ancient yew trees in St George's churchyard, including one said to be one of the oldest in the country, being well over 1,000 years old.

● Brickmakers Arms

Tandridge Lane, RH8 9NS
OS: 377480
☎ (01342) 892212 / 893042
11-3, 6-11 (12-10:30 Sunday)
Greene King IPA
Harveys Sussex Best Bitter
Guest Beers
Biddenden Medium Cider
Split level, single bar, country freehouse, with a log fire in each part. The building dates from the 15th century. The guest beers change every couple of weeks, and are often from breweries in the south-east, large and small. Outside drinking is limited to just a few benches outside. Walkers and dogs are welcome, with dog biscuits available on the bar. There is an attached restaurant, and candles on the tables in the bar. The food is home cooked, with meat and fish specials boards to supplement the normal menu, and is available in child-sized portions if required. Food is served Monday to Saturday from 12-2:30 and 7-9:30 and on Sunday 12-3 and 6-9:30, with Sunday evenings being an all you can eat buffet.

DORKING (B2)

Inhabited by settlers in both the Stone Age and Iron Age, Dorking High Street follows the line of Stane Street, built by the Romans to connect London with Chichester. The town is situated close to the crossroads of the A24 and A25 and close to the Pilgrim's Way. It is an attractive market town with a wide High Street and many specialist shops. Beneath it are many sandstone caves, some of which are open to the public on Heritage Open Days. St Martin's church was designed by the Victorian architect Henry Woodyer and has one of the highest parish church spires in England, at 210 feet (64 metres) tall. In 1903 Sir Edward Lutyens designed the high barrel-vaulted church of St Mary's in Pixham. Until 1907 a traditional mass football game was held on Shrove Tuesday, lasting all afternoon. Cotmandene became famous for its cricket during the 18th century, and Dorking players were prominent in the Surrey County Cricket Club when it was formed in 1844. Also during the 18th century Dorking developed a reputation as a health and holiday resort, and the many visitors could taste a local delicacy called "water souchy", prepared from perch, carp and tench from local mill-ponds and rivers, and served in local inns. The Nower, off Coldharbour Lane, was part of an 18th century country estate, and offers some attractive walks. The composer Ralph Vaughan Williams has connections with the town, and there is a statue to him outside Dorking Halls, home of the annual Leith Hill Music Festival. The emblem of the town is the five-clawed Dorking chicken, which emphasises the importance of Dorking as an agricultural centre. Today Dorking Football Club is still nicknamed "the Chicks". Denbies Estate to the north of town produces a number of wines, mainly white and sparkling, using several grape varieties that grow over 265 acres of land. It is easily the largest vineyard in Britain, and has excellent visitor facilities. In 2004 Dorking became the only town in Surrey to be awarded Fairtrade Town status.

● **Arty P's (Map 1)**
45 Dene Street, RH4 2DW
OS: 167494
☎ (01306) 882222
11-11 (12-10:30 Sunday)
Fuller's London Pride
Young's Bitter
Single bare boarded bar which describes itself as "Posh pub meets wine bar". Several original draw-

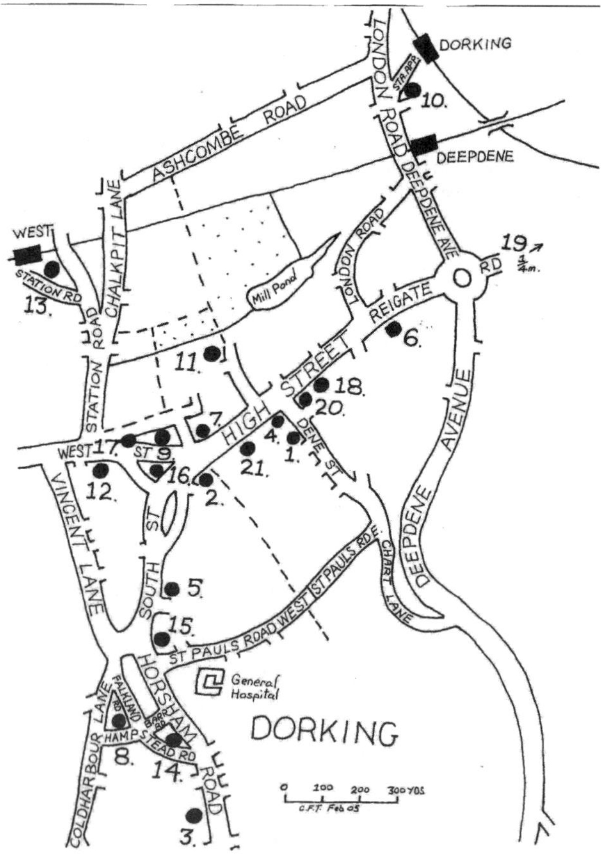

ings around the wall feature "pea" characters. All the food is home prepared and is of excellent quality. It is served all day until 9:30pm, except for Sundays when it finishes at 6pm. There is a very good tapas menu as well as the normal menu and tables can be booked. Families are welcome until 7pm. Outside is a covered decking area and pleasant patio garden, and there are some parking spaces in front of the pub. The pub was previously called JB's and was originally the Jolly Butchers.

◁▶ 🐴 🚗 ❆

Arundel Arms
Howard Road OS: 162493
A Friary Meux pub hidden away in Dorking's backstreets, the Arundel Arms had a reputation for serving a late pint! It closed in 1986.

Bell
57 West Street OS: 164492 (A25)
Another ex-Friary Meux inn, the building can still be easily recognised by the carved wooden bells just above head height outside it. A two bar pub, it closed in 1979.

● Bull's Head (Map 2)

11 South Street, RH4 2DY
OS: 164495 (A25)
☎ (01306) 885720
11-11 (12-10:30 Sunday)
Gale's Butser Bitter, Gales Best Bitter, HSB, seasonal beer
An old and attractive tile-hung pub on Pump Corner, the Bull's Head is a former coaching inn. Formerly a Friary Meux pub, it was bought by Gales in 1995. It is reached by climbing up a few steps from the main road, and internally features much wood paneling. Parts of the U-shaped bar area are designated as non-smoking at lunchtime when food is served (no food Sunday). Darts is played and Friday nights are open mic nights. Families are welcome until 9pm. The outside drinking area comprises two tables by the side of the pub.

◁ 🐴 ❆ 🚭 (when food served)

Bush (Map 3)

10 Horsham Road, RH4 2JL
OS: 166483 (A2003)
☎ (01306) 889830
Shepherd Neame Spitfire
Single bar pub, open all day, with an enclosed patio area behind which is used for families and summer barbecues. There are some old photos in the L shaped bar, plus darts and a pool table (with a set of snooker balls which can be used on it). There are also a couple of televisions. Live music and discos are held monthly and there are occasional food themed nights, such as curries. Food is served all afternoon on Sundays but not in the evening. On other days it is available each lunchtime and evening.

Café Rouge (Map 4)

170-172 High Street RH4 1BG
OS: 165495 (A25)
• (01306) 743400
No real ale
French style café, part of a national chain, with a strong emphasis on food, which is served from 10am in the morning till normal pub closing time. There is a separate breakfast menu and you can have a snack or three-course meal. The short list of bottled beers includes Hoegaarden and Leffe, not surprisingly at restaurant prices. The building used to be Murray's Wine Bar in the 1980s.

● Cricketers (Map 5)

81 South Street, RH4 2JU
OS: 164490 (A25)
☎ (01306) 889938
11-11 (12-10:30 Sunday)
Fuller's Chiswick, Discovery, London Pride, ESB, seasonal beer
Fuller's 1845 in bottle
This small pub has bare-brick walls that are covered in old photographs and Fuller's beer adverts.

Today there is one L-shaped bar, but etched glass on the unused exterior doors show that this was not always the case. A TV is in one corner and this is used for major sporting events. Darts is played down one end, and past this is one of the pub's best features, a fantastic walled Georgian garden. This is on two levels; the lower part is heated and is under a large umbrella. The upper part has well tended flowerbeds and is a real suntrap. Summer barbecues are held here. Food is currently only available weekday lunchtimes, but this may change.

◁☸

Dorking Halls (Map 6)
Reigate Road, RH4 1SG
OS: 170498 (A25)
☎ (01306) 881717
Worthington White Shield in bottle
A modern café bar attached to Dorking Halls, which hosts mainly arts related entertainment in its halls. As well as opening between 10am and 4pm Monday to Saturday, it also opens from 2 hours before the start of a show till just after the end of the interval. There is a second bar upstairs for users of the cinema, which opens from 30 minutes before the start of a film till 10 minutes after. The whole of the complex is non-smoking.

Falkland Arms (Map 8)
60 Falkland Road, RH4 3AD
OS: 164486
☎ (01306) 882428
Courage Best Bitter, Directors
The two handpumps are in the rear saloon bar of this genuine Irish pub. There is a pool table and a large screen for sports in the front bar, plus a smaller TV in each of the two bars. The pub does food from 9am till 9pm in the week and 9am till 6:30pm at weekend, with take-aways available including pizzas. There is live music on Saturday nights and Sunday afternoons.

Farola
112 High Street, RH4 1BA OS: 166495 (A25)
At the end of its life in the late 1990s, La Farola was a small bar at the front of a Spanish-style restaurant, and sold no real ale. It opened as OJ's in the mid 1990s, quickly changing name to Los Segades.

● **King's Arms (Map 9)**
45 West Street, RH4 1BU
OS: 163494 (A25)
☎ (01306) 883361
11-11 (12-3, 7-10:30 Sunday)
Fuller's London Pride
Greene King IPA
Guest Beers

It is appropriate that Dorking's oldest and perhaps most traditional pub is found in a street full of antique shops, and sells the best choice of traditional ales in town. Up to four guest beers are sold with the larger number usually available at weekends. These are mostly from microbreweries, from both near and far. The pub started off as three farmworkers' cottages, becoming a coaching inn during the 16th century. The split-level bar is well beamed and has leaded windows. At the rear of the pub is a smaller and quieter area. Down a few steps from here (and under an extremely low beam) is a cosy restaurant. It is in two parts, split by a fireplace. The food is all home produced, and is described as "traditional cosmopolitan with a modern twist". It is also of a very good quality, and is sold lunchtimes from 12-2:30 and from 6:30-9:30 from Tuesday to Saturday. On Wednesday and Sunday evenings a variety of live music is played.

◁▶ ✕ (evening only) 🚗 ❁

🚌 (Dorking West)

King's Head Coffee House (Map 7)

3 Old King's Head Court,
11 High St, RH4 1AR
OS: 166495
☎ (01306) 888849
No real ale

A small coffee house serving light meals, it also has a drinks licence from 11am. The King's Head ceased to be a pub long ago, and its pleasant courtyard is now surrounded by a selection of retail establishments, of which this is one. Formerly Emery's Café Bar, it closes at 5 (4 Thursday) in the evening and all day Sunday.

● Lincoln Arms Hotel (Map 10)

Station Approach, RH4 1TF
OS: 170503
☎ (01306) 882820
11-11 (12-10:30 Sunday)
Fuller's London Pride
Shepherd Neame Spitfire
Guest Beer

Much improved since the last edition of this guide, with a name more befitting a classic Victorian station hotel (the Happy Days Hotel featuring Deano's Diner didn't inspire confidence). The location on the edge of town (handy for both Dorking and Dorking Deepdene stations) means that the atmosphere is usually quite relaxed. There are two large bars – a lounge bar at the front and a wooden-floored public bar with a pool table at the back. A meeting room is available for hire and the public bar can be hired for functions. Both darts and pool are played in the latter bar. Accommodation consists of 20 rooms. Breakfast is served from 7-9am. A full menu is served each lunchtime from 12-3, and from 6-9 evenings (not Sunday). Basket meals are sold 3-6 Monday to Saturday and 3-9 Sunday. Families are welcome in the lounge bar until 7pm. Formerly the Star & Garter.

🛏 ◁▶ 🐴 🚗 ❁ 🚭 🚌 🚲

Malthouse (Map 11)

Mill Lane, RH4 1DX
OS: 165496
☎ (01306) 882393
No real ale

A Mr Qs pub with three pool tables, cash machine, several televisions, video juke box and DJs Friday and Saturday nights. Food, including a Kids' Menu, is available all day, every day, but stops at 8pm on Fridays and Saturdays. The pool tables are to the left, there is a raised seating area with some old local photos to the right and the area round the bar has some more seating. In the summer there is a bouncy castle in the garden for children. It is next to Dorking Football Club's ground and was formerly called the Evening Star. Unfortunately there is a possibility that the pub will be demolished as part of a new supermarket development.

Office

272 High Street, RH4 1QT
OS: 168497 (A25)

Originally Applejacks wine bar in the 1980s, this pub operated under a number of names including Arthur's, and R4s. After a short period of closure it reopened as the Office in 1996 by which stage it had become more pub-like, having a small split level bar, the upper part of which had a pool table. It closed in the late 1990s and is now an Italian restaurant. Real ale was sold during most of its life.

● Old House At Home (Map 12)

24 West Street, RH4 1BY
OS: 163493 (A25)
☎ (01306) 889664
11-11 (12-10:30 Sunday)
Young's Bitter, Special, seasonal beers

This 15th century pub has been very well renovated and it is now a successful mix of old and modern. Wooden floors, good solid tables throughout and subdued lighting help to create a warm atmosphere. There is a single bar, but with four separate areas coming off it, there are quiet parts to be found. Both the front and rear areas have wood paneling. Between these the walls are painted in subtle tones. Outside there is a very good garden and a separate function room. Dogs are allowed, but not during the lunch food hours of 12-2:30. No food is available weekend evenings. Originally a Courage pub, it was bought by Young's in 1989.

◁ ☸ 🚌 (Dorking West)

● Pilgrim (Map 13)

Station Road, RH4 1HF
OS: 161498
☎ (01306) 889951
11-11 (12-10:30 Sunday)
Adnams Bitter
Fuller's London Pride
Ringwood Best Bitter, Old Thumper

Locals' pub next to Dorking West station (check the timetable as not all trains stop here) that also caters for workers from the local estates at lunchtime. Food is served each lunchtime and all but Sunday evening (although food is available until 5pm that day). The pool table and dartboard are down a couple of steps on the right hand side of the single bar and the restaurant area is to the left. The pub is a meeting point for various clubs and societies from dog walkers to motorcycle owners. Accommodation consists of 5 rooms.

🛏 ◁ ▶ 🚗 ☸ 🚌 (Dorking West)

● Prince Of Wales (Map 14)

55 Hampstead Road, RH4 3AH
OS: 165487
☎ (01306) 889925
4-11, (3-11 Friday, 12-11 Saturday, and 12-4, 7-10:30 Sunday)
Caledonian Deuchars IPA
Fuller's London Pride

This small Victorian back street pub has a very attractive frontage. Standing proud at roof level is a large and colourful set of Prince of Wales' feathers. Inside is a single bar, the front part of which has some sofas by the window, surrounded by a number of plants. Note the old wooden clocking-in clock on the wall, rescued by the landlord from East London. Another old day and date calendar can be found at the end of the bar. The rear part of the pub is a small extension, and pool and darts are to be found here, with the pub running two pool teams. The pub is busy with workers at opening time during the week, and with local residents later on. Outside drinking consists of one table at the front.

☸

Puccino's
228-232 High Street, RH4 1QR
OS: 167497 (A25)
A modern café bar, this operated for a couple of years in the early 2000s. It is currently up for sale.

Punchbowl
Reigate Road, RH4 1QB
OS: 175499 (A25)
The Punchbowl was a Courage owned motel that was built using stone from Betchworth Castle. It comprised a drinkers' bar and a carvery, and when it closed in 1988 it was advertising itself, rather old-fashionedly, as a "motor hotel". It is now a Little Chef and Travelodge complex.

● Queen's Head (Map 15)
Horsham Road, RH4 2JS
OS: 164489 (A25)
☎ (01306) 883041
11-11 (12-10:30 Sunday)
Fuller's Chiswick Bitter, London Pride, ESB

This locals' pub with its tile-hung exterior is one of the most attractive in town. It dates from the 1780s and is a former coaching inn. The large bar has pool and darts in the rear part, and television for sport. A competing jukebox helps create a lively atmosphere. On the first Thursday of the month a quiz is held. Food is sold from 12-2:30 Monday to Friday and 12-6 Saturday. Outside there is a large garden with some play equipment and rabbits to entertain the children.

◁ 🚗 ☸

● Spotted Dog (Map 16)
42 South Street, RH4 2HQ
OS: 164494 (A25)
☎ (01306) 885218
11-11 (12-10:30 Sunday)
Courage Best Bitter
Fuller's London Pride
Young's Bitter
Pub with a single L-shaped bar selling some of the best value beer in Dorking. Note the two large and attractive bow windows, one either side of the central door. If the TV is switched off you can always watch the fish tank above the fireplace. The bar is in two parts, separated by a step. The lower part has a wooden floor and leads to the garden. This has two aviaries in it and gives impressive views towards Denbies vineyard and Ranmore Common. Although meals are usually only served at lunchtimes (not Monday), there are occasional special evenings featuring English food. Families are welcome until 7pm, and darts is played. A worthwhile place to visit on any tour of the pubs on the one-way system.

◁ ☸ 🐎

● Star Inn (Map 17)
36 West Street, RH4 1BU
OS: 162494 (A25)
☎ (01306) 889734
12-11 (12-10:30 Sunday)
Greene King IPA, Old Speckled Hen
Dating from the early 19th century, this small, attractively slate-hung pub punches above its weight in the entertainment stakes. Thursday night is Open Mic night for budding entertainers (the pub piano is

a cut above the usual), and the Culture Conspiracy on Tuesdays can feature anything from poetry to comedy, to Latin percussion. The tables on the pavement outside catch the evening sun and give a good view of the passing traffic. The Star was a Friary Meux pub until its sale to Greene King in 1990.

☸ 🚌 (Dorking West)

● Surrey Yeoman (Map 18)

220 High Street, RH4 1QR
OS: 168496 (A25)
☎ (01306) 741492
11-11 (12-10 Sunday)
Greene King IPA, Ruddles County, Abbot Ale, Old Speckled Hen
Hogs Back TEA

A former Friary Meux pub, the tile hung Surrey Yeoman features beams, flagstones, tiles and well-polished floorboards in its various areas, which are to be found on various levels. The pub takes its name from the Earl of Rothes who was a colonel of the Surrey Yeomanry in the early part of the 19th century and the hanging sign outside the pub is taken from an original picture held by the Royal Army museum. The original pub was extended when it was converted into a Hogshead, and it was refurbished again when bought by Greene King. The good garden at the back is not immediately obvious. Quiz night is Tuesday. Food is available each lunchtime from 12-3. If help is required getting in for the disabled, ring the bell on one of the doors. The pub can get very busy Friday and Saturday nights.

◁ ☸ ♿

● Watermill (Map 19)

Reigate Road, RH4 1NN
OS: 180502 (A25)
☎ (01306) 883248
11-11 (12-10:30 Sunday)
Courage Best Bitter, Directors
Guest Beers

The Watermill is a large, single bar pub with several separate seating areas, all but one of which are non-smoking. The guest beers, which vary in number from one to four depending on time of year and how busy the pub is, change weekly and are usually from the larger independent breweries. There are a couple of log fires and candles on the tables. It is food orientated, with an extensive choice of fish specials, varying in number from six to three times that number at busy times in the summer, when live lobsters and crabs from a tank may also be available. Food is available from 11-10 Monday to Saturday, and 12-9:30 Sunday, and there is a specials board as well as the seasonally changing main menu and the fish choices. Four roasts replace the specials board menu until 6pm on Sundays. Outside there is a patio garden to the side and rear, from which there are lovely views across to Box Hill.

◁ ▶ 🐴 🚗 ☸ 🚭 ♿

● White Hart (Map 20)

5 Dene Street, RH4 2DR

OS: 167495
☎ (01306) 881960
11-11 (12-10:30 Sunday)
Courage Best Bitter
Shepherd Neame Spitfire
Known locally as the Snakepit, this is a small but lively drinker's pub just off the High Street. There are two distinct areas on either side of a horseshoe shaped bar, one of which houses a pool table. Darts is also played. The walls are decorated with old adverts. The pub has no kitchen and the only food available is the excellent value bought in rolls and sandwiches. The cellars are built into local caves.

White Horse (Map 21)
High Street, RH4 1BE
OS: 166495 (A25)
www.whitehorsedorking.co.uk
☎ (0870) 4008282
Bass
An historic old coaching inn in the town centre, a building has been on this site since at least 1278, when it was known as the Cross House. In those days it was owned by the Hospitallers, who were derived from the Templars (groups of knights linked with the Crusades). Most of the current hotel is 18th century with more modern additions; there are parts, however, that survive from the 15th and 16th centuries. Open all day for drinks, the comfortable bar, with its real fire, is also open for teas and snacks during the afternoon. Full meals are served every lunchtime and evening in the bar and in the separate restaurant. Beer is, however, expensive. As well as the accommodation in the original building, there are two more modern "garden blocks", giving a total of 78 rooms.

Why Not's
Unit 4, Allen Court, RH4 1AY
OS: 165494
Hidden away off the High Street, up a flight of steps, Why Not's was a modern bar popular with the young, which opened around 1992. It changed its name to Steps in 1994, but closed shortly afterwards.

Windmill (Map 22)
Flint Hill, RH4 2LL
OS: 168478 (A2003)
A former Friary pub, the Windmill was a locals' pub on the southern edge of town. The one bar was split-level with a pool table up a few steps. It closed in 2004 permission has been granted to build eleven flats on the site.

DORMANS PARK (D3)

A residential development, which was commenced in a woodland setting around 1880, when it was called Bellagio. There are some Victorian and Edwardian houses around along with a number of Relatively pleasant modern development with some Edwardian and Victorian houses, and was originally called Bellagio in the 19th century. It is handy for Dormans Station, which opened in 1884.

Coach House
Wilderwick Road, RH19 3NT
OS: 401411
This was a one bar pub dating from the 20th century. It had a separate games area and there was a wood-burning stove in the bar. The pub was well known for its live music, which was played each Wednesday, Friday, Saturday, and Sunday night. The pub was demolished in 2004 with permission to put three houses on its site. It was a freehouse and sold a number of different real ales.

DORMANSLAND (D3)

Originally part of the parish of Lingfield, the village developed following enclosure of the local commons in 1815 and was extended following the arrival of the railway. There is evidence of an Iron Age fort close by which covered 26 acres, and was defended by three ditches. Greathed Manor was a Victorian manor house built in 1868 by Robert Kerr, the author of "The Gentleman's House".

● Old House At Home

63-65 West Street, RH7 6QP
OS: 402422
☎ (01342) 832117
11:30-30, 6-11 (12-4, 7-10:30 Sunday)
Shepherd Neame Master Brew Bitter, Best Bitter, Spitfire, seasonal beer (occasional)

This friendly old inn is hidden away on the western side of the village, but is worth visiting for its unspoilt architecture and equally good beer and food. Note that some of the beers are sold direct from casks behind the bar. The pub dates from the 16th century and is essentially one bar, with darts being played in a small room off to one side. The upper part of the pub houses a restaurant serving a wide range of good quality home made food, although note that this is not available Sunday evening. The well-beamed lounge area features a real fire and is very cosy in winter. No piped music is played in the pub, although there is occasionally some played live. Formerly a Friary Meux pub, it was bought by Shepherd Neame in 1991.

(Dormans)

Plough

44 Plough Road, RH7 6PS
OS: 406427 (B2028)
☎ (01342) 832933 (836283 restaurant)
Adnams Bitter
Fuller's London Pride
Gales Gales Best Bitter
Greene King IPA

Open all day, this 14th century pub is now open plan and has low beams and a large inglenook fireplace. Bar meals are served each lunchtime (traditional roasts on Sunday) from 12-3. A separate Thai Village Restaurant operates from 12-3 and 6-10 Tuesday to Sunday, and offers a choice of 65 Thai dishes plus set menus for 2, 4 or 6 people. Take away meals are also available. Outside there is a large garden where summer barbecues are held. Children are welcome and there are also facilities for the disabled.

● Royal Oak

57-61 High Street, RH7 6PU
OS: 403422
☎ (01342) 832383
11:30-11 (12-10:30 Sunday)
Adnams Broadside
Fuller's London Pride

A wide variety of homemade food is sold each lunchtime in this one bar pub, and the quality is excellent. In the evenings, food is only available by reservation, but enterprisingly the licensees offer a take away curry service seven days a week. The pub does much charity work and quiz nights are held on Thursdays. Darts and pool are also played.

◁ 🚗 ❄ 🚌 (Dormans)

DRIFT BRIDGE (B1)

Small residential area between Epsom Downs and Banstead.

Driftbridge
Reigate Road, KT17 1QZ
OS: 232600 (A240)
This large Mock Tudor pub was a former Toby Inn and restaurant. It also offered accommodation and function facilities. It dated from 1932, and featured timbers from HMS Ganges, which was built in Bombay in 1821. This was the last sailing ship to serve as a sea-going flagship. In the early days the pub used to have its own cinema. The pub was closed by pub-chain Mitchells & Butlers in 2004.

Omnia
215 Fir Tree Road, KT17 3LB
OS: 232599 (B291)
☎ (01737) 373776
No real ale
This modern steakhouse and bar is found is a parade of shops. The rather smart bar at the front, with a prominent television, serves a wide selection of cocktails. Bottled beers include the top-notch Belgian Duvel. The bar opens all day with food served each lunchtime and evening.

ELLENS GREEN (A3)

An isolated village on the West Sussex boundary, it dates from Elizabethan days, and has a green and some half-timbered houses.

● **Wheatsheaf Inn**
Horsham Road, RH12 3AJ
OS: 098359
☎ (01403) 822155
11-3, 6-11 (12-3; open all day Saturday in summer)
Badger K&B Sussex, Best
A 17th century, tile hung, brick built pub very close to the Sussex border, the Wheatsheaf has been refurbished following a change of tenant. This low beamed pub retains a cosy feel and has several pleasant drinking and eating areas off the little bar. There are three real fires including an attractive inglenook, and some of the original flooring remains. The pub is virtually no smoking with only a couple of tables and a small back room, with an old settle, designated for smokers. The beer quality has seen a significant improvement since the change of ownership and there is a big focus on high quality food from an extensive and imaginative menu. The pub caters mostly for a "well-heeled" and up market clientele, but all are made welcome; cyclists and walkers will find it a useful watering hole and families can take advantage of the large beer garden during the clement weather. Food is served from 12 - 2.30 all week including Sunday and 6.30 - 9.30 Monday to Saturday. Children are welcome away from the bar. Note that the pub is not open on Sunday evenings. Formerly a Watney pub, it was bought by King & Barnes in the late 1980s and is now owned by Badger. It still retains a fine King & Barnes pub sign.

◁ ▶ 🐴 🚗 ❄ 🚭

EPSOM (B1)

Dating from Saxon times, the town was once a spa with many springs and wells. The waters were said to cure indigestion and became popular with visitors in the 17th century, and are still remembered by the term "Epsom Salts". The area was enjoyed by royalty for sport and riding, and had fashionable visitors such as Samuel Pepys and Nell Gwynne. When the spa fell out of fashion in the 18th century, the town reverted to agriculture, but prosperity returned with the arrival of the railway in 1847. The High Street is the widest in Surrey, and still hosts a market.

Albion (Map 1)
134 High Street, KT19 8BT
OS: 205607 (A24)
☎ (01372) 744240
Greene King IPA, Abbot Ale, Old Speckled Hen
Guest Beers
18th century pub most notable for its listed "bas relief" frontage. There was once a courthouse on this site. The pub still shows signs of being a Hogshead Alehouse in its decor, and still keeps two guest beers, now supplied through owners Greene King. Food served all day from 12-7 and is all very good value.

● **Amato (Map 2)**
18 Chalk Lane, KT18 7AS
OS: 207597
☎ (01372) 721642
11-3, 5-11 (12-4, 7-10:30 Sunday)
Fuller's London Pride
Harveys Sussex Best Bitter
Young's Bitter
Guest Beer
A pub has been on this site since the 17th century, but has been burnt down and rebuilt on more than one occasion. The present pub is named after the 1838 Derby winner, which won its one and only

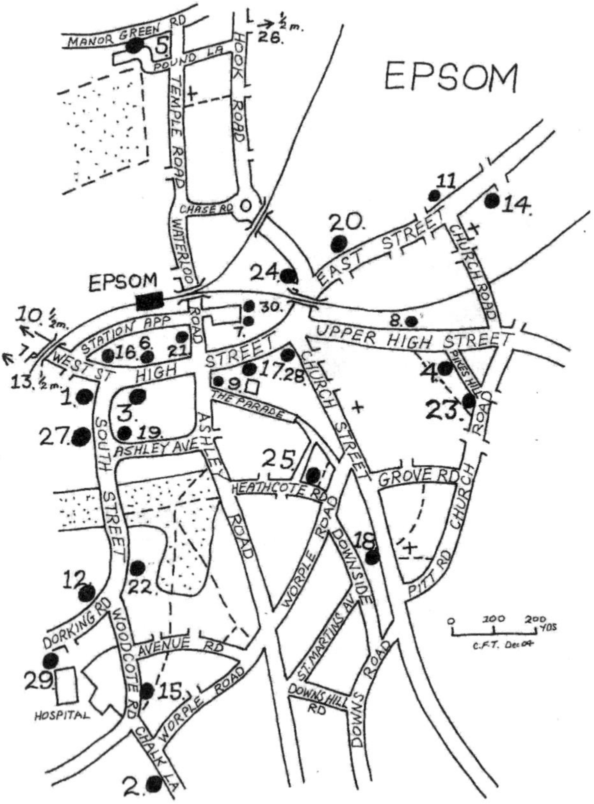

race. The pub is very civilised and is situated on a quiet road leading up to the Downs. There are two separate drinking areas in the bar. There is also a real fire, and on the walls are bits of equine memorabilia. The pub is known locally for its food (not served Sunday or Monday evening). Children are allowed in only if eating. One guest beer from Punch list is sold, which changes once in a while. According to legend, at dawn on certain Derby days, the name of the predicted winner mysteriously appears in chalk near the front of the pub.

◁▶ ☸ 🚭

● Assembly Rooms (Map 3)

147-153 High Street, KT19 8EH
OS: 206607 (A24)
☎ (01372) 737290
De Koninck Ambree
Fuller's London Pride
Greene King Abbot Ale
Marston's Burton Bitter, Pedigree
Guest Beer

Large Wetherspoon's pub with three distinct areas. The one by the entrance is carpeted. Steps lead up to a paved, bare brick wall area with high tables and stools. Up further steps is the long bar with a tiled floor. Originally built as Epsom's Assembly Rooms, which date from around 1710, the building was most recently a building society HQ before being converted to a pub in 2002. One constantly changing guest beer is available.

◁▶ ♿ 🚌

● Barley Mow (Map 4)

12 Pikes Hill, KT17 4EA
OS: 214609
☎ (01372) 721044
12-11 (12-10:30 Sunday)
Fuller's Chiswick Bitter, Discovery, London Pride, ESB, seasonal beer
Fuller's 1845 in bottle

Small back-street local hidden away off the Upper High Street. The pub is a conversion from three cottages and has several distinct drinking areas. A conservatory completes the indoor drinking areas and opens on to a large garden. Most of the food sold is prepared on the premises, and is complemented by barbecues in summer. The porthole to the right of the entrance gives a view of the cellar. The Upper High Street car park is free in the evenings and an alley makes it a very short walk to the pub.

◁▶ ☸ 🚌

Blenheim Arms (Map 5)

7 Manor Green Road, KT19 8RA
OS: 204616
☎ (01372) 720073
No real ale

This is one of Epsom's pubs which have suffered from a change of name over the last few years. It was built in 1933 and named the Blenheim after the Derby winner of that year. It became GGs in the 1980s, but regained its original name in the early 1990s. Open all day, the pub comprises one large bar area for the lager drinking locals.

Boogie Lounge (Map 21)
1a Waterloo Road, KT19 8AY
OS: 208609
www.boogielounge.com
☎ (01372) 749393
No real ale
Bar in a nightclub complex which is designed for "discerning thirty somethings". It is only open Tuesday to Saturday evenings from 8pm, with a late licence from Wednesday to Saturday. It has had other names over the years including Legends and Po-Na-Na.

Café Rouge (Map 6)
96-98 High Street, KT19 8BJ
OS: 207608 (A24)
☎ (01372) 749131
No real ale
Café bar which opens at 10am each day. French and Belgian bottled beers are sold.

Casa (Map 7)
10 Derby Square, KT19 8AX OS: 208608
☎ (01372) 729174
No real ale
Modern bar, open all day, which sells some Belgian bottled beers.

Chicago Rock Café (Map 9)
5/9 Spread Eagle Walk,
High Street, KT19 8DN.
OS: 208607
☎ (01372) 747499
No real ale
Large and smart bar hidden away off the High Street. It is decorated with Americana, and also features a restaurant. Opens Monday to Saturday evenings only from 5pm, and has a late licence.

Cricketers Inn (Map 10)
1 Stamford Green Road, KT18 7SR OS: 197607
☎ (01372) 729384
Fuller's London Pride
Greene King Old Speckled Hen
Young's Bitter
This weatherboarded pub with a brick extension is in an idyllic setting next to a pond with its waterfowl, and opposite the cricket green. It is 250 years old, and parts were once police stables, becoming a pub in 1836. Inside it has been modernised in typical Ember Inns fashion, with soft furnishings and the trademark pile of logs by the gas fire. There is one bar with a lounge area on several levels. Open all day.

Eclipse
26 West Hill, OS: 203608 (B280)
Away from the town centre, the Eclipse was a two bar Friary Meux pub. It took its name from a horse that was born under the sun's eclipse of 1763 and became a great champion and sire of many others. It closed in the early 1980s, but the building still stands and is used as offices.

Epsom Playhouse Bar (Map 19)
Ashley Avenue, KT18 5AL
OS: 206606 (A24)
☎ (01372) 742760
No real ale
Café bar in a theatre complex. Opening times may vary depending on the shows. The bar can be entered directly off South Street.

● Haywain (Map 12)
2-4 St Margaret's Drive, Dorking Road, KT18 7LB OS: 205603 (A24)
☎ (01372) 720691
11-11 (12-10:30 Sunday)
Beer range varies
Brewer's Fayre pub, restaurant, and motel that opened in July 1997 at a cost of £2.5 million. The building was originally built as a home for a Portuguese wine merchant, for which evidence still ex-

ists in the form of ceramic tiles showing the grape harvest. In 1928 it became a convent school. Inside it has many areas divided up to give a cosy atmosphere. Three real ales are sold, mainly from the family brewers.

● Jolly Coopers (Map 13)

84 Wheelers Lane, KT17 7SD
OS: 197605
☎ (01372) 723222
12-11 (12-10:30 Sunday)
Adnams Bitter
Harveys Sussex Best Bitter
Occasional **Guest Beer**

Three bar local which is over 200 years old. It is in the middle of a residential area, but has a more rural atmosphere. There is a cosy lounge with cream walls, beamed ceiling, half wood panels and red carpet. At the other side is the more basic public bar with a wooden floor and pool table. In between is a small bar with room for one table only. There are some tables outside at the front for the summer. No food is served Saturday evening or at all on Sunday.

● King's Arms (Map 14)

144 East Street, KT17 1EY
OS: 215613 (A24)
☎ (01372) 723892
11-11 (12-10:30 Sunday)
Young's Bitter, Special, seasonal beer
Traditional family-run Victorian pub with a friendly welcome. The lower bar has a darts board, while the quieter upper bar can be hired for functions. There is also a spacious landscaped garden in which

summer barbecues are held. A children's play area is also to be found here. The pub has football and darts teams, and also hosts a quiz on Sunday evenings. Additionally there is also a music quiz on the first Wednesday of each month. The cellar beams are reputedly from Men-of-war ships which fought at Trafalgar. Food is served 12-2:30 and 6-8 on Monday to Saturday 12-4 on Sunday.

● Ladas (Map 15)

13 Woodcote Road, KT18 7QS
OS: 206598
☎ (01372) 723780
11-11 (12-10:30 Sunday)
Fuller's London Pride
Young's Bitter, Special
Friendly welcoming pub which is named after the 1894 Derby winner which was owned by the Earl of Rosebery, and has its picture on a wall inside the pub. It is an old-fashioned community local, which is also home to the local football team. Being at the back of Epsom Hospital, regulars include some of their off-duty staff. It was runner up in a national competition run by Punch Taverns for beer quality, etc. A TV shows sporting fixtures. Darts, shut the box, dominoes and

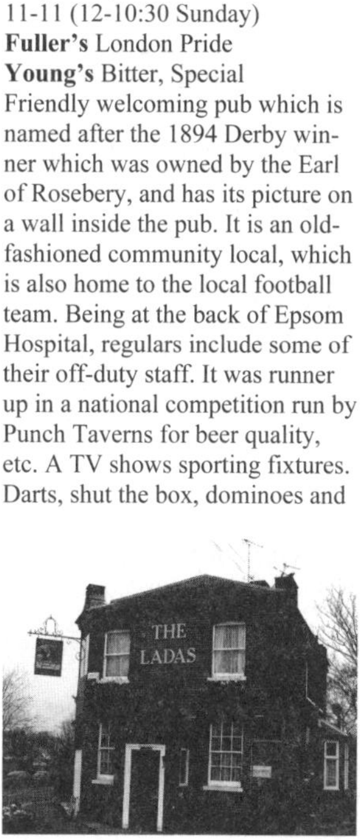

crib are played. Children are welcome at weekends. Lunches are served Monday to Friday only.

Lime Bar (Map 8)
11 Upper High Street, KT17 4QY
OS: 213608 (A2022)
☎ (01372)
No real ale
Formerly Casper's, this bar is due to reopen as the Lime Bar and restaurant.

Marquis Of Granby
(Map 16)
4 West Street, KT18 7RG
OS: 205608 (B280)
☎ (01372) 744278
Fuller's London Pride
Shepherd Neame Spitfire
300 year old pub which spent a while as the Flutter & Firkin. There are gardens to both the front and rear, and the back part of the pub is no smoking until 5pm Monday to Friday. Note the original Friary Meux inn sign in the fireplace.

Olde King's Head (Map 18)
26 Church Street, KT17 4QB
OS: 213604 (B284)
☎ (01372) 729125
Fuller's London Pride
Shepherd Neame Spitfire
Young's Bitter
This 300 year old local is Epsom's oldest pub and is popular with all ages. The pub is reputedly haunted by a female ghost. The small restaurant area at one end seems to compete with Sky Sports on above it. Open all day.

Plough & Harrow (Map 20)
27 East Street, KT17 1BD
OS: 211611 (A24)
☎ (01372) 740518
Greene King IPA
Young's Bitter
Attractive small and cosy pub which is open all day and has a late licence from Thursday to Saturday.

Queen's Head (Map 22)
77 South Street, KT18 7PY
OS: 205603 (A24)
☎ (01372) 720332
No real ale
Two drinking areas are served from the one bar. The games room at one end is fairly noisy and contains a pool table. The main bar is much quieter.

● Railway Guard (Map 23)
48 Church Road, KT17 4 DZ
OS: 214608
☎ (01372) 721143
11:30-11 (12-10:30 Sunday)
Fuller's London Pride
Guest Beers

This Victorian pub was originally built as three cottages. It has a very good atmosphere in its one bar, where big sporting events are shown on large-screen TV. At other times there is a jukebox. Three or four guest beers are available from the Enterprise Inns list, complemented by a good range of single malt whiskies. Outside there is a small triangular patio with seating. The pub hosts a golf society.

● Rifleman (Map 24)
5 East Street, KT17 1BB
OS: 210610 (A24)
☎ (01372) 726079
11-11 (12-10:30 Sunday)
Greene King IPA, Abbot Ale
The Rifleman is a tiny corner pub in the shadow of a bridge carrying the railway to and from London. It

was a Friary Meux pub until sold to Greene King in 1990. It is very much a locals' pub, but still welcomes passing trade. The interior is decorated with pictures of bygone Epsom, horse racing, and Chelsea Football Club, and a TV occupies part of the bar area, meaning the pub can get very busy Saturday afternoon. The garden is used for barbecues in summer. Simple meals are served Monday to Friday lunchtimes.

◁ ☸ 🚌

● Rising Sun (Map 25)

14 Heathcote Road, KT18 5DX
OS: 211605
☎ (01372) 743091
12-3, 5:30 (5 Friday)-11; (12-11 Saturday and 12-10:30 Sunday)
Pilgrim Surrey, Progress, seasonal beer
Guest Beer
Pilgrim Brewery's only tied house, and the first pub in Epsom to be totally non-smoking throughout. The one guest beer will be from another microbrewery. A tremendous range of quality foreign draught and bottled beers are also sold, with there being no place on the bar for the sort of Eurofizz sold elsewhere. A French cider is also sold. Beer festivals, held every three months, see even more imported beers on offer. The pub is smartly decorated throughout and has polished wood floors. The front bar area is for the drinkers, with diners using the rear area, but not to the exclusion of others. All food is prepared at the pub and is of excellent quality. Families are welcome until early evening. Cribbage and draughts can be played. The pub was the birthplace of the Society for the Preservation of Beer from the Wood in the 1960s.

◁ ▶ ☸ 🚭 🚌 ♿

Salthouse (Map 17)

45-53 High Street, KT19 8DD
OS: 208607 (A24)
☎ (01372) 740717
Courage Directors
Theakston Best Bitter
New town centre pub opened in February 1996 as the Old Banker, being originally a National Westminster bank. It's name changed shortly after this to the safer "Old Bank", and in June 2005 became Salthouse. It is a smart one bar pub with a garden to the rear. The original bank safes can be seen on one wall. All the food is home made and nothing is frozen. The pub is open all day with food served until around 9pm.

Sefton Arms (Map 26)

Sefton Road, Longmead, KT19 9JZ OS: 210623
No real ale
Modern two bar estate pub, which can get a bit lively at times.

Spread Eagle

89 High Street OS: 208607 (A24)
Large pub which is now the Spread Eagle Walk shopping precinct (see Chicago Rock Café). A grade II listed building that had been rebuilt in 1704, this former Friary Meux pub closed in the 1980s.

● Symonds Well (Map 27)

30 South Street, KT18 7PF
OS: 205606 (A24)
www.symondswell.co.uk
☎ (01372) 723158
12-3, 5-11 (12-11 Saturday and 12-10:30 Sunday)
Caledonian Deuchars IPA

Greene King Abbot Ale, Old Speckled Hen
Young's Bitter, Special
This old inn was mentioned by Samuel Pepys and was formerly called the Magpie. It is now named after John Symonds, an Epsom yeoman who in 1677 discovered a well nearby, with waters that were said to have medicinal properties. Now one can try the properties of the well looked after beers in this pleasant pub with one central bar. Etched windows give a good view of passing traffic, and there is a long bench in the front to sit on. The front area with polished wood floor leads to a more secluded carpeted lounge area to the rear. There is an open fire and the obligatory scenes of old Derby races. Darts can be played.
◁ ☸ 🚌 ♿

Vestry (Map 28)
2 Church Street, KT17 4NY
OS: 210608 (B284)
☎ (01372) 817750
Adnams Bitter
Fuller's London Pride
Marston's Pedigree
Occasional **Guest Beer**
As can be seen from the frontage, this used to be a cinema. More recently it was a Seeboard showroom, becoming a pub in 1996. The front bar area has a bit of a baronial hall feel to it with an upper balcony. The food trade during the day (12-9) gives way to a younger crowd later on, with a late licence on Friday and Saturday evenings.

Vibe (Map 11)
79 East Street, KT17 1DT
OS: 213612 (A24)
☎ (01372) 819945
No real ale
One bar pub popular with young people. The name has changed a few times (it used to be the Locomotive, and after that the Common Room, Bear's and Friends). Open all day, a late licence for Friday and Saturday has been applied for.

Wellington
High Street, OS: 207608 (A24)
Once a boisterous town pub, it now is an amusement arcade. Owned by Charrington's, this 19th century pub closed in the 1990s. Unusually, there was an upstairs snooker room.

White Hart
High Street, OS: 208607 (A24)
Now a shop and building society, this former Watney's pub and steak bar closed in the early 1980s.

● White Horse (Map 29)
53 Dorking Road, KT18 7JH
OS: 203599 (A24)
☎ (01372) 726622
11-11 (12-10:30 Sunday)
Fuller's London Pride
Young's Bitter
Friendly community local near the

hospital, which aims at attracting families. The Grade II listed building is decorated in a modern style with painted walls and white painted wood. There is a separate no-smoking and eating area to the rear. Evening meals feature both spicy dishes and traditional favourites. The menu is snackier at lunchtimes, but main meals are still served. On Sundays food is served until 4pm only. The garden features a children's playground. Jenga and Connect 4 are available to play indoors.

◁▶🐴🚗❄⊘♿

Yates's Wine Lodge (Map 30)
1 Derby Square, KT19 8AG
☎ (01372) 726622
No real ale
Open all day, this is a typical modern Yates bar, and is set in a new development area. A food trade during the day gives way to loud music for the younger set in the evening.

EPSOM DOWNS (B1)

Famous for the racecourse and the Derby, Epsom Downs is village of scattered buildings with views extending over much of London. The imposing racecourse grandstand has been extended and renovated several times. Racing has taken place on the Downs since the time of James I. The most famous race, first run in 1780, is reputed to have been called The Derby after the co-founders, Lord Derby and Lord Rosebery, tossed a coin and the former won.

Derby Arms
Derby Arms Road, KT18 5LE
OS: 216587
☎ (01372) 722330
Bass
Fuller's London Pride
Wadworth 6X
A large rambling 18th century pub opposite Epsom Downs grandstand, the accent is mainly on food. This is sold every day from 12-10 (9:30 Sunday). The pub has disabled facilities.

Rubbing House
The Downs, Langley Vale Road, KT18 5LJ.
OS: 215585
☎ (01372) 723245
Flowers IPA
Fuller's London Pride
The only pub in England situated on a racecourse, making it busy on race days. It is over 100 years old and was originally built as a place to rub down horses. Very food oriented, the pub is open all day.

Tattenham Corner
Tattenham Corner Road, KT18 5NY OS: 225585 (B290)
☎ (01372) 351454
Bass
Fuller's London Pride
This Out & Out branded pub restaurant, open all day, overlooks the racecourse and golf course. There are good views over the Downs from both the front no smoking conservatory and the garden, where summer barbecues are held. Built in 1928, the interior features wood paneling. Food is served each lunchtime and evening, and all day at weekends.

EWELL (B1)

Surrey's largest Roman town developed around natural springs. Ewell is at the source of the Hogsmill River, the waters of which were used in Victorian times for brewing, and also for powering corn, paper and gunpowder mills. The "Death of Ophelia", possibly John Millais' most famous painting, features willows by the Hogsmill River. The building of Nonsuch Palace began in 1538 to rival Hampton Court, and was eventually bought by Elizabeth I, but later fell into ruin. Today Nonsuch Park contains 300 acres of woods and parkland, and surrounds Nonsuch Manor House. The houses built before the 17th century have mostly gone, and Ewell has a more modern centre stretching towards the London suburbs.

● Eight Bells (Map 1)

78 Kingston Road, KT17 2DU
OS: 218632
☎ (020) 8393 9973
12-11 (12-10:30 Sunday)
Greene King IPA, Abbot Ale, seasonal beer

Friendly community local attracting a diverse age of clientele. Set back from the main road, the pub was rebuilt in 1905 on the site of an 18th century one. A former Charrington's pub, it was bought by Greene King in 1994. It comprises two separate drinking areas with a third zone for dining as well. A TV shows sport in the right hand area, the others are quieter. The large garden is very popular in summer. Live music every weekend. Quiz nights and meat raffles also held. The pub has a proud record of charity support.

◁▶ 🚗 ♿ 🚌 (Ewell West)

Green Man (Map 2)

71 High Street, KT17 1RX
OS: 220624
☎ (020) 8393 9779
Courage Best Bitter
Young's Bitter
Guest Beer (Summer only)
Imposing ex-Hodgson's pub built in the 1930s, it is open all day. The pub advertises itself as the "Famous Green Man", but nobody seems to know what it is famous for!

● Horton Park Country Club (Map 3)

Hook Road, KT19 8QG
OS: 203632 (B284)
www.hortonpark.com
☎ (020) 8393 8400
11-11 (12-10:30 Sunday)
Young's Bitter, Special

Lounge bar in golfing complex open to the public, with an adjoining restaurant that is open every day. There is a good "Sports Club" air to the bar, with golfers mingling with local drinkers popping in to enjoy the Young's ale. Busier towards the latter part of the week, with weekends, especially Sundays, being most popular. It may close early in winter months if trade is light.

◁▶ 🍴 🚗 ❄

Jim Thompson's Oriental Bar (Map 4)

65 London Road, KT17 2BL
OS: 222632 (A24)
☎ (020) 8393 2242
No real ale
Formerly the Organ Inn, beloved of double-entendrists everywhere. Now mainly a Thai Restaurant selling bottled beers from the Far East. Open all day.

Jolly Waggoners
112 Beggars Hill, OS: 218634
Demolished in 2001 / early 2002 in order to make way for a block of flats. Built circa 1950, it was best described as a one bar, down-to-earth estate type pub. It was owned by Courage, and a 1980s

pub guide described it as "pleasantly nicotined".

King William IV (Map 5)
17 High Street, KT17 1SB
OS: 220627 (B2200)
☎ (020) 8393 1294
Adnams Bitter
Greene King IPA
This 19th century pub has been restored to its original name after a spell as the Friend & Firkin, but retains its interior from that period. Very much sports oriented; two large screens plus smaller TVs are scattered throughout. There is a pool table at the rear. Open all day, barbecues are held in the garden in summer.

Kingfisher (Map 6)
Ruxley Lane, West Ewell, KT19 9JS OS: 201640 (B284)
☎ (020) 8397 5297
No real ale
A drinker's pub on a housing estate, the Kingfisher is open all day. Live TV sport is popular and the pool table is well utilised. The pub comprises two separate drinking areas and a garden that is popular with families in summer.

Plough (Map 7)
Plough Road, KT19 9RA
OS: 208630
☎ (020) 8394 2885
Tetley Bitter (occasional)
Open all day, this is a live TV sports and pool oriented pub, appealing to younger clientele. Real ale is only occasionally available.

Queen Adelaide (Map 8)
272 Kingston Road, KT19 0SH
OS: 214643 (A240)
☎ (020) 8393 2666
Courage Best Bitter, Directors
Originally a pub in its own right, it now forms part of a hotel lodge and restaurant combine. A Travelodge is situated to the rear of the premises, whilst a "Country Carvery" leads off the main bar, which is frequented mainly by the younger set. Open all day, the pub has disabled facilities.

● Spring Tavern (Map 9)
1 London Road, KT17 2AY
OS: 219628 (B2200)
☎ (020) 8786 0121
12-11 (12-10:30 Sunday)
Fuller's London Pride
Guest Beers

An attractive weatherboarded exterior belies the multicoloured interior. It is food oriented, but not to the exclusion of drinkers, who have three guest beers from the Ember Inns list to choose from. These tend to be from the family brewers and change every few months. Food is served all day until 8pm. The Rolling Stones apparently stayed here in the 1970s and a former landlord was hanged a few hundred yards from here for murdering his wife.
◁▶ ❅ ⊘ ♿ 🚉 (Ewell West)

Star (Map 10)
2 Cheam Road, KT17 1SA
OS: 221625 (B2200)
☎ (020) 8786 8413
Badger K&B Sussex, Best, Tanglefoot, seasonal beer
This former wine bar has had a multitude of names over the years. These include After Hours, Pipps, Marbles, and the Loose Box. It was acquired by Hall & Woodhouse in 2001 and given more of a pub feel. There are several distinct areas, including a small snug by the entrance. Pleasant bar staff. It is open all day.

Toby Carvery (Map 12)
45 Cheam Road, KT17 1QZ
OS: 226623 (A232)
☎ (020) 8786 8166
Fuller's London Pride
The former Glyn Arms is now a nondescript carvery pub. In 1991 this lovely old inn had the ignominy of becoming TJ's Rib Place, and unsurprisingly stopped selling a decent pint. Today real ale is not prominent, and what is offered may change. There is a good collection of Bamforth postcards in the gents' loo, however. Open all day.

● Wheatsheaf (Map 13)
34 Kingston Road, KT17 2AA
OS: 219627
☎ (020) 8393 2879
11-11 (12-10:30 Sunday)
Webster's Green Label Best
Young's Bitter
Guest Beer

The Wheatsheaf has a comfortable modernised interior and fine leaded "Isleworth Brewery" windows. There are two comfortable carpeted rooms with open fires, served by a single bar. Prints and old photos of the area complete the decor. The pub was built in 1858 and stands opposite the scenic Hogsmill river. A pub has been on this site since 1456. A true community local with both Morris men and the Epsom Male Voice Choir meeting here. Darts, crib, shove halfpenny and shut the box are all played. Occasionally sport, particularly rugby, may be shown on TV. There is live music at weekends, mostly easy listening. Good homemade lunches are served 12-2 from Monday to Saturday.
◁ ❁ 🚌 (Ewell West)

EWHURST (A3)

A small village below the Surrey Hills, with an unusual village sign that was erected to commemorate the Coronation in 1953. The Norman church has medieval windows, an ancient font, and a Jacobean pulpit. In 1956 a Roman villa was discovered at Rapsley, when a local copse was being replanted. The archaeological examination finished in 1968. The mill at Ewhurst was a notable landmark, and was situated 800 feet (244 metres) above sea level. It ceased to work in 1885 and was converted into a house a few years later. In 1983, Baryonyx, a type of fish-eating dinosaur, was discovered in the local clay, and the skeleton can now be seen at the Natural History Museum in London.

Bull's Head
The Street, GU6 7QD
OS: 093408 (B2127)
☎ (01483) 277447
Adnams Bitter
Flowers IPA
Marston's Pedigree
This quiet one bar pub has a non-smoking area "fenced off" to the left hand side by agricultural implements. The outside skittle alley can be booked, but requires at least 30 people who must also pay for a set meal. Six basic bedrooms are available.

Windmill Inn
Ride Way, Pitch Hill GU6 7NN
OS: 080424
www.gastro-windmill.com
☎ (01483) 277566
No real ale

The sign advertising the inn name as "W" tells you that this is not a conventional pub. However, despite the lack of real ale, there is much to admire about this old pub that used to be a smuggler's look-out. Although very much a restaurant, there are several comfortable seats for drinkers, but, unusually, no tables. There are two parts to the bar, separated by a fireplace, and two suits of armour guard over them. An excellent menu is offered with a wide variety of fresh home-cooked dishes available. This is run as a brasserie operation lunchtime and from Monday to Wednesday evening, with a full à la carte menu available Thursday to Saturday evening. Perhaps the most impressive feature of the pub is the fantastic garden. This is multi-levelled, and good use has been made of decking. From here superb views of the surrounding countryside can be had. There is a separate outside bar at a lower level, and a grill menu is served here in the summer. Open all day Sundays and summer Saturdays, this place would be a cracker if it sold some Real Ale in a Bottle.

FARLEIGH (D1)

Close to the Greater London border and only saved from becoming part of the Borough of Croydon by a spirited fight from its residents during the local government changes of the 1970s. The Norman church remains almost completely unrestored.

● Harrow Inn

309 Farleigh Road, CR6 9EL
OS: 365597
☎ (01883) 629031
11-11 (12-10:30 Sunday)
Bass
Fuller's London Pride
Occasional **Guest Beer**

One main bar, from which lead several areas for eating and drinking. This Vintage Inn is heavily geared up as a food venue and there is an ancient flint barn attached to the main pub which is exclusively for diners. Nevertheless, it is an attractive building and inside there is a mix of flagstones, quarry tiles and wooden floorboards to complement the comfortable seating, with a huge outdoor area for eating and drinking. The pub is on the 409 bus route. Food is available from 12-10 Monday to Saturday and 12-9:30 Sunday. A guest beer may be available in summer.

◁▶ ✕ ♞ 🚗 ❁ ⊘ ♿

FELBRIDGE (D3)

Village which is becoming an extension of East Grinstead on the other side of the Sussex border. Its millponds are a reminder of the days when it was part of the iron industry

Felbridge Hotel

London Road, RH19 2BH
OS: 374397 (A22)
☎ (01342) 326992
No real ale

140 room hotel and conference centre just over the Sussex border. The one no smoking bar shows televised sport and has a pool table. Open all day.

Star Inn

London Road, RH19 2QR
OS: 373396 (A22)
☎ (01342) 323239
Marston's Pedigree
Occasional **Guest Beer**

Serving food all day, the 18th century Star has been greatly extended over the years. Although featuring fake timber, there are some genuinely old parts to the pub, but you have to hunt to find them. The name of the pub comes from the badge of the Earls of Surrey and Sussex. Full disabled facilities are available, and there is a family room in operation until 9 p.m..

Woodcock
Woodcock Hill, RH19 2RE
OS: 366411 (A22)
An attractive beamed bar attached to an 18th century restaurant, food was very much a feature here. The building only became a pub in the mid 1980s and was a freehouse selling a variety of beers. Originally called the Lincoln Imp, it soon changed its name to the Woodcock. The small bar featured stone flagging and leaded windows. Accommodation comprised five letting rooms. Unfortunately the pub closed in the late 1990s.

FETCHAM (B1)

Fetcham has expanded towards Leatherhead, with the River Mole between them, and has relatively few old properties. It has been inhabited since Saxon times and the walls of St Mary's church contain Roman bricks and other pre-Conquest masonry. Bockett's Farm, just off the A246, is a working family farm with interesting breeds of farm animals and poultry, with a tea-room in an 18th century barn. Fetcham's millponds and its spring have been scheduled as a Site of Special Scientific Interest.

● Bell

Bell Lane, KT22 9ND OS: 148859
☎ (01372) 372624
11-11 (12-10:30 Sunday)
Young's Bitter, Special, seasonal beers
Young's Golden Champion, Special London Ale in bottle.
Large 1930s pub set away from the village centre, the Bell was built on the site of an earlier pub. The recently refurbished single bar is divided into three areas by large pillars. Food is a prominent part of the business and is served all day until 9:30, with changing specials and a children's menu. Families are welcome until 9:30pm. A large tiered terrace runs the width of the front of the pub for the warmer months. Dominoes and board games are available to play. Originally a Hodgson's of Kingston house, it was sold to the Magic Pub Company who were then bought by Greene King. It was bought by Young's in 2004.

Cheers
145 Cobham Road, OS: 148564
This wine bar, which closed in the early 1990s, is now a tile shop. This means there is no drinking establishment in central Fetcham. A number of real ales were sold. Towards the end of its life it became Friends Wine Bar, and finally it became Al's Pasta & Café Bar.

Rising Sun
Hawks Hill, OS: 160560 (B2122)
Once a classic 1930s Hodgson's Kingston Brewery brick built pub, the façade was hidden by wooden cladding in later years as a Harvester pub-restaurant. Previous to this it had been a lively two-bar Courage pub. Boule was played in the garden in the 1990s. The pub was demolished for housing in 2005.

FICKLESHOLE (D1)

Small collection of houses on the Greater London border near to Biggin Hill Airport.

● White Bear

Fairchildes Lane, CR6 9PH
OS: 389603
☎ (01959) 573166
11-11 (12-10:30 Sunday)

Everard Tiger
Fuller's London Pride
Wells Bombardier
Occasional **Guest Beer**
A large, attractive Grade II listed 16th Century pub which started life at the right-hand end of a terrace and gradually expanded into successive adjoining cottages over the years. The building's evolution has led to a warren of interconnecting low-ceilinged rooms on different floor levels, three with real fires, and a couple of inglenooks; and all with much heavy antique furniture and fittings. Fittingly, given the building's age, two ghosts are said to haunt the pub. Note the two very attractive J. T Davies mirrors and also the coloured leaded lights in some windows. The pub is proud of its civilised atmosphere which it helps retain by a complete ban on electronic games, TV, sports etc, and with music kept to a discreet level. The origins of the stone bear at the front are unclear. One source has it that it arrived here from Piccadilly Circus; another says it replaced an earlier design in wood and is said to be around 200 years old. One thing is certain; it narrowly escaped being "kidnapped" by Polish pilots from Biggin Hill at the end of World War Two! Voted Pub/Restaurant of the Year (2004) by the Surrey Guardian. The emphasis is very much on food, but no less welcoming for the casual drinker too. The majority of the pub is no smoking. Food is served 12-3 and 6-9, Monday to Thursday and 12 – 9:30 Friday to Sunday. Views of planes taking of from Biggin Hill Airport can be had from the garden. Hard to find for the uninitiated but a pub well worth seeking out!
◁▶✂🚗❁⊗♿

FOREST GREEN (B3)

A small hamlet overlooked by Leith Hill and Holmbury Hill and with a large green on the main road. A track from Forest Green over the back of Leith Hill was known as Smugglers' Way, and much contraband was transported towards London through the well-wooded countryside. The village forge was renovated in 1985, and the chapel was built for use by nonconformists towards the end of the 19th century. A song sung by a labourer to Dr Ralph Vaughan Williams when he was collecting folk songs later became "O Little Town of Bethlehem".

● Parrot Inn

Horsham Road, RH5 5RZ
OS: 124413
☎ (01306) 621339
11-11 (12-10:30 Sunday)
Courage Best Bitter
Fuller's London Pride
Hog's Back TEA
Marston's Pedigree
Guest Beer
This large rural pub is in a very attractive position overlooking the green and was a former Surrey Trust Company house. The name is thought to come from smuggling. The beamed area in front of the bar has some large flagstones on the floor and a large inglenook and some polished brass. There are a number of other areas around, including an area to the rear where pool can be played. There is also a piano here, and a raised brick built stage area watches over both items. Next to this is a public telephone, sitting in a genuine red booth. All the food is home-

cooked and is available each lunchtime and evening, with a carvery in operation for Sunday lunch. Outside are large gardens including a children's play area – children are allowed into the pub until 9pm. To the rear of the pub is a function room which is licenced to hold weddings. The guest beer often comes from King's. Sunday night features a quiz.

◁▶ ✂ 🐴 🚗 ❁ 🚭 ♿ 🚲

FRIDAY STREET (A2)

A beautiful hamlet in a steep wooded valley, which is reached by narrow roads, it contains a pond, some old stone cottages and an inn. In the 11th century the mill ground corn, and in later years iron, wire and gunpowder were made in the valley. Built during the reign of Henry VIII, the powder mill is said to be the first of its kind in England.

● Stephan Langton

Friday Street, RH5 6JR
OS: 128456
☎ (01306) 730775
11-3 (not Monday), 5-11 (11-11 Saturday, 12-8 Sunday)
Adnams Bitter
Fuller's London Pride
Hogs Back TEA
Westons Old Rosie Cider

This gastro-pub, with the only Michelin "bib gourmand" in Surrey, is named after a local man who became the Archbishop of Canterbury in 1206 and who was involved in the writing of Magna Carta. Stephan Langton, reputedly born in Friday Street and brought up in nearby Broadmoor, inspired the book of his name by Martin Tupper. Only built in the 1930s, the bar has a welcoming open fire, and dogs are welcome if kept on a lead. Situated in good walking country, by an old hammer pond, it gets especially busy in the summer, and booking is often essential if you want Sunday lunch, and is advisable at all times. There is a daily changing menu and all food is freshly cooked, even the bread. Food is available each lunchtime except Monday (when the pub is closed) from 12:30-3, and Tuesday to Saturday evenings from 7-10. It might be best to use the nearby walkers' car park to the west if the limited parking is full. Outside is a patio garden.

◁▶ ✂ 🚗 ❁

GATWICK AIRPORT (C3)

Once part of Surrey, but transferred to West Sussex in 1974 under the terms of the 1972 Local Government Act. The former Gatwick Racecourse was used for the running of the Grand National during the First World War. Gatwick Airport has greatly expanded since then and has once more crept up to the Surrey boundaries. Although there are several bars at the airport, only one of the landside ones sells real ale. However, a number of pubs in this guide are accessible to those who are here for a while. See the separate article in this guide for details.

Village Inn

Gatwick Village, South Terminal RH6 0NN
OS: 288413
☎ (01293) 579800
Courage Directors
Marston's Burton Bitter, Pedigree

Included in this guide only for completeness; if you are stuck at the airport for a short while, you will probably find your way here. Although operated by Wetherspoon's, don't expect cheap beer or guest ales. Its major attraction is that it is open all day from 4 in the morning (perhaps slightly later in winter) until 11 in the evening (10:30 on Sunday). There is Sky Sports on TV, and food available all day. The "pub" at the North Terminal, the "Bridge Bar", is keg beer only.

GODSTONE (C2)

Godstone is a village built around a large tree-lined green, with a small nature reserve around Bay Pond run by the Surrey Wildlife Trust. Stone was mined beneath the North Downs, and there are around 300 miles of tunnels between Godstone and Reigate, some of which were used to store brandy and to grow mushrooms before the Second World War. Sand has also been quarried locally and there has been surveying for oil carried out. There were originally two villages – one at Godstone Green, and the other where the church stands, to the east of the current village. In Saxon times the second village was referred to as Wolcnestede and it was also mentioned in the Domesday Book as a homestead where cloth was "walked" (trampled) in vats with local Fuller's Earth. Godstone was also a centre for the leather industry and ironwork. In the churchyard lies the body of "Walker Miles", who was well known for promoting rambling as a pastime. Sir George Gilbert Scott designed the Tudor-style almshouses in Church Lane in 1872, and also rebuilt the 12th century church. The church contains the black and white marble tomb of Sir John Evelyn and his wife. The Evelyn family owned the mill used to manufacture gunpowder in 1588 for the fight against the Spanish Armada. Godstone Vineyards are nearby, as is Godstone Farm, which gives the opportunity to see farm animals, a nature trail and picnic area.

● Bell Inn

128 High Street, RH9 8DX
OS: 350515 (B2236)
☎ (01883) 741877
12-11 (12-10:30 Sunday)
Bass
Fuller's London Pride
Occasional **Guest Beer**

This is the oldest pub in Godstone and dates from 1393, although it has been much modified over the years. As a coaching inn, this was where the travellers stayed, with the grooms and coachmen staying at the long gone Rose & Crown. Tunnels underneath the Bell connect it to the White Hart up the road. Today there is an agreeable drinking ambience to the pub, with a good range of food available in the bar and in the small restaurant at the back of the pub. This is served all sessions during the week, and from 12-9 on Saturday and 12-6 on Sunday. Dominoes and jenga can be played in the bar.

◁▶✂🚗☸

● Hare & Hounds

Needles Bank, Bletchingley Road
RH9 8LN
OS: 350517 (A25)
☎ (01883) 742296
11-11 (12-10:30 Sunday)
Fuller's London Pride
Harveys Sussex Best Bitter
Young's Special

Facing the village green from an elevated position, this 400 year old pub used to be part of the Westerham Brewery estate. Although good food is available each lunchtime and evening, this is still very much a pub and the beer quality is equally good. Food is also available all day on weekends. Inside there are three distinct bar areas, and dominoes and shove halfpenny can both be played.

◁ ▶ 🚗 ☸ 🚭 ♿ (public toilets outside pub)

Old Surrey Hounds
Godstone Hill, RH9 8AP
OS: 350523
An old and attractive Friary Meux pub, it was situated next to the also demolished Godstone bus garage. In the 1970s it was a basic two bar pub, but sold Ind Coope bitter direct from casks behind the bar. Around 1990 it was sold to the free trade and was renamed the Old Surrey, but was pulled down for housing in 1995.

● White Hart

71 High Street, RH9 8DU
OS: 351516 (B2236)
☎ (01883) 742521
11-11 (12-10:30 Sunday)
Fuller's London Pride
Greene King IPA
Wadworth 6X

A highwayman reputedly haunts this old well-beamed coaching inn, and Queen Victoria stayed here on her way to Brighton. Underground tunnels connect the White Hart to the nearby Bell Inn. Opposite the pub is the village green on which cricket is played in summer. Bar food is served all day with more substantial meals being sold in the restaurant which is open every lunchtime and evening (and all day Sunday). Children are welcome in the non-smoking bar. Elsewhere in the pub darts and pool are played.

◁ ▶ ✂ 🚗 ☸ 🚭 ♿

White Swan
60 High Street OS: 350518 (A25)
Still standing as offices, the White Swan was a Friary Meux house which closed in 1984. It dates from the mid 17th century, and was a traditional two-bar pub with an inglenook. Under the bar was a well which was used by smugglers.

GOMSHALL (A2)

Gomshall was the site of 11th century leatherworks. These continued for hundreds of years, eventually combining to form one large tannery. Tanning only ceased in 1988, with the site now used for housing. The railway was opened in 1846, and a local tale holds that people were encouraged to wait for the train by the offer of free beer from the Black Horse so that a station would be built at Gomshall. The original water mill was mentioned in the Domesday Book and spans the Tillingbourne. It had two waterwheels, the larger of which was the biggest in the south of England. The restored Gomshall Mill is now a restaurant.

Black Horse

55 Station Road, GU5 9NP
OS: 086478 (A25)
☎ (01483) 202242
Fuller's London Pride
Greene King IPA

This Thai restaurant has an attached bar with pool and darts upstairs, and a raised garden outside. The bar is open all day, but, other than Sundays, food is only available at lunchtime and in the evening. Alternate Tuesdays are Indian Buffet Curry nights, where you may eat as much as you like. Sunday lunchtime, till 5pm, is a carvery rather than Thai. Originally a malt house in the late 17th century, it did not become a pub until the early 19th century. John Reffell's brewery used to be situated at the back of the inn, and brewed mild, bitter and a Farmer's Brew here. William Gladstone is said to have had a meeting here. Young's of Wandsworth bought the pub in 1926 and closed the brewery three years later. The pub was known as a smart country hotel up until its sale to Whitbread in 1989, who then ran it as a Mulligans fish restaurant. Thankfully it has now returned to being a pub.

● Compasses

50 Station Road, GU5 9LA
OS: 085478 (A25)
☎ (01483) 202506
11-11 (12-10:30 Sunday)
Marston's Pedigree
Guest Beers

Situated on the A25 this is an excellent spot to break your journey. Dating from 1830, this former Surrey Trust Company pub stands on the banks of the Tillingbourne and has a separate bar and restaurant, which serves homemade food, cooked to order. This is available each day, from 12-9 Monday to Saturday and 12-6 on Sunday. Additionally, an à la carte menu is served in the non-smoking restaurant from Wednesday to Sunday evening. The pub was originally called God Encompasses, but over time this was shortened to the current, easier to pronounce name. The three guest beers change monthly and generally come from micro-breweries. Live music in the form of a duo (blues, rock or folk) is featured every Friday evening from 9pm. The garden is reached by a bridge over the stream. The resident ghost is of a girl in her twenties who drowned in the Tillingbourne after trying to escape a fire in the pub. Luckily she is friendly and is known to turn the pub taps on, and to skip across the water. Accommodation is two twin en-suite rooms.

GREAT BOOKHAM (B2)

In the centre of the village is the Grade I listed St Nicholas church which was originally Saxon, but was rebuilt by the Normans in the 12th century. The chancel was built by the Abbot of Chertsey, John Rutherwick, in 1341 and there is some impressive 15th century stained glass. Jane Austen, whose godfather was rector, is among a number of well known people who have worshipped here. Another was Fanny Burney who was living in Great Bookham when she wrote "Camilla". Nearby is Polesden Lacey, a Regency mansion which was extensively altered in the early 1900s. The future King George VI spent some of his honeymoon here in 1923. The house and the 1,400 acre grounds are now owned by the National Trust. The gardens host Shakespearean plays in summer.

● Anchor

161 Lower Road, KT23 4AH
OS: 139548
☎ (01372) 452429
11-3 (3:30 Saturday), 5:30-11 (12-3, 7-10:30 Sunday)
Courage Best Bitter, Directors
Guest Beer

16th Century, Grade II listed pub which is in contrast to the suburbia that surrounds it. The pub is traditionally decorated and has exposed

brickwork, oak beams, and a large inglenook fireplace. Quality food is served between 12 and 2, Monday to Saturday. Cards and dominos are played. The guest beer tends to be from the family brewers and may stay the same for some time if it proves popular.

◁ 🚗 ☸

Old Crown
1 High Street, KT23 4AA
OS: 135545
☎ (01372) 458119
Fuller's London Pride

The pub only occupies what was the saloon bar of the original building, with the eastern end now being a French restaurant and the western end a hairdressers. The bar is decorated in a modern style. The western end features some wonderful tiling from Hodgson's Kingston brewery, who built it back in the 1930s.

Preston Cross Hotel and Country Club
Rectory Lane, KT23 4DY
OS: 126543
www.prestoncrosshotel.co.uk
☎ (01372) 456642
Guest Beer

A Victorian country house set in spacious grounds; it was converted into a country club and hotel in the 1960s. It features full restaurant facilities and 22 en-suite bedrooms. It is open to non-residents and general drinkers are welcome in the bar provided they dress to suit the environment. Good quality live jazz is played each Sunday lunchtime in the separate Sovereign Suite, for which a small admission is charged. The one beer changes regularly and is often form a regional brewer. Large car park and some sporting facilities.

● Royal Oak
16 High Street, KT23 4AG
OS: 135544
☎ (01372) 452533
11-11 (12-10:30 Sunday)
Beer range varies

A small two bar local which dates from 1570 and has a low ceiling and plenty of beams in the cosy and warm lounge. A flagged floor and inglenook complete the country village pub feel. The public has darts and background music or jukebox. Very much a locals' pub that can get noisy, it is friendly at the same time. Snacks and meals are offered through the day. 5-6 real ales are rotated off a list of about 8 beers from regional brewers.

◁ ▶ 🚗 ☸

HAMSEY GREEN (D1)

A small residential area adjoining Croydon, with parts in Greater London and parts in Surrey. Hamsey Green Pond is thought to have been in existence since Neolithic times.

● Good Companions
Limpsfield Road, CR6 9RH
OS: 350595 (B269)
☎ (020) 8657 6655
www.thegoodcompanions.com
11-11 (12-10:30 Sunday)
Westerham Black Eagle SPA, British Bulldog, 1965 Special Bitter Ale, Sevenoaks 7X, seasonal beer

Built in the 1930s to serve the new housing development around Hamsey Green, the "Goodies" is a much altered example of Brewer's Tudor, and is reputed to be named after J B Priestley's eponymous novel. Prior to the fad for ripping out partitions, the various bars were actually named after characters from the book. Now with one large open plan bar and a separate no-smoking restaurant, this former Watney's house is bidding fair to build up an excellent reputation with drinkers and diners alike. Although not tied to them, all the beers come from the Westerham brewery. The Special Bitter and the Sevenoaks alternate. The pub's previous reputation has now been swept aside by the forward thinking family who now hold the lease and it is a pleasure to discover a total absence of national ale brands. There is also a comfortable non-smoking area within the main bar. Large screen TVs show the major sporting events. Tuesday is open mic night, and there is a disco on the last Saturday of the month. Pool and darts are both played, and families are welcome until 9pm. There is also a children's play area in the garden. Food is available from 12-9 Monday to Thursday, 12-10 Friday and Saturday, and 12-7 Sunday. Disabled access is possible to both the bar and the upper restaurant area. A pub well worth seeking out.

HAXTED (D2)

Near the Kent border, Haxted is known for its double-fronted mill on the river Eden, which was built in two halves in 1580 and 1794. It has been restored and now houses a museum and picture gallery.

Haxted Mill
Haxted Road, TN8 6PU
OS: 418455
www.haxtedmill.co.uk
☎ (01732) 862914
Greene King Hen's Tooth in bottle
Working water mill on the River Eden which is now part of Haxted Mill Museum. It is situated on the Surrey Cycleway. The bar is part of the restaurant and is closed Sunday evening and all day Monday (and winter Tuesdays). Only bottled beer is sold but this does include one Real Ale in a Bottle. An excellent wine selection is also available.

HEADLEY (B2)

Surrounded by the National Trust owned Headley Heath, the village is popular with walkers and horse-riders. Headley Grove was once the home of Sir Malcolm Campbell, and Headley Court became the headquarters of Canadian forces in Europe during the Second World War. It is now the Defence Services Medical Rehabilitation Unit.

● **Cock Inn**
Church Lane, KT18 6LE
OS: 204548
☎ (01372) 377258
12-11 (12-10:30 Sunday)
Beer range varies
Family run pub, which has recently benefited from a bit of well needed TLC after being run down by a succession of PubCos. The pub is around 250 years old and has some of the old features from its past still intact. It is good to see that the pub has returned to its

original name after a few years being unnecessarily called The Cock Horse. The traditional public bar has been reinstated for pub games and can also be hired for functions. The main bar is aimed at the food trade, but not to the exclusion of drinkers. It has painted walls and woodwork, with pictures to break things up. To those who remember the cult children's TV show "The Clangers", the metal chickens around the place should seem familiar. There are wonderful views across the valley opposite from the pub and garden. It is hoped to expand the range of real ales to four from the Coors list. Children are only allowed in the restaurant area when eating. Food served until 5 on Sundays.

◁▶✕🚗❁⊗♿

HOLMBURY ST MARY (A3)

Known as Felday until 1879, Holmbury St Mary is mainly a 19th century development, and is named after Holmbury Hill, from which there are panoramic views of the North and South Downs. An Iron Age hill fort can be found here. St Mary's church dates from 1879 and was built by George Edmund Street, designer of the London Law Courts. The area was used by smugglers and poachers, and many of the cottages had large cellars in which their ill-gotten gains were hidden. The area was described in E M Forster's novel "A Room With a View".

● King's Head

Pitland Street, RH5 6NP
OS: 112442
☎ (01306) 730282
12-11 (12-10:30 Sunday)
Greene King IPA, Old Speckled Hen
King Horsham Best Bitter
Guest Beer

One of Surrey's "Best Kept Secrets" is tucked away up a back lane at the southern end of the village and is popular with walkers. The building dates from the 17th century, and the pub used to brew its own beer. It later became a Friary pub until they sold it in 1979. Today families are welcome in the bar of this free house, which has an open fire between the two bars. The far wall of the front bar area has a large number of shooting prints on display. The rear part of the pub has a wooden floor and is split level. The right hand side of this has bare-brick walls decorated with agricultural artefacts. Home cooked meals are served each lunchtime and evening apart from Sunday evening and all day Monday. This is served from 12-2:30 (3 Sunday) and 6-9 and features a number of fish specials. Takeaway food is available on Monday and Friday evenings between 6-8, the latter night's speciality being fish and chips. There is a gently sloping beer garden at the rear. Rare for Surrey, the pub still has an outside gents. The guest beer changes monthly.

◁▶🐴🚗❁

● Royal Oak

The Glade, Felday Road, RH5 6PF
OS: 110444
☎ (01306) 730120
11-3, 6-11 (12-3, 7-10:30 Sunday)
Adnams Bitter
Bass
Greene King IPA
Young's Bitter

In a beautiful setting between the picturesque church and village green, the 17th century Royal Oak is situated in the centre of the village, and is a lovely place to sit outside on a summer's day. There is a small entrance porch containing a couple of tables leading to a small and cosy bar where home-made meals are served at every session, except Sunday evening and Monday, with fish dishes being a speciality. Food is served from 12-2 and 6-9, but these hours are slightly flexible. At one end of the bar is an attractive fire. At the other end of the bar, down a small step, is a small tiled area. The pub is a popular destination with walkers and cyclists. There is a separate room for families.

HOOKWOOD (C3)

Small village on the outskirts of Horley which now includes a superstore.

● Black Horse

Reigate Road, RH6 0HU
OS: 264431 (A217)
☎ (01293) 773611
11-11 (12-10:30 Sunday)
Badger K&B Sussex, Best,

Tanglefoot, seasonal beer
A large pub on the outskirts of Horley, the Black Horse has been well renovated and is now a popular dining pub. Originally a Friary Meux pub, then a free house, it was bought by Hall & Woodhouse in 1994. Internally there are large solid tables to sit at, and the walls are adorned with old photographs. Food is served each day until 9:30 (9 Sunday) and the pub is a good stop on the way to Gatwick Airport. Families are welcome until 9pm.

HOOLEY (C1)

Main road village near the end of the M23 and by a railway cutting on the Brighton line.

Star
Brighton Road OS: 289568 (A23)
Just north of the village centre and opposite Star Bridge, this two bar Charrington's house was entered directly off the narrow pavement on the A23. Former regulars remember a traditional public bar with heavy wrought iron marble topped tables, and a more comfortable saloon. They pub was demolished in the autumn of 1977 as part of a road widening scheme, leaving the area without a pub.

HORLEY (C3)

Horley changed from a tiny village to a town with the arrival of the railway in 1841. The first iron works in Surrey was documented here in 1371. The original centre was around St Bartholomew's church, which dates from the 14th century, but was almost entirely rebuilt in 1881. In the 14th century the district was known as Thunderfield in the Forest, where it is thought there may have been an Anglo-Saxon pre-Christian shrine. Horley was due to be transferred to West Sussex under the 1972 Local Government Act, but stayed in Surrey following local protests. The town lies close to Gatwick Airport and there are plans to build around 3,000 more houses in the area.

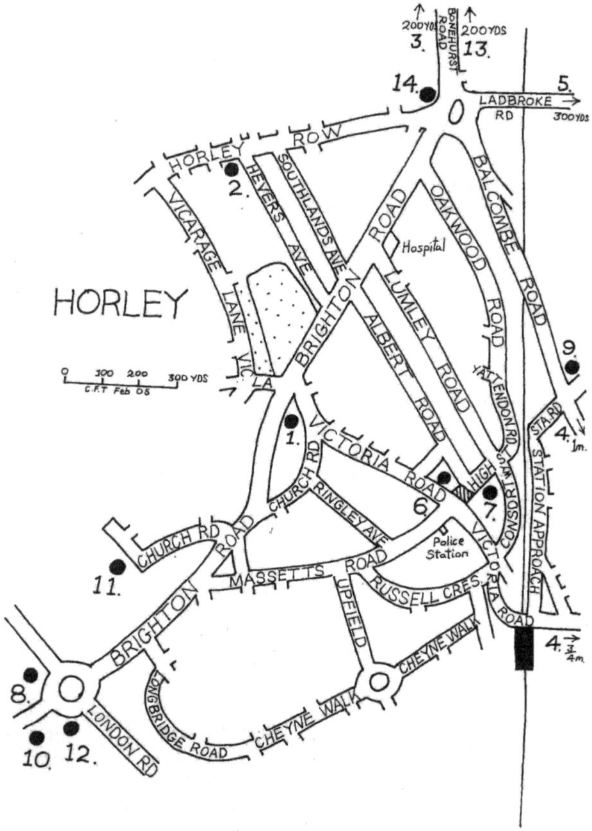

Air Balloon (Map 1)
60 Brighton Road, RH6 7HE
OS: 280433 (A23)
☎ (01293) 823726
No real ale
Open all day, the Air Balloon occupies a prime site on the main road. Originally built as the Thorns, later becoming the Game Bird, it re-opened under its current name in March 2003. Now aimed squarely at families, there is a Wacky Warehouse for the kids, but sadly no real ale for the parents. The pub has two gardens, one with children's play equipment, the other adult only.

● **Bull (Map 2)**
Horley Row, RH6 8DE
OS: 278439
☎ (01293) 783701
12-11 (12-10:30 Sunday)
Harveys Sussex Best Bitter
Guest Beer
Built as two cottages, the pub was originally called the Rainbow. It was renamed the Bull in the early 1990s after the landlord, Fred Bull. It is a true drinkers' pub with no food served apart from outdoor barbecues in the summer. Pub games enthusiasts can play pool and darts as well as dominoes and chess. The walls are decorated with much sporting memorabilia including golf clubs, tennis racquets, and several signed cricket bats. Also to be found are some royal telegrams amongst many other items of bric-a-brac. The guest beer changes monthly and is

from a list supplied by the pub company.

Cambridge Hotel (Map 3)
Brighton Road, RH6 8PP
OS: 284447 (A23)
www.thecambridgehotel.co.uk
☎ (01293) 783990
No real ale
37 room hotel with two bars in separate buildings. The front part of the hotel was built as a house for the 2nd Duke of Cambridge in 1865 and is grade II listed.

Chancer's
Station Arches, The Drive, RH6 7NQ OS: 286426
Originally a bar and restaurant called Tracks, which opened in 1992, and was impressively built in the arches under Horley Station. The walls were bare brick as might be expected giving its location. It changed its name to Chancer's in 1995 and became more a young persons' venue, opening evenings only. It closed a few years later. Parts of the premises are still boarded up, with the left hand arch now being part of the Archway Theatre.

● **Coppingham Arms (Map 4)**
263 Balcombe Road, RH6 9EF
OS: 293417 (B2036)
www.coppinghamarms.co.uk
☎ (01293) 782283
11:30-11 (12-10:30 Sunday)
Greene King Old Speckled Hen
Harveys Sussex Best Bitter

A traditional 300 year old pub, built from two cottages, the Coppingham Arms had its origins as a cider house. Families are welcome in the pub, which is well known locally for the quality of its food. This is served Monday to Friday from 12-2:30 and 6-10, Saturday 12-10 and Sunday 12-9. Although there is only one bar, there are distinct public and saloon areas, the former containing a pool table. Four bed and breakfast rooms are available, one of which is en-suite.

● **Farmhouse (Map 5)**
Ladbroke Road, RH6 8PB
OS: 290441
www.thefarmhousepub.co.uk
☎ (01293) 782146
12-11 (12-10:30 Sunday)
Courage Best Bitter
Fuller's London Pride
Shepherd Neame Spitfire
Guest Beer

Originally this was built as a farmhouse for Hewitt's farm in the 17th century, and the bar area of the pub dates from this time. The ghost of Mabel Hewett is believed to haunt the pub. In the 1930s the solicitor who acted on behalf of Mrs Simpson lived here, and it is said that King Edward VIII's abdication papers were signed here. Willow trees from the area were used to make cricket bats sold under the Stuart Surridge name – he was an England cricketer who lived nearby. The building became a pub in October 1985 and boasts many original timbers and inglenooks. Darts is played and the pub runs its own cricket team. Food is available every day from 12-9. Outside there is a large garden. This is used for a charity six a side cricket match against the Bull every June. Families are welcome in the Farmhouse until 9pm. The guest beer changes weekly.

◁▶

Foresters (Map 6)

88 Victoria Road, RH6 7AB OS: 284430
☎ (01293) 827041
Greene King IPA
Fuller's London Pride
This attractive town centre pub dates from the 19th century. It has much external weatherboarding, and unsurprisingly is known locally as the Wooden Hut. It has been extended over the years, but only has one bar - this is open all day. Photos of old Horley adorn most of the walls. There is a DJ on Thursday and Friday night when the pub can get very loud and very busy. Food is available all day until 9pm. The pub is on the Surrey Cycleway.

● Gatwick (Map 7)

42 High Street, RH6 7BB
OS: 285431
☎ (01293) 783801
11-11 (12-10:30 Sunday)
Badger K&B Sussex, Best, First Gold, Tanglefoot,
seasonal beer
The Gatwick is the best bet for beer in Horley town centre. This one bar pub has distinct public and lounge areas, and was named after the long gone Gatwick Racecourse. Real ale is popular in this former King & Barnes pub, and it is all served from 18-gallon kilderkins, which is rare these days. Darts is played in the public side of the bar. Food is available Monday to Saturday from 12-2:30 and 5-9:15.

◁▶

Gatwick Moat House (Map 10)

Longbridge Roundabout, RH6 0AB OS: 266425
☎ (01293) 899988
No real ale
124 room hotel with seven meeting rooms. The non-resident's bar is called Harriet's Bar.

Greyhound

Radford Road, Tinsley Green, RH10 3NS OS: 290396
☎ (01293) 884220
Adnams Broadside
Tetley Bitter
Now in West Sussex, the Greyhound was part of Surrey until 1974, and still has a rural feel to it, despite its proximity to Gatwick Airport and Crawley's industrial estates. There are two separate bars to this 1930s pub, plus an upstairs function room. The public has two pool tables and a dartboard. The lounge includes a semicircular part to the front which has a number of old photographs pertaining to marbles, for the Greyhound is well known as the venue for the World Marbles Championship every Good Friday. The six-foot raised ring they play on can be seen in the car park. The pub is open all day, with food served 12-8. Sport is shown on big screen TVs and outside there is a large garden.

Holiday Inn Gatwick Airport (Map 8)

Povey Cross Road, RH6 0BA
OS: 266426
☎ (0870) 4009030
No real ale
214 room Gatwick hotel with nine meeting rooms. The Hub Bar is open to non-residents. A carvery food operation can be found in Traders Restaurant. Previous names have been the Post House and the Forte Crest.

● King's Head (Map 9)

63 Balcombe Road, RH6 9HY

OS: 287433 (B2036)
☎ (01293) 827051
12-11 (12-10:30 Sunday)
Fuller's London Pride
Shepherd Neame Spitfire
Young's Bitter
Large, comfortable pub at the junction between Balcombe Road and Smallfield Road. Inside, everything has been knocked through to leave a U shaped room with the bar forming an L shape in the middle. The end result is 2-3 distinct drinking areas. Parts of the original interior were originally panelled but these, along with the rest of the walls have been painted in that creamy/orangey colour that is becoming prevalent in the current wave of pub refurbishment. Scattered throughout the pub are several gaming machines, which ensure the solitary drinker has more than one way to spend his money. Outside there is a large beer garden to the rear, while there are two or three table benches to the front for those who like to drink on the street. Over 21s only after 9pm and no work clothes at any time. Food is served from Monday to Saturday from 12-2:30 and 5-8:30 and on Sunday from 12-4. Disabled customers will find entering easier from the car park entrance.

◁▶ 🚗 🚭 ♿ 🚌

● Olde Six Bells (Map 11)
Church Road, RH6 8AD
OS: 276428
☎ (01293) 789911
11-11 (12-10:30 Sunday)
Adnams Bitter
Bass
Fuller's London Pride
Dating from 1403, this pub has valid claims to be one of Britain's oldest. This pub rests on wooden piles, some of which date from the year 827. Most of the pub is 16th century, however, but there are stone flags, some very low beams, and a welcoming inglenook fireplace. The pub is listed, as is the barn next to it. This is today the cellar for the bar. The pub rambles over two floors and there are many nooks and crannies in which to sit in comfort. A queen post is used to hold the roof up on the upper level – apparently only one other pub in England has this feature. The walls are covered in old photos showing historical views of Horley. Food is available every day from 12-10. The pub is to be found at the bottom Church road and the garden stretches down to the River Mole, although this is fenced off.

◁▶ 🚗 ❁ 🚭

Renaissance London Gatwick Hotel (Map 12)
Povey Cross Road, RH6 0BE
OS: 266425
☎ (01293) 820169
No real ale
254 room hotel with 12 meeting rooms. It opened in June 1978 and is now part of the Marriott Group. Previous names have been the Ramada, Gatwick Penta, and the Gatwick Park. The main bar is the Atlas Bar but it sells no real ale.

Skylane Hotel (Map 13)
34 Bonehurst Road, RH6 8QG
OS: 285445 (A23)
www.skylanehotel.co.uk
☎ (01293) 786971
Webster's Yorkshire Bitter
73 room family run hotel with real ale in the Wheel Bar which is open all day. There is a restaurant attached to the bar, and the hotel has a function room.

Station
Station Approach, RH6 7HQ

OS: 287428
Despite its name, this former Charrington's pub was a few hundred yards from the station, overlooking the railway line. Towards the end of its life it was a popular live music venue. It closed around 1993 and was later demolished for housing.

Thistle London Gatwick (Map 14)
Brighton Road, RH6 8PH
OS: 285441 (A23)
☎ (01293) 786992
Flowers Original
The public bar of this large 104 room hotel is the Chequers pub. This attractive bar dates from 1537 when it was a beer house for the village. It later became a coaching inn for a change of horses on the London to Brighton run. Today it still functions as a locals' bar, and has two giant 42" plasma screens for TV sport. Darts is also available and live music is played most weekends. Food is served from 12-7 daily, with the bar open all day.

HORNE (C2)

Horne is a small village with an extensively restored and altered church. John Kidgell, its parson in the 1770s, was, according to Horace Walpole, "much in vogue among the old ladies for his gossiping and quaint sermons" until he fled to Europe leaving behind large debts.

● **Jolly Farmer**
Whitewood Lane, RH9 8JR
OS: 347450
☎ (01342) 842867
12-3, 5:30-11 (12-11 Saturday and 12-10:30 Sunday)
Courage Best Bitter
Fuller's London Pride
Harveys Sussex Best Bitter
Guest Beer
The owner of this 270 year old pub has redecorated throughout without changing the cosy atmosphere which benefits from having two open fires. Years ago the pub was used for the registry of births, marriages and deaths, and later it became a bakery. The non-smoking restaurant has its own bar for busy periods and offers a range of good value dishes including traditional English and Thai dishes. Snacks and traditional pub meals are also available from the bar. Food is available all opening hours except Sunday and Monday evening. The Jolly Farmer is home to golf, fishing and shooting societies and boasts its own cricket ground, home to a thriving team. Darts and bar billiards are also available for those who prefer games without leaving the bar. Families are welcome throughout the pub. Unusually for this area Courage Best is the most popular ale available. A guest ale is not always available, but when it is, it tends to be from a microbrewery.

HURST GREEN (D2)

Joined to Oxted but still with its own railway station. Although the church was built in a medieval style, it only dates from 1912.

Diamond
Holland Road, RH8 9BQ
OS: 407503
☎ (01883) 716040
Greene King IPA
Originally three cottages, the Diamond was named after Queen Victoria's jubilee. Darts is played

in the one bar which also features an open log fire. Live music is played once a month. The pub is open all day and children are welcome until 9pm. A second beer is sometimes available. The pub was called the Kingsman for a while but this proved unpopular with the locals and so the original name was restored.

KINGSWOOD (B1)

A very upmarket residential area whose church, with its tall spire, was built in 1852 as a copy of the 14th century church in Shottesbrooke, Berkshire. A recent survey found that more millionaires live in Kingswood that anywhere else of comparable size. The manor house in Kingswood Warren was once the home of Sir Cosmo Bonsor, chairman of both the brewery group Watney, Combe & Reid, and the South Eastern Railway Company, with the latter having a special carriage constructed to take him to the very grandiose station.

● Kingswood Arms

Waterhouse Lane, KT20 6EB
OS: 247566
www.kingswoodarms.co.uk
☎ (01737) 354053
11-11 (12-10:30 Sunday)
Adnams Bitter
Courage Directors
Fuller's London Pride
Greene King Old Speckled Hen
Shepherd Neame Spitfire

This huge mock-Tudor pile was built around 1900 as the Station Hotel to serve the adjacent Kingswood Station on the Tattenham Corner branch. By the mid-60s it had become the Pigeon Pair and assumed its present title in the 1980s. Over the years, exposed brick has given way to painted render, whilst the amount of first floor black and white facing has grown. To the front of the interior is the main wood-beamed drinking bar - look out for the old silver cash register and a pre-decimal Watney's price list on display. Other artefacts include old agricultural implements and stuffed birds and fish in glass cases. A separate area known as the "Study" is available for hire, whilst to the right is a very large, more recent conservatory extension, capable of accommodating 120 diners. Food is served until 9:30pm all week (6pm Sunday). The pub was winner of the 1983 Evening Standard Pub of the Year Award and the licensees have been here ever since. A strong golfing society gathers in here, encouraged, no doubt, by the landlord's predilection for the game!

LEATHERHEAD (B1)

Originally a small market town, Leatherhead lies on the River Mole and has been extensively modernised. The market dates from a grant from Henry VIII in 1248. St John's School, originally for the sons of clergymen, was moved to Leatherhead in the mid 19th century. The County Court was said to have been held in the town before moving to Guildford in the 13th century. St Mary and St Nicholas church was mentioned in the Domesday Book. The Royal School for the Blind, founded in 1799, is situated here, as was the Thorndike Theatre, which originally opened in 1969. It closed in the 1997, but has recently reopened as the more modest Leatherhead Theatre. The birthcontol campaigner, Marie Stopes, wrote her controversial book "Married Love" in 1918 in Leatherhead, and lived locally. Vaughan Williams set John Shelton's poem "The Tunning of Elinour Rumming" about the landlady of the Running Horse to music in 1936. A local tradition was that the carrying of a dead body established a right of way. The owner of the 19th century Swan Brewery charged one penny for carrying a corpse through the brewery yard in order to prevent a right of way being established. Anthony Hope Hawkins, author of the "Prisoner of Zenda", is buried at the parish church of St Mary and St Nicholas. An attractive riverside walk leads to old mill ponds which are home to many water birds.

Brahms & Liszt
31 High Street, OS: 166565
This former modern bar is now an Indian restaurant. It was built as Muswells, a chain of café bars operated by Allied Breweries. It changed its name to Brahms & Liszt in 1992 and started selling real ale. It ceased being a pub in the late 1990s.

Brennan's
The Courtyard, Swan Centre
OS: 167565
This small Irish bar and restaurant has been replaced by a shop. It closed in the late 1990s.

Bull Hotel
41 North Street, OS: 163565 (A245)
Formerly a large residential hotel with three bars. The site is now flattened and surrounded by hoardings. Dating from 1926, it was originally owned by Young's of Dorking. At one stage it was Friary Meux's busiest outlet.

Duke's Head
57 High Street, KT22 8AG
OS: 167564
☎ (01372) 372076
Adnams Bitter
A large rambling pub, it is set back from the main road. The pub itself dates from the 17th century, but the frontage is 19th century. In the early 20th century the town band used to play in front of the pub. Open all day, it is now stuck at the top end of the sad pedestrianised High Street. The pub is mainly frequented by younger people in the evening and weekends, with sport shown on large screen TVs. Food is available each day from 12-8 and children are welcome until 9. The pub features a real fire and has a large conservatory.

● **Edmund Tylney**
30-34 High Street, KT22 8AW
OS: 166564
☎ (01372) 362715
10-11 (12-10:30 Sunday)
Courage Directors
Fuller's London Pride
Greene King Abbot Ale
Marston's Burton Bitter, Pedigree
Guest Beer
Former Woolworth store, this typical Wetherspoon's pub provided a good addition to Leatherhead's drinking scene when it opened in the late 1990s. Edmund Tylney, a Leatherhead man, was Master of the Revels to Queen Elizabeth I. This post had the power to licence plays. The height of the interior gives it a spacious feel. Children are allowed in until 8pm (6pm Fri & Sat) if they are eating. The one guest beer changes twice a week.

◁▶ 🚭 ♿ 🚌

Mole's Wine Bar
14, Bridge Street,
OS: 164564

This former bar is now yet another Indian restaurant. During the winter months in the 1980s, a cask of Fuller's ESB would be set up on the bar. By 1989 it was called Hamiltons and was selling no real ale.

● Penny Black

5 North Street, KT22 7AX
OS: 165565
☎ (01372) 386719
11-11 (12-10:30 Sunday)
Young's Bitter, Special, seasonal beers

What was a Hogshead alehouse conversion of the old Post Office in 1996 is now part of Young's tied estate. The building dates from 1895, but ceased being a post office in 1995. The decor is a mixture of bare brick, and painted walls and ceiling. Sports events are shown on the large TVs and tend to dominate the pub. A large patio area to the side of the pub is popular in the warmer months.
◁▶ ❁ ♿ 🚌

Plough

93 Kingston Road, KT22 7SU
OS: 165573 (A245)
☎ (01372) 377608
Fuller's London Pride
Greene King IPA
Wood panelled bars help create a pleasant atmosphere. The lounge with its conservatory is more suited to conversation than the public where games include darts and shove halfpenny. Open all day.

Prince of Wales

Lower Fairfield Road,
OS: 166565
A Courage pub that was demolished to make way for the Swan Centre in the late 1970s. It never sold real ale; however, most unusually, Directors was sold under gas pressure.

Railway Arms

85 Kingston Road,
OS: 164573 (A245)
Small and basic one bar Courage pub that dated from 1906. It was demolished in the late 1990s and replaced by apartments.

Royal Oak

265 Kingston Road, KT22 7PJ
OS: 163579 (B2430)
☎ (01372) 811988
Greene King IPA
A large and comfortable community pub on the outskirts of town, the Royal Oak was formerly owned by Charrington's, and became part of the Greene King estate in 1994. The one bar, which is open all day, has both pool and darts, and also big screen TV for sporting events. One guest beer may be introduced soon. At lunchtime the pub is popular with office staff from the nearby industrial estates and food is available each lunchtime from 12-3, and Monday to Friday evening, 6-8. Outside are a large patio area and a beer garden.

● Running Horse

38 Bridge Street, KT22 8BZ
OS: 163563
☎ (01372) 372081
11:30-11 (12-10:30 Sunday)
Fuller's London Pride
Greene King IPA, Old Speckled Hen
Taylor Landlord
Young's Bitter
Guest Beer
This historic Grade II* listed pub can trace its roots back to at least 1520. It was built on land belong-

ing to the church and was originally known as Rummings House, after the Elinour Rumming, who was written about by Henry VIII's poet, John Skelton. The poem can be found on a wall in the pub. Elinour was not the most attractive of women (according to the poem she was "scurvy and lousy …wondrously wrinkled like a roast pig's ear"). The beer (called "noppy ale" in the poem) does not sound that great, as hens ran loose around the brewhouse and would "go to roost, straight over the ale joust, and dung when it comes, in the ale tuns". History has it that Elizabeth I spent a night at the pub when flooding made the River Mole impossible to cross. Today the old lounge has been extended into a back room making it split level, with several areas. This rear area is mainly, but not exclusively, for food and has table service. A courtyard is available for summer drinking, as well as a garden at the back. The smaller public bar has live sport on TV, as well as darts and pool. At one time the pub was threatened with a ludicrous scheme to turn it into a Firkin pub. The guest beer changes every two to three months and is from the Punch list. No food Sunday evening. The pub car park is very small, but there is a public car park close by.

◁▶ 🚗 ❄ ⊘ ♿ 🚌

LEATHERHEAD COMMON (B1)

Small collection of buildings north of Leatherhead near Pachesham Park.

● Star

Kingston Road, KT22 0DP
OS: 166599 (A243)
☎ (01372) 824416
11-11 (12-10:30 Sunday)
Courage Best Bitter
Greene King IPA, Abbot Ale

Large pub on the Surrey and Greater London boundary. It is very popular with diners, but not to the exclusion of drinkers. There are dark red painted wood panels to waist level, with cream walls above, punctuated by pictures. Several log fires make for a cosy atmosphere in winter. The flower arrangements are a nice touch. High chairs are available. Its proximity to Chessington World of Adventures tends to make it busy at weekends.

◁▶ 🚗 ❄ ⊘

LEIGH (B2)

A pretty village with a pub, church and medieval houses surrounding a small village green. The village is pronounced "Lie" after an old word for a forest clearing. The Priest's House was built by Newark Priory, and is a 14th century timbered building with a Horsham stone roof. Leigh Place, a moated house with a decorative clock tower and battlements over the front door, was rebuilt in 1810. In the 17th century nearby Shellwood Common was the scene of a pitched battle between the old Commonwealth supporters and Royalists.

● Plough

Church Road, RH2 8NJ
OS: 224468
☎ (01306) 611348
11-11 (12-10:30 Sunday)
Badger K&B Sussex, Best, Tanglefoot, seasonal beer

Set in an attractive position opposite the church, the Plough has two contrasting bars. The weather-boarded part to the right of the pub is the oldest. This dates from the 15th century and contains some low beams and is now the pub lounge and no-smoking restaurant. The public bar is a Victorian addition and is where darts is played along with a large number of board games – ask at the bar for details. Note the fallow deer skull above the bar. A wide variety of home made food is served, including a number of daily specials. Food is served all day from 12-10 Monday to Saturday and from 12-9 on Sunday. Outside is a small patio garden.

● Seven Stars

Bunts Common Road, Dawes Green, RH2 8NP OS: 217472
☎ (01306) 611254
11-11 (12-10:30 Sunday)
Fuller's London Pride
Greene King Old Speckled Hen
Young's Bitter

This very attractive two bar tile-hung inn has been a pub since at least 1637. Evidence of this can be found in the saloon bar where part of the wall, covered by glass for protection, has written on it "Gentlemen, you are welcome to sit at your ease, pay what you call for and drink what you please", William Eades, 1637. It is rumoured that the Seven Stars was mentioned by Ben Johnson, the first Poet Laureate, who is said to have lived for a while at nearby Swaynes Farm. As Ben Johnson died in 1637, this would make the pub even older. The original pub was just the small top part of the bar, and the original entrance can be seen from the front of the building by the painted central door. Externally the pub is covered in hanging baskets and window boxes and there are extensive gardens. The saloon bar, which is dog friendly, is split level with a large inglenook at one end and a log burning stove at the other. The lounge bar was rebuilt in 1995 using 17th century oak timbers and contains some very low beams, many of which are draped with hops. This bar contains the restaurant and is entirely non-smoking. All the food is home cooked and there are a number of daily specials available. On Sunday only traditional lunches are served, with no food in the evening. Tuesday is tapas night when a large number of such dishes are served.

LIMPSFIELD (D2)

Limpsfield is an attractive village with a mixture of buildings, several half-timbered, ranging from the 15th to the 20th centuries. In 1924 the combined sound of a cello and a nightingale was broadcast by the BBC, when the cellist Beatrice Harrison played in the woods near her home. For a number of years Nightingale Festivals were held when the public could enjoy the gardens and nightingales for a shilling. Beatrice is buried, along with two sisters, in St Peter's churchyard, which is also the resting place of the composer Frederick Delius, Sir Thomas Beecham and Eileen Joyce, the Australian pianist.

● **Bull Inn**
High Street, RH8 0DR
OS: 416530 (B269)
☎ (01883) 713402
11-11 (12-10:30 Sunday)
Adnams Bitter
Marston's Pedigree
This 16th century community pub was formerly a coaching inn. It is situated in the centre of the village, and is Grade II listed. There are three separate rooms, one of which has a dining area off it, where food is available each lunchtime from 12-2:30. Evening food is only available if booked in advance. The pub has a cash machine, juke box, darts and shove-halfpenny. There is live music once a month, and, occasionally, karaoke. Sport is shown on big screen TVs and families are welcome in the bar until 8.

◁▶

LIMPSFIELD CHART (D2)

Good walking country in an attractive area of heathland and mixed woodland, much of which is owned by the National Trust and the Forestry Commission. Joseph Conrad lived here, and Baden-Powell and Buffalo Bill are said to have flown man-lifting kites on the common.

Carpenters Arms
12 Tally Road, RH8 0TG
OS: 424518
☎ (01883) 722209
Greene King IPA
Young's Bitter
L shaped bar with the area at the side used as a restaurant, or occasionally for functions, and the front for drinking. As well as being a meeting place for locals, its situation on the National Trust Limpsfield Common means that it is used by walkers, with or without dogs, and horse riders. Darts is played and the pub holds fortnightly quiz nights on Sundays. No food Mondays or Sunday evenings. Look for the pub sign at the end of Tally Road on the B269.

LINGFIELD (D3)

Known for its all weather surface racecourse, the Wealden village of Lingfield has a large 15th century church within a conservation area of old timbered houses. Inside the church is one of the finest collections of brasses in Surrey, and a series of monuments to the Cobham family. Near the pond is St Peter's Cross, which was built in 1437 as a boundary marker between Puttenden and Billeshurst manors. An unusual stone cage dating from 1773 was used as the village lock-up until 1882. The floor of the cage was higher than the ground outside, so prisoners had to be thrown upstairs rather than down. The public library is situated in the Guest House, which is the only surviving part of the college that was founded by the third Lord Cobham who fought in the Battle of Agincourt.

● Greyhound Inn

Plaistow Street, RH7 6AU
OS: 386435 (B2028)
☎ (01342) 832147
11-11 (12-10:30 Sunday)
Adnams Bitter
Greene King IPA

Dating from 1584, this old pub is reputedly haunted. The one bar area has bare wooden floors and pine furniture with darts being played in one area. Traditional home made food is sold and there is a separate restaurant. There used to be a tunnel connecting the pub to the church. Food is served every lunchtime and all but Sunday evening, and children are allowed in the pub until 9pm.

● Hare & Hounds Inn

Lingfield Common Road, RH7 6BZ OS: 387447
☎ (01342) 832351
11:30-11 (12-8 Sunday)
Flowers Original
Greene King IPA, Old Speckled Hen
Formerly a cottage, this country pub was only licenced around

1930. Very well known for the quality of its food, this is also a relaxing place for drinkers to visit, with chess and domino sets available for playing. Food is available all sessions, but note that the pub is closed on Sunday evening. Children are welcome at all times.

Lingfield
11 Godstone Road,
OS: 384436 (B2029)
A Friary Meux pub, it was known locally as "the Hotel" although it had not been so for many years. It was built in 1895, when its owner was a certain E Osbourne, and for some time there was a skittle alley at the rear. A large pub, it was set back from the main road. It closed around June 1988. The site is now the entrance to a modern housing development (Jenny Lane).

● Old Cage

Plaistow Street, RH7 6AU
OS: 385436 (B2028)
☎ (01342) 834271
11-11 (12-10:30 Sunday)
Greene King Old Speckled Hen
Harveys Sussex Best Bitter
John Smith Bitter
Young's Special
House Beer
The Old Cage is a grade II listed building, and dates from 1592. The building only became a pub in 1970 but had previously been a bakery, a shop, a restaurant, and a private residence. There are many genuine antiques around the pub including some wonderful blowlamps. The one bar is stone flagged and has many little areas

off it including one which has a real fire housed in a magnificent inglenook. Food is served every day from 12-9, with breakfast available from 9 in the morning. There is a patio for outside drinking. The guest beer in this free house changes weekly and is usually from local suppliers; however it is sold under the house name of Jailer. The three bedrooms are all en-suite.

● Star Inn

Church Road, RH7 6AH
OS: 385436
www.starinnlingfield.com
☎ (01342) 832364
11-11 (12-10:30 Sunday)
Brakspear Bitter
Flowers Original
Fuller's London Pride
Gales HSB
Greene King Old Speckled Hen
Wells Bombardier

The original pub was in a building opposite (now Church House). The current pub is around 100 years old, and is to be found away from the main road in an attractive area close to the parish church. Old photographs show that the pub used to be owned by Kelseys of Tunbridge Wells, a brewery that closed in 1956. Today the pub comprises a single L-shaped bar with pool and darts, and a real fire burns in winter. Open for breakfast, the Star sells food all sessions until 9:30 in the evening. Accommodation comprises of seven double rooms, all with en-suite facilities. Live music is performed on Friday nights. The beer range changes from time to time.

LITTLE BOOKHAM (A1)

The church here dates from the 12th century and contains several examples of medieval architecture. An 17th century tithe barn stands nearby, and there are buildings dating from Tudor times to the present day. In the 17th century, John Aubrey wrote of Great Bookham "Near this place is Little Bookham wherein nothing occurs worthy notice". The National Trust owned commons contain 12 ponds, which are home to all three types of British newt including the rare great crested newt. The five largest ponds were man-made for fish production in the 17th century.

Bookham Grange Hotel

The Approach, The Common, KT23 3HS OS: 124557
☎ (01372) 452742
No real ale
Hidden away 18 room hotel with a bar open to non-residents. It is surrounded by National Trust commonland.

Olde Windsor Castle

25 Little Bookham Street, KT23 3AA OS: 125545
☎ (01372) 452226
Courage Best Bitter
Guest Beers
The front part of this pub dates from the early 15th century. It was extended in 1914 with the addition of a saloon bar. With further extensions over the years, it provides ample space for drinkers and diners alike. A beamed ceiling and stone flagged floor remind you of the pub's history. Two guest beers

are sold from the Spirit list. Open all day.

LOWER KINGSWOOD (C2)

A small village of mainly Victorian dwellings, much character was lost when the A217 was widened and split it in half. The Grade I listed Church of Jesus Christ the Wisdom of God was built in 1891 by two Victorian archaeologists, Dr Edwin Freshfield and Sir Henry Cosmo Bonsor. Dr Freshfield brought nine Byzantine treasures from Ephesus and Constantinople for the church. The interior is decorated with different marbles and there is spectacular decoration around the altar. Outside there is an unusual separate bell tower.

● Fox on the Hill

Brighton Road, KT20 6SU
OS: 248538 (A217)
☎ (01737) 832638
Winter: 11-2:30, 5-11 (11-11 Friday and Saturday, 12-2:30, 5-10:30 Sunday)
Summer: 11-11 (12-10:30)
Adnams Bitter
Young's Bitter

Originally known as the Fox Hotel, then the Fox until 1996 when it received its present, geographically accurate, epithet. It is a large white, pebble-dashed building with some weather-boarding. There is a large garden and car park. In more tranquil days, before road widening, there was an old pond opposite the pub. It was used by traction engines to fill up with water after labouring up Reigate Hill. The current owners have revived its former use as a hotel with the inclusion of 12 en suite letting bedrooms. There is a heavy emphasis on Indian food, and the pub incorporates a non-smoking restaurant called Lal Akash, from which a take-away and home delivery service is available. Originally owned by R & F Pagden, Epsom, it became one of 14 pubs to be acquired by Mellersh & Neale in 1931 following their takeover of said brewery. It ended its brewery owned days under Carlsberg Tetley and is now a Punch leasehold. Note that the pub is open all day from May to September. Food is served in the restaurant until 10.00 Sunday to Thursday and until 11.00 Friday and Saturday. Diners and residents can enjoy a later drink.

🛏 ◁▶ ✗ 🚗 ☸ ♿

● Mint Arms

83 Buckland Road, KT20 7EF
OS: 247533
☎ (01737) 242957
12-11 (12-10:30 Sunday)
Fuller's London Pride
Guest Beers

A pleasant brick and tile-hung exterior belies a rather uninspiring interior, in which no original features have survived, following a savage refit several years ago. Now with a change of ownership, the enthusiastic new management is seeking to breathe life back into what had been considered a fading establishment and until recently was feared to be under threat of closure. A Thai restaurant has been established in the modern extension at the rear of the pub and we understand the pool table is due for eviction, opening up the whole of the place for drinkers and diners. The name derives from the crop which was grown in the vicinity from the late 18th century and whose oil went to sweet factories in Mitcham. Up to 1922 this pub was owned by the Swan Brewery of Leatherhead until taken over by Mellersh & Neale of Reigate. With the latter's demise in 1938, it operated under the Meux banner, switching to Friary Meux in the late 1950s. Sold off by Carlsberg Tetley in the 1990s, it now trades as a genuine free house and up to three guest beers are available, often from regional family or micro-brewers. Darts played. Food is served Monday to Saturday, 12-3 and 6-10, and Sunday from 12-3. A new venture which deserves support.

◁▶✕♘🚗❁♿

MARSH GREEN (D2)

This small village is just in Kent, and dates from at least Elizabethan times. In 1886 it was scheduled to be the venue for the last bare-knuckle fight in England. However, rumours that the police were going to intervene scared off the boxers and their supporters, and the fight did not take place.

● Wheatsheaf

Marsh Green Road, TN8 5QL
OS: 437441 (B2028)
☎ (01732) 864091
www.thewheatsheaf.net
11-11 (12-10:30 Sunday)
Everard Tiger
Harveys Sussex Best Bitter
Guest Beers
Biddenden Medium Cider

Just over the Kent border, the Wheatsheaf is a must for beer drinkers. Up to eight different beers are sold and these are constantly changing – around 3,000 different beers have been sold in the last ten years. They usually include a mild and beers from local brewers such as Larkins and Westerham. There are five drinking areas, and half the pub plus the conservatory restaurant are non-smoking. A beer festival is held in the summer – this will coincide with the village fête. Very good quality food is served each lunchtime and evening. Shove half-penny is played. Outside there is a garden where barbecues take place in good weather. Civilised children are welcome.

◁▶♘🚗❁🚭♿

MERSTHAM (C2)

This large village has been known since medieval times for mining and quarrying. The horse-drawn Surrey Iron Railway was the first public railway in England and the southern extension, completed in 1805, was used to carry firestone to London where it was used in the construction of such buildings as the Royal Palace of Westminster, Henry VII's chapel in Westminster Abbey, London Bridge and Windsor Castle. Remains of the track have been preserved in Merstham High Street. Alfred Nobel used one of the local quarries for testing dynamite. The village greatly increased in size after the Second World War when it was one of the sites chosen by London County Council to house people who had lost their homes in the air raids. The 13th century St Katharine's church is built using local flint and sandstone, and its lychgate is made from parts of an old windmill. Quality Street contains a number of old buildings and is the scene of an annual fair. Merstham railway tunnel was the scene of the first railway murder, on 24th September 1905. The mutilated body of Mary Money was found in the tunnel and it was discovered that she had been thrown from a train. The murderer was never found. Gatton Park, towards Redhill, covers over 500 acres and was designed by Capability Brown.

YOUNG'S
BITTER

THE RAM BREWERY
EST. 1831
WANDSWORTH
YOUNG'S

A warm welcome and great beers await at a Young's pub near you

Home Cottage
Redstone Hill
Redhill
Surrey
RH1 4AW
Tel: 01737 762771

Chequers
Chequers Lane
Walton-on-the-Hill
Surrey
KT20 7SF
01737 812364

Penny Black
5 North Street
Leatherhead
Surrey
KT22 7AX
Tel: 01372 386719

The Bear
Leatherhead Road
Oxshott
Surrey
KT22 0JE
Tel: 01372 842747

The Bells
124 Church Street
Staines
Middlesex
TW18 4ZB
Tel: 01784 454240

The Bell
Bell Lane
Fetcham
Surrey
KT22 9ND
Tel: 01372 372624

● Feathers

36 High Street, RH1 3EA
OS: 290534 (A23)
☎ (01737) 645643
11-11 (12-10:30 Sunday)
Adnams Bitter
Greene King Old Speckled Hen
Shepherd Neame Spitfire
Taylor Landlord
Wells Bombardier
Guest Beer
Addlestones Cloudy Cider

Imposing multi-balconied and half-timbered edifice which displays much evidence of the arts and crafts movement. Although the multitude of tiny wood-framed ground floor windows with their circular dimples seem in keeping with the architecture, two attractive frosted and etched door windows (one exterior, one interior) depicting the Prince of Wales's feathers hint at the existence of an earlier scheme. Other stained and leaded examples on the north side suggest a later extension has been incorporated into the pub proper. Though internal divisions have long-gone, careful retention and modification of the original heavy wooden bar, plus differing styles of décor, help divide the pub up into distinctive areas, including a rear no smoking room. Other features worthy of note are a superb mirror, plus a large number of small cast-iron fireplaces which "shout" Art Nouveau! The mix of contemporary seems to work here and the pub is popular with young and old alike. There is an interesting selection of bottled foreign beers on sale and the guest beer changes regularly. Families are welcome before 6pm. Food is served 12-3 and 6-9:30 Monday to Friday and 12-9:30 Saturday and Sunday.

◁▶

Iron Horse

27a Bletchingley Road, RH1 3HU
OS: 295528
☎ (01737) 642874
No real ale

A symmetrical 1950s pub with red brick ground floor and tile-hung upper storey built by Charrington's to serve the London County Council's post-war Merstham overspill estate. Whilst retaining 3 bars and most of its original fitments, real ale has not been a feature for a number of years; though in one bar beautifully polished handpumps and a copious display of pump-clips serve as a reminder of better days. The name may allude to the Croydon, Merstham & Godstone Iron Railway (an extension to the Surrey Iron Railway), though this was a strictly equine-hauled operation.

● Limes

58 Albury Road, RH1 3LJ
OS: 293525
☎ (01737) 642085
12-11 (12-10:30 Sunday)
Greene King IPA
Young's Bitter

This 1960s bow-windowed building was originally called the Griffin and was built on the bowling green of an earlier pub of the same name. Very typical in design of its time, the inside of today's pub consists of a single gantry and bar in light-coloured wood serving three distinct areas. There is a main front bar, plus a left-hand adjoining room and a right-hand section used respectively for bar billiards and pool. Darts is also played. Outside, a late-period Whitbread hanging sign "Hind's Head" finial reveals the pub's former ownership. The original plan was to change the name to "The Beeches", only to be thwarted by the lack of such flora in the immediate vicinity. Only snacks are served.

● **Railway Arms**
London Road North, RH1 3BG
OS: 291534 (A23)
☎ (01737) 642289
12-11 (12-7 Sunday)
Greene King IPA, Abbot Ale
This former Charrington's pub is 200 years old and comprises one main L-shaped public bar, plus a separate later saloon section panelled in dark wood abutting on the right. The latter was originally a butcher's shop into which the pub was later extended and you can still see the old knife sharpening stone outside. The two bars are quite a contrast and remind one of what the divisions were originally intended for. The public is very much a locals' bar, full of characters and buzzing with activity with pool and darts both played, whilst the saloon is the place for a quiet chat in more comfortable surroundings (the latter is non smoking). The origin of the pub's name is a little mysterious; the present Merstham station site dates from 1844 and replaced an earlier one of 1841, but the building is much older than that. Perhaps then this is another local reference to the Croydon, Merstham & Godstone Iron Railway (as with the Iron Horse), which reached the area from Croydon in 1805? To add to the confusion, the pub's sign depicts the coat-of-arms of the much later Southern Railway which did not come into being until 1923! Food is served 12-2:30 Monday to Friday and 12-2 Saturday and Sunday. Note the early closing on Sunday nights. Families are welcome until 8pm.

Rookwood House Hotel
13 London Road South, RH1 3AZ
OS: 289529 (A23)
A family run hotel on the main road, it had a small bar which contained a pool table, making it a local for nearby residents. There were ten bedrooms, and the hotel had its own Chinese restaurant, the Golden Cloud. The building was demolished for housing in 2004.

Shepherd's Pen
229 London Road North, RH1 3BN OS: 290543 (A23)
In the 1970s this was a freehouse called the Jolliffe Arms, and was a large three bar pub. By 1990 it had changed its name to Detroits, and was decorated with loads of Americana including a car. Seemingly the people of Merstham were not ready for this, and it closed for office development. However, the right hand part of the building reopened as the Shepherd's Pen around 1992. This was a small Victorian bar with a wooden floor and an open fire. A tiny snug area was to be found by the spiral staircase. Real ale was a major feature; however the pub closed in the late 1990s. It is now the Vojan Indian restaurant, although there is a proposal to put housing on the site.

MICKLEHAM (B2)

Situated on the east bank of the River Mole, Mickleham was bypassed by the A24 in 1934. Juniper Hall is an 18th century mansion and is now owned by the National Trust. It was rebuilt in 1870. Aristocratic French refugees used the hall as a meeting place during the French Revolution. It is now used as a centre for a wide range of environmental courses. Fanny Burney, the novelist, was married in St Michael's church to one of the refugees, General Alexandre d'Arblay.

● **King William IV**
4 Byttom Hill, RH5 6EL

OS: 174538
☎ (01372) 372590
www.kingwilliamiv.com
11-3, 6-11 (12-10:30 Sunday)
Adnams Bitter
Badger Best Bitter
Hog's Back TEA
Guest Beer
Hog's Back TEA in bottle.
Marvellous two roomed pub which nestles on the slopes of the North Downs. It was built in the late 18th century and became the alehouse for the staff of the Beaverbrook estate. The building was extended in Victorian times. The attractive multi-layered garden has lovely views out over Norbury Park and the Mole Valley and is very popular in the summer. The extensive menu, featuring a large number of vegetarian choices, gives a restaurant feel early evening. Food is served Monday to Saturday from 12-2 and 7-9:30. There are no evening meals on Sundays, when meals are served through to 5pm instead. The guest beer changes every month or so and is usually from one of the local small brewers, but may not be available during the quieter times of the year. Access is difficult for the infirm as the main entrance is up some steep steps. Parking is available outside the Italian restaurant, just off the main road.

◁▶☸

● **Running Horses**
Old London Road, RH5 6DU

OS: 170535 (B2209)
☎ (01372) 372279
www.therunninghorses.co.uk
11:30-11 (12-10:30 Sunday)
Adnams Bitter
Fuller's London Pride
Greene King Abbot Ale
Young's Bitter
Large and attractive 16th century inn on the old route to the coast from London. As shown on the double-sided inn sign, it is named after a run-off of the Derby in 1828 after there was a dead heat in the original race. Racehorses were stabled here then. The pub is in good walking country with Mickleham Downs just above it. The main bar is dominated by a large fireplace, where a real fire blazes away in winter. Beams and horse brasses abound. The front patio is popular when the weather is good. There are 5 letting rooms and a restaurant, which is no smoking. If driving, remember than the pub is on the regular 465 bus route, and park accordingly.

🛏◁▶✗☸♿

MOGADOR (B2)

Tiny village which is surrounded by attractive commonland, making it popular with horse riders. It is the home of several rich and famous people including, until recently, George Best.

● **Sportsman**
Mogador Road, KT20 7ES
OS: 241533
☎ (01737) 246655
11-3, 5:30-11 (11-11 summer Saturdays; 12-10:30 Sunday)

Courage Best Bitter
Fuller's London Pride
Wadworth 6X
Young's Bitter
Guest Beer

A little gem of a pub, well off the beaten track, situated on the edge of Walton Heath amidst excellent walking and horse riding country. Parts of the pub date from the 16th century, although most of the current building is of later construction - possibly early Victorian. There is an attractive tiled portico running the length of the façade with bench seating to keep the rain off. It was built as a lodge on Royal hunting grounds and would almost certainly have been used by Henry VIII and his entourage. Today it is a cosy and welcoming split-levelled one bar establishment with a 25 seat non-smoking restaurant serving good and interesting food. At times, especially warm weekends, it can get very busy, with an eclectic mix - walkers, cyclists, dedicated drinkers, diners, etc… yet at other times, it will be very quiet with a loyal band of regulars propping up the bar and soaking up the atmosphere along with the fine ale! Look out for the interesting pub map of Surrey inside the bar dated 1958 - a most useful source of reference for this surveyor! The new leaseholders are "testing the water" with opening hours at present but it is a safe bet to say that the pub will be open all day on Saturdays and Sundays throughout the summer months. It may be advisable to ring ahead to check for extensions to stated opening hours during the rest of the week. Food is served 12-2:30 and 7-9:30 Monday to Saturday, and from 12-4 on Sunday. Note the once common but now rare illuminated Courage cockerel sign on the exterior belying its former ownership. Darts is played. This is not an easy pub to find but we recommend you make the effort.

◁▶✕🚗☸

MOORHOUSE (D2)

Hamlet on main A25 on the edge of Limpsfield Chart, and close to the Kent border.

Grasshopper Inn

Westerham Road, TN16 2EU
OS: 428534 (A25)
www.grasshopperinn.co.uk
☎ (01959) 563136
M & B Brew XI
Guest Beer

This large establishment has a bar for drinkers, which is attached to a carvery. There is a separate restaurant and the function room is used as a nightclub three nights a week (smart dress and jacket and ties on two of them), with DJs and a disco. It was originally a couple of cottages in the 13th century, one of which was used as a beer house. It was considerably extended in the 1950s, including using materials originally from the Houses of Parliament and the old Coventry Cathedral. The M&B Brew XI is sold under the house name of Grasshopper Inn Ale and the guest changes monthly and may be a national or local beer. The large car park has spaces for coaches and is also used by various car clubs. Food is served each weekday session and all day on Saturday and Sunday.

MUGSWELL (C2)

Hamlet in attractive countryside to the east of the A217. Close by in one of Surrey's 10 surviving windmills, but only the roundhouse survives as it was partly demolished in 1912 and is now a private dwelling. It bears the inscription "532", its height above sea level.

● Well House Inn

Chipstead Lane, CR5 3SQ
OS: 258553
www.wellhouseinn.com
☎ (01737) 830640

12-11 (12-10:30 Sunday)
Archers Best
Fuller's London Pride
Hogs Back Hair of the Hog
Wadworth 6X
Weltons Old Cocky
Guest Beer
Moles Black Rat Cider
A rural gem nestled away in attractive countryside down a narrow lane, yet, surprisingly not far from the M25 and the towns of Reigate and Coulsdon. The building dates from at least the 16th century, and in the garden is St Margaret's Well or Mag's Well which is reputedly mentioned in the Domesday Book, and gives the area its name. There are three bars each with its own log fire and a newly built non-smoking conservatory has been added at the rear. Food is of a high standard and Sunday lunches are served until 4pm (6pm in the summer), but there is no food Sunday evening. The guest beer changes frequently and can often be something interesting. Families are welcome until 9pm. A popular quiz is held on Tuesday night, and there is occasional live music.

◁▶

NEWCHAPEL (D3)

The first European church of the Latter Day Saints (Mormons), the London Temple, was built here in 1958. The large temple is open only to members, but the public are admitted to the visitor's centre and grounds. Newchapel House was built in 1908 for the owner of Pear's Soap.

● Blacksmith's Head

Newchapel Road, RH7 6LE
OS: 366425 (B2028)
www.theblacksmithshead.co.uk
☎ (01342) 833697
11-3, 5:30-11 (Opens 6 Saturday and only 12-3 Sunday)
Fuller's London Pride

Harveys Sussex Best Bitter
Guest Beers
Country pub near the Mormon Temple, it was built in the 1920s on the site of a former forge. There is a restaurant area to the side, while drinkers use the area round the bar, which has a couple of wood burning stoves. The guests are usually from small independents or micros and change frequently. The large number of pump clips on the wall behind the bar are a testament to the landlord's interest in beer, and the darts trophies won by the two darts teams are on display. The previous occupation of the owners as landscape gardeners is shown in the carefully planned garden, and the collection of bottles dug up during that time are now ranged around the top of the pub walls. The monthly quiz is on the first Tuesday of each month. There are three menus, an a la carte menu for the restaurant and a bar menu. There is also a tapas menu, which is available whenever the other menus are, apart from Saturday evenings. All food is freshly prepared and the pub is open to the public, as well as residents, for breakfast each day. Food is available from 12-2:30 each lunchtime and from 6-9:30 Monday to Friday and 6-10 Saturday evenings. The five non-smoking bedrooms are all en suite, and are of a high standard, shown by the fact that the accommodation has received four red diamonds from the AA, putting it in the top ten percent of their bed and breakfast listings. Note that the pub is closed Sunday evening.

◁▶

Peacock
Eastbourne Road, RH7 6HL
OS: 364414 (A22)
☎ (01342) 832596
No real ale
Single bar, food orientated pub, which does food all day. Most of the pub is laid for diners with a few tables for drinkers in the smaller, smoking part. There is a cash machine, nappy changing in the disabled toilet, a function room with a bar and a children's play area in the large garden.

● **Wiremill Inn**
Wire Mill Lane, RH7 6HJ
OS: 364418
11-11 (12-10:30 Sunday)
☎ (01342) 832263
Courage Best Bitter, Directors
Shepherd Neame Spitfire
Wells Bombardier
This split-level pub is found down a track off the main road. It was originally built as a wire and nail mill in 1602 and supplied these items for St Paul's Cathedral in London. In addition, bronze cannons were produced, and in the 17th century it was a flour mill. Since then the building has been used as a women's refuge and a place for members of the RAF to stay in the World Wars. Today the pub overlooks a lake used by a water skiing club and there is a patio with tables outside by the water. The main pub area is the top lakeside bar; the restaurant is down one level and the toilets and a small seating area are a further level down. The restaurant is French, and food, which is served every lunchtime and evening, is home cooked. On some summer Mondays there is a jazz trio playing. The pub may close during weekday afternoons in winter.
◁▶✗🚗☸

NEWDIGATE (B3)
In the 16th century Newdigate became the first village in Surrey to have an ironworks. Christopher Darrell set up his foundry just north of the village at Ewood in 1553 when he was able to make use of exemption from an Elizabethan Act forbidding the felling of trees over a certain age. Local oaks were also used for shipbuilding and house building. Evidence of the latter can be seen in the many restored half- timbered buildings found locally. St Peter's church dates partly from the 12th century and features a wooden tower supported by four 17-inch square oak posts, and an octagonal spire. Hogspudding Lane used to have brickworks on it, and between 1934 and 1981 the Schermuly factory in Parkgate made rocket-propelled safety equipment. Both these locations are now used for housing.

Rusper Golf Club
Rusper Road, RH5 5BX
OS: 198396
www.ruspergolfclub.co.uk
☎ (01293) 871871
Badger K&B Sussex
Guest Beers
Large bar attached to an eighteen-hole golf course which is close to the Sussex border. It is open to all for food and drink starting with breakfast at 7, with drinks served from 11 until it is dark or the last golfer leaves. Adjoining the bar is an attractive covered patio, with more tables outside. Food is served all day, and on Sunday, roasts are served. The guest beers change frequently, and are usually from local microbreweries such as Weltons and Kings.

● Six Bells

Village Street, RH5 5DH
OS: 197420
☎ (01306) 631276
10:30-11 (12-10:30 Sunday)
Badger K&B Sussex, Best, Tanglefoot, seasonal beer

Dating in parts from the 17th century, the pub is to be found opposite the village church. Originally built as two cottages, the pub has been extended over the years. The pub was called the Five Bells, but when the church bells were recast in 1803 and six bells installed instead, the pub changed its name. At the end of the 19th century, the last Manorial Courts of Cudworth met in the Six Bells. The interior rambles around the bar to provide a number of cosy areas to drink. Down a few steps to the left of the bar is a tile-floored area with an inglenook fireplace. The pub does have a second fireplace, but this is still hidden behind boards. The main bar area has floorboards and beams, and has a dartboard. Outside is a large garden with children's play equipment and a wishing well. To the rear of the pub is a large separate restaurant area. The menu is to be found on a blackboard and is constantly changing. The food is all home-cooked and is good old-fashioned English pub grub. A selection of interesting vegetarian meals is also offered. The pub organises many themed food weeks with menus reflecting the cuisine of a region supplementing the normal menu. Food is available from 12-3 and 6-9 Monday to Saturday, and 12-9 Sunday. The restaurant can be converted into a skittle alley if it is pre-booked by groups of 20 people or more.

● Surrey Oaks

Parkgate Road, Parkgate, RH5 5DZ OS: 205436
www.surreyoaks.co.uk
☎ (01306) 631200
11:30-2:30, 5:30-11 (11:30-3, 6-11 Saturday, 12-3, 7-10:30 Sunday)
Caledonian Deuchars IPA
Harveys Sussex Best Bitter
Taylor Landlord
Guest Beers
Moles Black Rat Medium Cider

The Soaks has done more to support micro-breweries than any other pub in this guide. Two guest beers are available and these are constantly changing. On average a new beer to the pub comes on sale every day. In the summer months golden ales and wheat beers are popular. In winter expect to find porters, stouts and old ales. A mild will always be available in May. A beer festival in a marquee takes place over the August Bank Holiday when the pub is open all day. With real cider, served direct from the cellar, plus a number of bottle conditioned Belgian and Dutch beers always on sale, it is unsurprising that the Surrey Oaks has

been voted the East and Mid Surrey Camra Pub of the Year on numerous occasions. The middle non-smoking "Members Bar" has many framed certificates on the wall to give testament to this, along with a number of animal paintings. The building itself dates in part from the 16th century, but only became a pub in 1850 having previously been a wheelwright's cottage. Internally there are a number of distinct drinking areas. To the left is the Georgian restaurant and bar which is all non-smoking. To the right of the serving area is a low-beamed flagstone bar which has a large inglenook fireplace complete with wood burning stove, and low beams covered in pumpclips. Fresh flowers are used to decorate the bar area and dried hops can be found throughout the pub. Finally there is a separate pool room. Home-made food is also a feature and a number of daily specials are always available – particularly recommended are the chef's pies and the landlady's pâtés. No food is sold either Sunday or Monday evenings. Outside is a large garden with goats and an aviary and a children's play area. Also to be found here is a boule pitch. Locals use this in the summer months with perhaps more enthusiasm than skill! Check out the website for details of forthcoming guest beers. The Camra Surrey Pub of the Year 2005.

NORWOOD HILL (B3)

Small group of buildings named after the hill on top of which they stand.

● Fox Revived

Norwood Hill, RH6 0ET
OS: 240435
11-3, 5:30-11 (11-11 Friday and Saturday, 12-10:30 Sunday)
☎ (01293) 863030

Fuller's London Pride
Harveys Sussex Best Bitter
Wadworth 6X
Wells Bombardier

After the Fox burnt down, a new pub was built close by, hence the name of the Fox Revived. There is a picture of the pub, showing ownership by Mellersh & Neale, by the bar. The current building is built in a ranch style. The small entrance hall leads to a bar lined by bookcases, and in the corner can be found a stuffed fox sitting down having a drink. The front bit of the bar has wooden floors and a couple of comfy chairs. Throughout the drinking area are a number of good solid wood tables. Beyond this is a restaurant and two conservatories where traditional home-cooked English food is served every lunchtime and evening. Note the pennies sculpture on the bar – these are given to charity after a large pile has been collected. Outside is an excellent garden containing fruit trees, and there are good views towards Betchworth and the North Downs. Don't miss the old green and red Massey tractor.

NUTFIELD (C2)

Fuller's earth has been extracted to the north of the village since Roman times, and was used in the preparation of woollen and worsted cloth from the 15th to 17th centuries. So important was Fuller's earth that its export was prohibited during the reign of Edward II. Production finally ceased in the late 1990s.

● Crown Inn

1 High Street, RH1 4HH
OS: 310506 (A25)
☎ (01737) 823240
4-11 (12-11 Friday and Saturday, 12-10:30 Sunday)

Greene King IPA, Old Speckled Hen

A lively village local with lots of activity, parts of the building are over 400 years old. This former Friary Meux pub was sold to Greene King in 1990. The emphasis is on sport and music but there are also regular quizzes as well as thriving darts and pool teams. Newspapers and magazines are available to help pass the time while you enjoy your drink or the Saturday lunchtime fry-up! Food is available lunchtimes from Friday to Sunday, and each evening except Sunday. There is a small function room available for parties etc free of charge. Children are welcome away from the bar and outside there is a courtyard garden.

● Queen's Head

13 High Street, RH1 4HH
OS: 306505 (A25)
☎ (01737) 823619
11-11 (11-3 winter Monday, opens 12-6 Sunday)
Fuller's London Pride
Guest Beers

The Queens Head advertises itself as a "restaurant and bar" and that is a very appropriate description. Although the emphasis is on food, drinkers are welcomed. The pub is on split levels with a few steps leading up from the bare floorboards of the central bar area to the carpeted restaurant. The menu is varied and includes traditional British as well as French and Oriental influences, and is served every session except Sunday evening when the pub is closed. The oak tree in the car park was planted to commemorate Queen Victoria's jubilee in 1877.

NUTFIELD MARSH (C2)

Small area between Nutfield and Merstham that is currently under threat from quarrying. A 55-acre lake, surrounded by a country park, is used for water sports.

● Inn On The Pond

Nutfield Marsh Road, RH1 4EU
OS: 303515
☎ (01737) 643000
11-3, 5:30-11 (11-11 Saturday and 12-10:30 Sunday)
Fuller's London Pride
Greene King IPA, Ruddles County
Harveys Sussex Best Bitter
Guest Beer

Situated in the little hamlet of Nutfield Marsh, in an area of the Holmesdale Valley where the quarrying of Fullers Earth was once the major source of industry, this attractive large white-painted building faces a cricket pitch and eponymous pond which dates back to 1603. It only entered pub use in 1988 having formerly spent many years as the Lancelyn Club. There are plenty of wooden beams, a real fire and low ceilings in the front drinking areas, whilst at the rear there is a popular no smoking restaurant on a higher level. Note the superb collection of traditional 1950s/60s model cars in various glass cases around the walls, which claims to be the largest on display in Southern England. The large rather austere building behind the pub is the former club's squash courts and can now be hired as a function room. Very much a family oriented pub, it extends a genuinely warm welcome to all. It hosts many charity events, at some of which a Tapas spread is laid on by the landlady. There is extensive outdoor seating in the pleasant garden, ideal for watching the cricket in the summer months. Food is served Monday to Saturday 12-2:30 and 6:30-9 (9:30 Friday and Saturday); Sunday 12-3:30. Off the beaten track, but well worth finding.

◁▶✕♞🚗❄♿

OAKWOOD HILL (B3)

The church of St John the Baptist is in a wood some distance from the village, and is the most isolated church in Surrey. Dating from the 13th century, it was enlarged 1879 by the addition of the north aisle. The older spelling of Okewoodhill, from a local stream once known as the Oke, is still to be seen on some sign posts.

● Punchbowl

Oakwood Hill Lane, RH5 5PU
OS: 133375
☎ (01306) 627249
11-11 (12-10:30 Sunday)
Badger Best, Tanglefoot, seasonal beer

Attractive tile hung building with a large brick inglenook in the flag stoned lounge. Parts of the building date from 14th century, although most is newer. Previously a freehouse, Hall & Woodhouse bought the pub in 1991. There is a separate bar which has pool and darts. Traditional pub games (shut the box and cribbage) are also available. A large and varied menu featuring home made food is always available. There is a function room upstairs and children are welcome in the bar. The Pub is the meeting place for the Surrey Union Hunt.

◁▶✕♞🚗❄🚲

OCKLEY (B3)

Ockley stands on Stane Street, the old Roman road between London and Chichester. The long green has scattered tile-hung cottages, a cricket pitch and a duck pond. It has been suggested that in 851 the Danes were routed by Ethelwulf of Wessex in a fierce battle at Ockley and up the slopes of Leith Hill. In 1822 many human remains were unearthed at Etherley Farm just below Leith Hill. In 2001, well-preserved bones of Iguanodons were found in clay pits at Smokejacks Brickyard. The Hannah Peschar Sculpture Garden on Standon Lane is open to the public, and features an ever-changing display of mainly European sculptures in landscaped gardens.

Cricketers Arms

Stane Street, RH5 5TP
OS: 146397 (A29)
☎ (01306) 627205
Fuller's London Pride
Hogs Back TEA
Ringwood Best Bitter
Guest Beer

This is an attractive 16th century pub that has a huge inglenook fireplace and large flagstones and polished brass on the beams. Hops surround the fireplace, and to the left of it is a gurning ring. To the right of the bar, down a few steps, is a small games area with a dartboard.

Gatton Manor

Standon Lane, RH5 5PQ

OS: 128389
www.gattonmanor.co.uk
☎ (01306) 627555
Hogs Back TEA
Occasional **Guest Beer**
The bar and restaurant are attached to this 18th century 18-room hotel that used to be part of the Albury Estate. It sits in 200 acres of land and contains an 18-hole golf course that crosses the River Arun on several occasions.

● Inn on the Green

Stane Street, RH5 5TD
OS: 147403 (A29)
www.inn-onthegreen.co.uk
☎ (01306) 711032
11:30-3, 5-11 (11:30-11 Friday and Saturday and 12-10:30 Sunday; open 11-11 Monday to Saturday in summer)
Beer range varies
Formerly the Red Lion, this large pub dates in parts from the 15th century, although several extensions hide the antiquity very well. The front part of the bar is decorated with cricketing prints, and to the left of this is a games room with pool and darts. A raised area to the right of the bar can be used by families. By ducking under a well disguised beam the bar opens out to an area with comfy sofas, and there is a more contemporary feel to this part of the pub. This area is a more modern addition, being 17th century, and has an impressive fireplace. Beyond this is a large restaurant where a wide variety of good homemade food is served. The standard menu is supplemented by a seasonal à la carte selection. A conservatory looks out over the enclosed rear garden where there is a play area for children. Five en-suite bedrooms are available for letting. Three beers are sold. These change quite frequently and tend to be from the regional brewers.

● King's Arms Inn

Stane Street, RH5 5TS
OS: 149505 (A29)
☎ (01306) 711224
11-2:30 (3 Saturday), 6-11 (12-3, 7-10:30 Sunday)
Bass
Flowers IPA
Greene King Old Speckled Hen
This absolutely charming 300 year old inn is perhaps better described as a dining house and hotel. From the main road the pub is entered via a small porch. Candles on all the tables help set the scene. The bar area is in two main parts, the rear bit being no-smoking. Old photos and paintings take up every bit of space on the walls, with mugs hanging from the beams. The beams are also covered in horse brasses. An incredible collection of bric-a-brac is displayed on tables and ledges, with items varying from china to a model ship and an old typewriter. The main bar also includes an old inglenook in which a real fire burns in winter. The pub is very well known for its top quality food. This is served 12-2 each lunchtime and in the evenings from 7-9 (10 Friday and Saturday). The food is all homemade and is mainly English. The menu changes frequently and often includes such specials as pheasant breast. Tables cannot be booked in the bar, so get there early. The hungry will appreciate the fact that the pub does not appear to be aware of portion control! An a là carte menu is served in the separate restaurant where there is another old fireplace. Tables can be booked here. Accommodation comprises six en-suite rooms (one twin and five doubles), one of

which has a four-poster bed. Outside the pub are some very well kept gardens. There are 18 tables here, making it popular for al fresco summer dining. The pub has a civilised atmosphere and boisterous behaviour has no place in it. Even the ghost is quiet and friendly.

● Old School House

Stane Street, RH5 5TH
OS: 145395 (A29)
☎ (01306) 627430
www.bryces.co.uk
11-3, 6-11 (12-3, 6-10:30 Sunday)
Fuller's London Pride
Gales Gales Best Bitter
Hepworth Traditional Sussex Bitter

Formerly a Victorian schoolhouse which was renovated in 1963, this became a pub in July 1965. It was owned by King & Barnes of Horsham at this time, but became a free house in the 1990s. It is now a very well known fish restaurant, but a cosy bar is still maintained where there are beams and an inglenook fireplace. Very high quality food is served in the separate restaurant. Most, but not all, is fish based, and is prepared using excellent quality fresh produce, and booking is recommended. A separate bar menu is also served featuring a number of "fish and chips" meals (again home made, and also very good). Between the bar and the restaurant is a small cocktail bar for diners. Food is served in the bar each day from 12-2:30 and 6:30-9:30 and in the restaurant from 12-2 and 7-9. 16 wines are available by the glass with many more by the bottle.

OUTWOOD (C2)

Until November 1960 two windmills were to be seen in Outwood, but now only one remains. This is a post mill, built in 1665 and restored by the Society for the Protection of Ancient Buildings. The whole of the wooden body carrying the sails rotates around a central wooden post, and is turned to face the wind. This mill is the oldest working one in England. The other mill, built in the late 18th century, was a smock mill, but blew down in a storm. The National Trust owns Outwood Common which surrounds the village.

● Bell Inn

Outwood Lane, RH1 5PN
OS: 328457
☎ (01342) 842989
12-11 (12-10:30 Sunday)
Fuller's Chiswick Bitter, Discovery, London Pride, ESB, seasonal beer
Fuller's 1845 in a bottle
Dating from 1635 the Bell was previously a coaching stop on the route from London to Brighton, and the former stables now house the pub's toilets. Until a few years ago there was a hanging tree in the garden that was reputedly used for despatching witches! The bell from which the pub takes its name is displayed by the front door. It is said to have been made from melted down ships' cannons from the time of Charles II and weighs around a quarter of a ton. Fullers bought the pub in the autumn of 2004 and have sympathetically refurbished it, opening out a fine inglenook fireplace which now

boasts a cosy log fire. A number of milk churns have been converted into seating around the bar, and there a number of large prints of the local area on the walls. Although the emphasis is definitely on food, the Bell provides a welcoming stop for drinkers also. A wide variety of food is available each day from 12-9:30 (apart from Sunday when it is served all day from 12-9), but there will always be a number of fresh fish specials. Although there is only one bar, there are a number of separate drinking and dining areas around. The Chiswick, Discovery and ESB will not all be available at the same time, but further variety is provided by the bottled 1845 listed above.

● Castle Inn

Millers Lane, RH1 5QB
OS: 317453
☎ (01342) 842754
12-3, 5:30-11 (12-11 Saturday and 12-8 Sunday)
Adnams Broadside
Fuller's London Pride
Harveys Sussex Best Bitter
Guest Beer

Cosy and welcoming pub with three distinct drinking areas including a small no-smoking snug. Log fires and lively conversation add to the atmosphere which is free from TV and piped music. There is a strong emphasis on locally sourced food but this is also a drinker's pub which welcomes locals and visitors including cyclists and ramblers. Boule is played in the garden area and a Ford GT40 Enthusiasts club meets here monthly. Darts is played and families are welcome at lunchtimes. The landlord is an Arsenal fan and was once on their books as a player. Guest beers are usually available, often from microbreweries. The pub was once owned by the Youell & Elkin brewery of Horley.

● Dog & Duck

Prince Of Wales Road, RH1 5QU
OS: 313460
☎ (01342) 842964
12-11 (12-10:30 Sunday)
Badger K&B Sussex, Best, Tanglefoot, seasonal beer

This rural pub used to called the Prince of Wales (the address does rather give this away). A number of tables outside the pub allow for summer drinking. On entering the bar you arrive at a small well-beamed area with darts to one side. Beyond this, past the double-sided fireplace, complete with wood-burning stoves, is a brick fronted bar. Above the fireplace can be found the very rare game of ringing the bull. Further on from the bar is a small restaurant area and a large wooden floored no-smoking area. This has dark wood paneling, some large solid tables, and walls decorated with wild bird prints. Outside, overlooking a pond, is another outdoor drinking area, this one with children's play equipment. Food is served from 12-2:30 and 7-9:30 Monday to Saturday, and from 12-6 Sunday.

OXTED (D2)

Old Oxted was recorded in the Domesday Book. There has been extensive development around the new town, to the north, since the arrival of the railway. St Mary's church has a short 12th century tower with

14th century stained glass windows depicting the four evangelists.

● Crown Inn

53 High Street, Old Oxted, RH8 9LN OS: 386522
☎ (01883) 717853
12-3, 5:30-11 (12-11 Saturday and 12-10:30 Sunday)
Adnams Bitter
Fuller's London Pride
Greene King IPA
Guest Beer

Dating from the 17th century, the Crown was extended in the 1800s. A woman, perhaps a former landlady, reputedly haunts the pub and a ghostly man has also been seen. There are bars on two levels, the lower one being more traditional and contains a log fire. The bars operate different hours, with the upper one open 12-3 and 7-11 during the week, and all day at weekends. The small lower bar is closed on Saturday and opens at 5:30 during the week and at 7 on Sunday, although the pub does tend to stay open longer in summer. The guest beer changes four times a year and is often from the Westerham brewery. The pub name comes from it being on the crown of a hill and the pub has a number of attractive features including different shaped windows and Victorian wooden paneling. A number of board games can be played including chess, draughts, dominoes and backgammon. Home-cooked food is served every session and all day on Sunday, and a speciality is fresh seafood. The pub is family orientated with children welcome inside if under supervision. Outside is a good garden with a children's play area.

◁▶ 🐴 ❄

● George Inn

52 High Street, Old Oxted RH8 9LP OS: 385522
www.thegeorge-inn.com
☎ (01883) 713453

11-11 (12-10:30 Sunday)
Badger K&B Sussex, Best, Tanglefoot, seasonal beer

This 500 year-old pub has been well refurbished throughout its two relaxing bars, and is both elegant and contemporary. It is very food oriented with good quality meals served in the bar and restaurant every lunchtime and evening, and all day from Friday to Sunday. The furniture is a mixture of good solid chairs and tables, and comfortable sofas, and the floors are bare wooden boards. Outside there is a decked area for drinking. The website offers a virtual tour of the pub.

◁▶ 🚗 ❄

Hoskins Arms
Station Road West, RH8 9EB OS: 392527
The original Hoskins Arms was a hotel dating from 1886. It had three bars, a public, a lounge, and a cocktail bar, and was a Friary Meux pub by the 1960s. This was demolished and replaced by an unusual hexadecagonal building in 1974. This was a free house selling a number of real ales. The building was on three levels, and incorporated two bars, a coffee shop, a restaurant and twelve letting rooms. It closed in early 1993, and was later badly damaged by fire. A similarly shaped block of apartments stands on the site. This meant that until the Oxted Inn opened in 1997, the modern part of Oxted had no pub.

● Old Bell

68 High Street, Old Oxted RH8 9LP OS: 384522
☎ (01883) 712181
11-11 (12-10:30 Sunday)
Greene King Old Speckled Hen
Wells Bombardier
Guest Beer

Extended in 2002, the Old Bell is a traditional pub dating from the 15th century. It is furnished with traditional old world fittings and is now a comfortable pub with three log fires. All food is prepared on the premises. Snacks are available Monday to Saturday until 6pm, with restaurant meals sold all day every day. A children's menu is also available. The guest beer changes every week. A female ghost lights candles when the pub is closed.

● Oxted Inn

Units 1-4 Station Road West, RH8 9HR OS 395528
☎ (01883) 723440
10-11 (12-10:30 Sunday)
Greene King Abbot Ale
Hop Back Summer Lightning
Marston's Burton Bitter, Pedigree
Guest Beers

This purpose-built Wetherspoon's pub was opened in July 1997 on the site of a former builders' merchant. It is less than one minute's walk from Oxted station. To help plan your return journey, there is a live train departure screen behind the bar. As Oxted is on the Greenwich meridian, the pub is decorated with over 20 working clocks, showing the time in London, and other places such as Cairo, Nairobi, Tehran, Calcutta, Sydney, and Anchorage. Also, the pub, which is the only one in the new part of town, is decorated with many local photos from the 1905-1910 era, including the George Inn (Crowleys Ale), Old Bell (the sign being in the shape of a large bell), Crown and local shops and roads. Other displays give historical information about the area including one about industrial unrest caused by the importation of labour from Belgium to speed up construction of Oxted tunnel. A number of genuine imported beers are sold on draught. Food is served all day and the pub also opens at 10am on Sunday for breakfast.

Troggs Wine Bar
111 Station Road East, RH8 0AX OS: 394528
A wine bar that sold no real ale, Troggs closed in the mid 1990s. It is now the Gurkha Kitchen, a Nepalese restaurant.

Wheatsheaf Inn
9-11 High Street, Old Oxted RH8 9LN OS: 387523
☎ (01883) 713154
Fuller's London Pride

A former mill house, the Wheatsheaf is a sports minded local with darts and pool both played, and there is big screen TV for sport. To the rear is a riverside garden. It is open all day Saturday and Sunday.

PEASLAKE (A2)

A hidden village on the slopes of Hurtwood Common, with

locally quarried stone used in the construction of many of the properties. The church, built from local sandstone, was carved by village craftsmen in 1889. There is also a special burial ground for Quakers. The surrounding countryside is enjoyed by large numbers of walkers and horse riders.

● Hurtwood Inn
Walking Bottom, GU5 9RR
OS: 086446
www.hurtwoodinn.com
☎ (01306) 730851
12-3, 5:30-11 (12-11 Saturday and 12-10:30 Sunday)
Hog's Back TEA
King Horsham Best Bitter
Young's Bitter
Guest Beer

The Hurtwood Bar in this traditional hotel serves as a guest bar, walkers' rest and the local. There variety of seating ranges from plush sofas to bar stools as well as tables and chairs. As well as a very good quality restaurant, there is also a separate bar menu. The hotel was built in 1920 on the site of an old off-licence that was due to be sold at auction. Locals were so worried that they would have nowhere to buy their beer that they persuaded the Surrey Trust Public House Trust Company to build a hotel. The name came from the whortleberries or "hurts" that grew locally. The Hurtwood Inn has been awarded an AA rosette for the quality of its food and a silver accolade by the English Tourist Authority. 21 en-suite rooms are available. There are three function rooms and the inn is a popular place for wedding receptions. Ramblers are welcome if they remove their muddy boots.

◁▶ ✕(not Sunday)

RANMORE COMMON (A2)

Ranmore Common is a village of scattered houses around a long green with excellent views towards Dorking and the surrounding countryside. St Barnabas church was built in 1859 in a Gothic style for George Cubitt (first Lord Ashcombe), and was designed by Sir George Gilbert Scott. Much of the common is owned by the National Trust.

Ranmore Arms
Crocknorth Road, RH5 6SX OS: 112501
The Ranmore Arms was an isolated pub set in six acres of land on the Pilgrim's Way and the Surrey Cycleway. Previously the Ranmore Country Club, it only became a pub in 1972. It was not the most attractive of pubs, basically being little more than a bungalow. However it was a rarity in the area, being a true free house. Even better, it sold good beer. On Saturday night live music was performed, sometimes featuring nationally known musicians. The pub closed around 2000 and is currently derelict, although an application has been made to build two houses on the site.

REDHILL (C2)

Originally known as Reigate Foreign, Redhill developed rapidly with the arrival of the railway in 1841, after this was turned down by Reigate. The area around the station became known as Warwick Town, changing its name to Redhill some time later. The town attracted both industry and commerce, and grew towards Reigate. The modernised town centre contains the Harlequin Theatre, but many of the town's original Victorian buildings have been demolished.

Abbot (Map 1)
14 Station Road, RH1 8BD
OS: 280506 (A25)
☎ (01737) 765218
Greene King IPA, Abbot Ale, Old Speckled Hen

A lively, modern, youngsters' pub opposite the railway station, which dates from 1997 and is built to a faux Victorian redbrick pastiche. The multi-levelled interior has the "benefit" of plasma and big screen projection TV, plus the sort of ride-on electronic games machines usually found in amusement arcades. The pub is open all day with a late licence to 12 on Thursday and Friday and to 1 on Friday and Saturday, with an admission charge after 9 on Friday and Saturday (when smart casual dress is required). Food is available every day from 12-8.

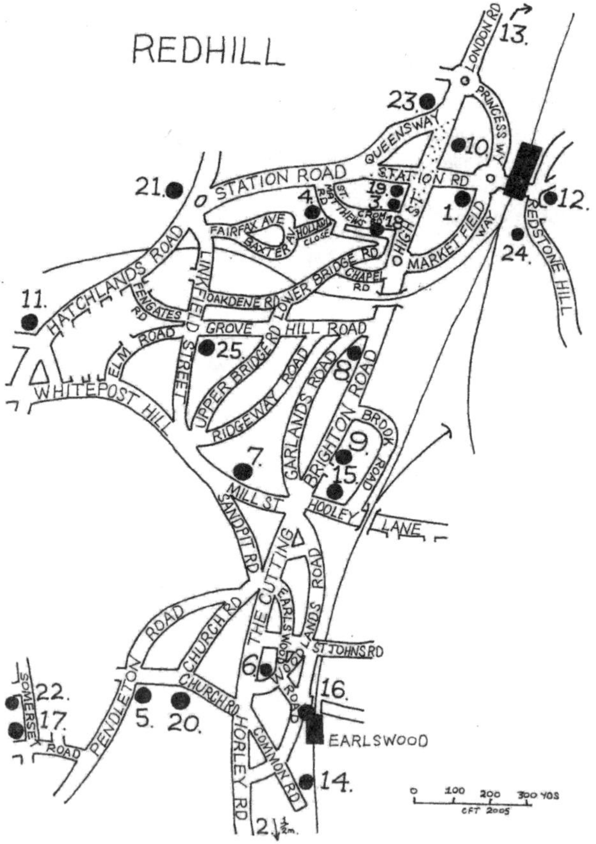

● Causeway (Map 2)

1 Horley Road, Earlswood,
RH1 5AL OS: 278480 (A23)
☎ (01737) 764538
11-11 (12-10:30 Sunday)
Courage Best Bitter, Directors
This is a large multi-area purpose built pub and steakhouse for all the family, and contains "Pirate Pete's Playden" for children. There are also baby- changing facilities. Families are welcome until 9pm. The pub opened in May 1997 on the site of the Nag's Head, which was demolished in 1996. The pub is opposite Kiln Brow, the home of Redhill Football Club, and is close to East Surrey Hospital. Live football is shown on TV, and there is karaoke or live music on Saturday night. Pool is played. Food is available all day.

◁▶✕♞🚗❄♿🚲

Dog & Duck (Map 3)

33 High Street, RH1 1RD
OS: 280504
☎ (01737) 770316
Marston's Pedigree
A multi-levelled street corner town pub with live football shown on TVs, and with occasional live music. Now owned by Wolverhampton & Dudley Breweries, the pub has had a number of names in recent history. Originally it was a Courage pub called the Tower, then it became Crocks, then the Office, before adopting its current name. Popular with shoppers during the day, in the evening it is part of the Redhill drinking "circuit". Darts played.

● Dragon (Map 4)

39 Holland Close, RH1 1HT
OS: 278504

☎ (01737) 770324
12-3, 5-11 (12-10:30 Sunday)
Shepherd Neame Best Bitter, Spitfire, seasonal beer
Originally a Friary Meux pub called the George & Dragon, the pub is just off the town centre. There is a single bar with pool and darts to one side. To the left of the pub is a large split-level conservatory where children are welcome. The lower level has bare boards, and affords great views of the ugly façade of the Belfry centre and the traffic queuing on the A25 one-way system. Pine furniture is used and this helps make the pub look light. Sky Sports shows football and horse racing. The pub is popular with office workers at lunchtimes and with locals in the evening. Food is served weekday lunchtimes from 12-3.

◁♞❄🚌

● Elmshades (Map 5)

26 Pendleton Road, St Johns,
RH1 6QF OS: 273492
☎ (01737) 766502
12-3, 5:30-11 (12-11 Friday and Saturday, 12-10:30 Sunday)
Shepherd Neame Best Bitter, Spitfire, seasonal beer
A good locals' pub, which, in 1995, had its name changed to the Earlswood Arms. Following an outcry from residents and pub goers alike, it eventually got its original name back in July 2002. It is a one bar open plan pub, with equal emphasis on both food and drink. There is a designated no smoking area for drinkers and diners. Bar billiards is played in here and there is a regular quiz every Sunday night. Live music is

played on various nights. Originally a Bushell Watkins & Smith's, Westerham Brewery house it passed into Ind Coope's ownership in 1965, ending up as a Shep's house in the mid 90s. Food served 12-3 and 6:30-9 Monday to Saturday, and 12-7 Sunday.

◁▶ 🚗 ❁ 🚭 🚌 (Earlswood)

● Flying Scud (Map 6)

90 Woodlands Road, Earlswood, RH1 6HB
OS: 276493 (A23)
☎ (01737) 763652
12-3, 6-11 (12-11 Friday and Saturday; 12-10:30 Sunday)
Courage Best Bitter
Wadworth 6X
Guest Beer

Half-timbered 19th Century pub once in the ownership of Courage and still displaying the latter's red and gold illuminated cockerel sign outside. The interior is comfortable but much altered, and the brick-built bar with its ceramic top is quite clearly of a relatively recent provenance. The pub has a nautical theme, which is appropriate given that the Flying Scud was a famous ship of the Victorian era. However, to the right of the bar is a large collection of model aeroplanes. An area to the left of the bar is designated for non-smokers. Pub games include bar billiards, crib and dominoes and there is a quiz every Thursday night. The pub prides itself on its "home prepared" food which is available Thursday and Friday from 12-2, Saturday 12-5 and 7-9, and Sunday 12-4 and 7-9, and other times by prior arrangement. Beer is well kept with one ever changing guest ale. Although it started off life as a Mellersh & Neale pub, Courage acquired it through pub swaps in the 1970s and it is now part of the Enterprise Inns chain.

◁▶ 🚗 ❁ ♿ 🚌 (Earlswood)

● Garibaldi (Map 7)

29 Mill Street, RH1 6PA
OS: 275499
☎ (01737) 761239
12-11 (12-10:30 Sunday)
Fuller's London Pride
Young's Bitter
Guest Beer

It's a steep climb to reach this small single room pub, which is notable for its tiled-roofed front and side veranda and whose garden affords fine views of Redhill. It is around 150 years old and was named after the Italian soldier and popular hero, credited more than any other for laying the foundation of Italy's unification. He also visited England on a couple of occasions and several pubs were named in his honour. It was one of the last pubs in the area to gain a full licence. The new licensee is planning a complete internal refurbishment which should not alter the character of the pub. Presently there is a minute non-smoking area to the rear of the pub. Thai food is available either to eat in or as a takeaway. Standard pub fayre is also available each session. Two guest beers a week are sold, and these can be unusual for the area. Many regulars and previous landlords have seen the ghost of Albert, an old coachman who used to tie his horse up outside. However, he means no harm and just sits on a stool at the left hand side of the bar.

◁▶ ❁ 🚭

● Garland (Map 8)

5 Brighton Road, RH1 6PP
OS: 279502 (A23)

☎ (01737) 760377
11-11 (12-3, 7-10:30 Sunday)
Harveys XX Mild Ale, Long Man Pale Ale, Sussex Best Bitter, Armada Ale, seasonal beer
Harveys Imperial Russian Stout in bottle
A classic Victorian street corner local dating from 1865, the Garland is just south of the town centre. It was originally built as the Anchor but changed its name shortly before Harveys acquired it from Ind Coope in 1992. Originally it was a Mellersh & Neale of Reigate pub. The full range of Harveys ales are sold including every seasonal beer and one-off brews the landlord can get hold of. Eight handpumps dispense these – if there is a ninth beer then it is sold straight from the cellar. Even bottled beers have their own menu on the tables. Much charity work is undertaken with three guide dogs having been bought. Now the pub collects for a different charity each year. Darts is very popular here, with two boards, one of which is in a separate room that can also be used for functions. Note the huge collection of clowns that can be found around the bar. Not immediately apparent, there are in fact over two thousand of them. Lunchtime food is available during the week and the pub is close to several late-night eating places. It is worth noting that the Garland is the only pub in this guide serving mild all the time. Voted the Camra Surrey and Sussex Pub of the Year in 2002, the Garland is a great pub.

Gatton Point
171 London Road, RH1 2JH
OS: 281520 (A23)
A Friary Meux pub on the outskirts of Redhill, this was a large Edwardian building that was demolished for housing in 1997.

Greyhound (Map 9)
82 Brighton Road, RH1 6QP
OS: 278499 (A23)
☎ (01737) 767147
Shepherd Neame Master Brew Bitter, Spitfire, seasonal beer
Rather basic one bar pub dating from 1864 that is on the busy main road. It features regular live music and karaoke. Music on Fridays and Saturdays features a variety of styles ranging from folk to jazz, usually in the main bar, to blues and rock of varying shades of heaviness in the function room at the back. Alternate Wednesdays are open mic nights and there's a quiz on Sunday evening. The pub hosts free pool competitions every Wednesday night and there is a quiz every Sunday, with darts also available. There are outdoor drinking areas at front and rear on patios. Built by Nalder & Collyer of Croydon, it was bought by Mellersh & Neale by 1884 and eventually absorbed into the Allied Breweries conglomerate, until sold off to Shepherd Neame in the early 1990s. No food is sold. Open all day.

Harlequin Theatre (Map 10)
Warwick Quadrant, London Road, RH1 1NN OS: 280506
☎ (01737) 773721
No real ale
Bar in the foyer of the Harlequin Theatre and Cinema complex. The opening hours are irregular, but it is open weekday lunchtimes and usually when events are staged in the evening.

● Hatch (Map 11)

44 Hatchlands Road, RH1 6AT
OS: 270502 (A25)
☎ (01737) 764593
12-3, 5-11 (12-10:30 Sunday)
Shepherd Neame Best Bitter, Spitfire, Bishops Finger, seasonal beer

The Hatch dates from the 17th century, and is a former workhouse with a hayloft for horses. There is one L-shaped bar on which sit a bank of eight handpumps. To the left of the bar is a small room with more seating. Above the fireplace here, on a beam, can be seen the former name of the pub, the Foresters Arms. It was in 1991 that the name was changed to the Hatch. Beyond this, up a few steps and quite hidden away, is a pool room. Darts is also played. A number of Edwardian style prints decorate the walls of this smart pub. Homemade food is available lunchtimes Monday to Saturday from 12-2, and from 12-4 Sunday. Evening food, served 6:30-9, is only available on Friday and Saturday. A pop quiz is held on Monday night and there are occasional jazz nights on Sunday.

◁▶☸

Hobo's

4-5 Berkeley House, 51 High Street, RH1 1RX
OS: 278504 (A25)

A modern bar opened in 1994, when it was called Joe's, selling two real ales. It comprised a raised bar area surrounded by an L-shaped restaurant. It later became Hobo's and is now a restaurant.

● Home Cottage (Map 12)

3 Redstone Hill, RH1 4AW
OS: 284505 (A25)
☎ (01737) 762771
10:30-11 (12-10:30 Sunday)
Young's Bitter, Special, seasonal beers
Young's Golden Champion, Special London Ale in bottle.

This double-fronted, bow-windowed, cream-painted building dates from the mid 19th century with a significant addition in 1904. The original premises are recalled in a photograph of 1880 displayed inside. Surviving etched glass windows lettered "public bar", "saloon bar", "club room" and "coffee room" help give some idea how the building would have been divided and operated around 100 years ago. The front bar has an amazing and possibly now unique set of five stubby ceramic-handled handpumps which sit on a pewter base inscribed "Hurst & Co. of Southwark" and are worth a visit in themselves. A Young's house since 1978, it was a formerly free house owned and run by Miss Sybil Starr who was born in the pub in 1901, and was licensee for 39 years from 1939. A pub frequented by loyal Young's drinkers and others who appreciate good beer and the pleasant atmosphere that pervades this hostelry. There is a large non-smoking conservatory/dining room at the rear of the pub. Food is served 12-3 and 6-9 Monday to Friday, 12-5 on Saturday, and 12-4 on Sunday.

◁▶✕🐴🚗☸🚭🚌

● Jolly Brickmakers (Map 13)

60 Frenches Road, RH1 2JD
OS: 287522
☎ (01737) 789388
11-11 (12-10:30)
Everard Tiger
Wells Bombardier

Basic yet friendly locals' pub which forms one end of a terrace of houses and whose previous existence as a Charrington's house is evidenced by its leaded (but now clear) windows and tiled lower exterior façade (albeit now painted green). The wood-panelled interior is effectively still two-bar with a public section to the left which contains some unusual moulded heraldic wall badges and an attractive grape vine coving. The saloon area to the right is distinguished by an attractive Bass mirror, a bar billiard table, plus a "library" of paperback books! Pub game fans will also find pool and darts here. A good community pub, selling a decent pint. No food.

● Joshua Tree (Map 14)

30 Common Road, Earlswood, RH1 6HJ OS: 277491
www.thejoshuatree.biz
☎ (01737) 211994
11-11 (12-10:30 Sunday)
Adnams Broadside
Greene King IPA

Overlooking Earlswood Common, this used to be a Friary Meux pub called the Railway. It later became known as the Albatross and was for a while a Shepherd Neame pub. Evidence of the latter's ownership can be seen by the lanterns outside the pub. Today it is a smart one bar pub which is well colour co-ordinated. Subtle tones of orange and brown have been used for the walls, ceiling and also the soft furnishings, and there is modern art on the walls. The L-shaped bar leads to a striking separate domed and rounded restaurant. The licensee is a former chef and so it is not surprising that the pub is well known for good quality food, for which fresh produce is used. This is served from 12-2:30 and 6:30-9 Monday to Saturday and from 12-3 Sunday. There is also a decent wine list. Bar skittles and shove halfpenny can be played.

(Earlswood)

Locomotive
21 Ladbroke Road, OS: 282507
Dating from the late 19th century, this Charrington's pub was demolished in the 1980s for the rebuilding of Redhill town centre.

Marquis Of Granby (Map 15)

8 Hooley Lane, RH1 6ET
OS: 277497
☎ (01737) 761959
No real ale

Impressive Brewers' Tudor ex-Friary Meux pub which unfortunately has not found real ale a viable option for some time. A small amount of wood carving from what seems to be the interior's original décor survives on one end of the glass gantry. The present pub replaced the earlier 17th century one, which stood in front of it, in the 1930s. Open all day Saturday and Sunday.

Monson Arms
Green Lane, Batts Hill,
OS: 272513
A 1950s pub built for the nearby housing estate, this Friary Meux pub closed in 1991 due to subsidence and more housing was built on the site.

Nags Head
1 Horley Road, Earlswood, RH1 5AL OS: 278480 (A23)
Situated on the junction of Horley Road and Three Arch Road, The Nags Head was a two-bar Charrington pub in which darts was popular. It was unusual in having a putting green in the garden in the 1980s. By the time it closed in 1996 it was a fairly basic freehouse offering accommodation. The Causeway is now on the site, although the two pubs are not connected.

New Inn
147 Brighton Road, RH1 6PS
OS: 277497 (A23)
The New Inn dated from the 19th century, and was a Friary Meux pub that was popular with bikers. Although small, it was in a very prominent position on the junction of Garlands Road. It was one of a number of pubs sold to Greene King in 1990, but closed in 1997.The building still stands and is now a plumbing shop.

Noah's Ark
100 Brighton Road OS: 277493 (A23)
A 19th century beerhouse that only received a full licence in 1945, the Noah's Ark was another Friary Meux pub. It closed in 1977 and was finally demolished in 1992.

Old Chestnut (Map 16)
12 Station Approach West, Earlswood, RH1 6HP OS: 278492
☎ (01737) 779937
Courage Best Bitter
Fuller's London Pride
Built around 1864, this community local was originally called the Station Hotel. It consists of one room around a very large bar. To one end is a pool table and darts is played away from this. The pub also runs its own golf society. The floor is made up of a variety of surfaces, all bare, including wooden boards and tiles to give the pub a more modern look. It is next door to the well known Ruchita Indian Restaurant. The pub is open all day.

Old Oak (Map 17)
40 Somerset Road, Meadvale, RH1 6LT OS: 267490
☎ (01737) 241987
Fuller's London Pride
Hog's Back TEA
Young's Bitter
Guest Beer
A tile-hung locals' haunt in a residential area. Friary Meux lanterns still adorn the exterior. One large bar with few vestiges of its multi-bar past. Longest serving landlord in the area (over 35 years) who must have seen many changes between being a brewery tenant and a leaseholder with Punch. Perhaps a tad adventurous in stocking four real ales. Bar billiards and darts played. No food.

Oliver's (Map 18)
8 Cromwell Road, RH1 1RT
OS: 278504 (A25)
☎ (01737) 767040
No real ale
Small wine bar in a former shop unit, it is only open at the moment Monday to Friday from 12-9, although it is often used for private parties. It was previously called Bar Renoir. Changes are possible in the near future as the lease was up for sale while this guide was being compiled.

O'Neill's (Map 19)
1 High Street, RH1 1RD
OS: 280506
☎ (01737) 769298
No real ale
Standing in the centre of town on what was once the crossroads of the A25 and A23, this listed building dates from 1902. The pub's original name of the Wheatsheaf is still to be seen at the top of the building, and on the gable ends the name of the original owner, Nalder & Collyer, is proudly displayed.

No such evidence of its time as the Firlot & Firkin is to be found, however. Today it is part of a fake Irish Bar chain and is popular with the young and features occasional live music. Lovers of such pubs beware, as baseball caps may not be worn. Open all day.

● Plough Inn (Map 20)

11 Church Road, St Johns, RH1 6QE OS: 275492
☎ (01737) 766686
11-3, 5:30-11 (12-4 Sunday)
Adnams Bitter
Bass
Marston's Pedigree
Tetley Bitter

Parts of this welcoming white-rendered pub date back to the 16th century and over time the premises have seen the typical expansion into adjoining properties and outhouses, gaining all sorts of nooks and crannies in the process. The ceiling in parts is extremely low, even for buildings of this kind; whilst a set of flagstones in the back bar are said to be around 400 years old and were reputedly used as an influence in the set design of a Harry Potter film. There are several real fires. The back restaurant (which also has an incredibly low ceiling!) is non-smoking. At the back there is a delightful garden with additional seating. The pub was originally owned by Mellersh & Neale, Reigate brewers, eventually becoming a Friary Meux badged pub before being bought by Punch Taverns. There is a nice old photo of the pub in its Mellersh & Neale livery in the restaurant. A charming, characterful, and cosy pub selling good beer and which sticks to traditional hours, Monday to Saturday and does not open on Sunday evenings. Food served 12-2:30 and 6:30-9:30, Monday to Saturday, and 12-3 on Sunday.

◁▶ ✕ ☸ 🚌 (Earlswood)

Prince Albert
108 Horley Road, Earlswood, RH1 5AA OS: 278475 (A23)
The Prince Albert was a two-bar Friary Meux pub set back from the main road. In the late 1990s it became a Mongolian barbecue, and is now a drive through McDonald's burger "restaurant".

● Red Lion (Map 21)

48 Linkfield Lane, RH1 1DP
OS: 274506 (A25)
☎ (01737) 778633
12-11 (12-10:30)
Fuller's London Pride
Guest Beers

An old-fashioned listed pub, the Red Lion contrasts with the modern Donyngs leisure centre behind it and the tyre centre next door. One end of the L-shaped beamed bar has an inglenook fireplace. More seating is to be found to the right of the bar on two different levels. A partial fake ceiling allows space for a number of rustic artefacts including sacking and barrels and on the far wall is a huge clock. Outside the pub is a small patio garden which features a fine floral display making it a pleasant place to sit despite being close to the main road. Food is served from Tuesday to Saturday, 12-3 and 6:30-9:30, and Sunday lunch from 1-4. Only snacks are available Monday. Two guest beers are sold, mainly from the larger regional brewers. The pub used to be former local lad Ronnie Biggs' local until 1963.

◁▶ 🚗 ☸

● Ship Inn (Map 22)

23 Copse Road, Meadvale, RH1 6NW OS: 266492
☎ (01737) 244589
11:30-11 (12-10:30 Sunday)
Fuller's London Pride
Greene King IPA

An amazingly intact classic 1952 estate pub which typifies the final era of traditional English pub architecture. The public bar, complete with bar billiard table as well as pool and darts, runs from left-to-right across the main frontage, whilst the saloon occupies the right-hand end and short leg of the combined L-shape. Originally it seems there was no internal connection between the two for patrons but an arched doorway has since been cut through to link the rooms. Both bars retain their original vertical wood paneling, with that in the saloon being subtly more ornate, though the walls in the public have since succumbed to paint. Further period features include the original Formica counter top, plus a glass-bricked wall in the public and also what may have been a bell button to call for service. Other incredible survivors include a large cut-glass saloon bar mirror bearing a stylised "ship" motif, a theme also repeated in differing ways on two circular port-hole-like door windows and on a side window of the saloon bar entrance. Evidence of changes of brewery ownership can be seen in the wooden bar back in both rooms, which features the pub's name spelt out in typical 1960s illuminated Allied Brewery lettering and, outside, a plaque adjacent to the left-hand entrance makes reference to Charrington's. The Ship was a Westerham Brewery house until 1965. The beer is well kept. Hot "Lazerfood" and snacks are available at all times.

◁▶ 🐴 🚗 ☸

Somers Arms

Reffels Bridge, OS: 273505
Another old Ind Coope pub, the Somers Arms was built in 1853, but was closed in the mid 1970s.

South Eastern

9 Station Road, OS: 282505
A large Ind Coope owned pub on the corner of Ladbroke Road, it was named after the South Eastern Railway. The pub closed in 1977 as part of the town centre redevelopment.

Sultan

London Road, OS: 280506
The Sultan is unusual in having been demolished twice. The original pub dated from the 19th century, but this was replaced by a modern building in the 1960s. This Friary Meux pub was itself demolished in the late 1970s for a road scheme.

● Sun (Map 23)

17-21 London Road, RH1 1LY
OS: 279506 (A25)
☎ (01737) 766886
10-11 (12-10:30 Sunday)
De Koninck Ambree
Greene King IPA
Marston's Burton Bitter, Pedigree
Shepherd Neame Spitfire
Guest Beers

When the Sun opened in August 1996, it was Wetherspoon's 150th pub. It is on the site of a former Magnet kitchen store, and has been built as a huge brick slab with windows along the whole frontage at a lower level. Inside there is one long bar serving one vast open space. A non-smoking area is to be found at the left hand side of the bar, and this includes a raised dining area. A total of four pillars provide the only relief from the openness of the pub, and one of these is surrounded by fruit machines. A bookcase fills part of the right hand wall, and there are many prints telling stories of famous local people. A number of modern paintings by local artist Robert Jones depicting life in Redhill are also displayed. Families are welcome until 6pm, and food is served all day from 10-10 Monday to Saturday, and from 12-9:30 Sunday.

◁▶ ♘ ⊗ ♿ 🚌

● Toby Lodge (Map 24)

2 Redstone Hill, RH1 4BL
OS: 284504 (A25)
☎ (01737) 768434
12-11 (12-10:30 Sunday)
Harveys Sussex Best Bitter
Greene King IPA

Still known to locals as Lakers, unfortunately the marketing department at Mitchells & Butlers, the pub company now owning the property, have decided to apply corporate branding to this large pub. The interior of this Victorian bar-cum-hotel has been so thoroughly modernised that not a single original feature appears to have survived and it is now impossible to discern the original layout. Having said that, today's pastel-shaded and light-wooded decoration is still in a traditional vein and the many wooden dividing screens help break the large interior up into more secluded and intimate drinking areas. Heavily food oriented, as the name would suggest, meals are available every day from 12-10. Attached is a 37 bedroom hotel. "Bob's Bar", now the administrative offices, once rivalled the Home Cottage for popularity in the 70s. Earliest parts of the building date from 1846 when it was originally called the Reigate Junction Railway Hotel in "Reigate Foreign" (as Redhill was called in those days) and owned by one Richard Laker. Renamed the Railway Hotel when Redhill finally became a town it became known as Laker's Hotel from the turn of the 20th century. Charrington's took it over in the early 1960s and it is now part of the huge M&B chain.

🛏 ◁▶ ✕ ♘ 🚗 ❄
⊗ ♿ 🚌

● White Lion (Map 25)

40 Linkfield Street, RH1 6BY
OS: 275502
☎ (01737) 764045
12-11 (12-10:30 Sunday)
Greene King IPA, Abbot Ale

This street corner local on a quiet street is one of the oldest pubs in the area. It dates back to when Linkfield Street was the main north-south road around these parts. The multi-levelled interior has many exposed beams and cosy areas that help indicate the antiquity of the building. Above the bar is a collection of old plates, teapots and potties. Of particular note are the magnificent stained glass windows and screens, which are best appreciated from inside the pub with a pint. Darts and pool are played and there is a quiz on Tuesdays. The White Lion was one of a batch of 87 pubs sold by Allied Breweries to Greene King in 1990.

🚗 ❄

REIGATE (C2)

The original settlement of Reigate was some distance to the east of the present town, and was known as Cherchefelle in the Domesday Book. It is thought that the original castle was built soon after the Norman Conquest, and the new town grew around it. A market existed in 1276 and the town was constituted as a borough by Royal Charter in 1863. The railway arrived in 1849 and there is an 18th century market house in the centre. The old road tunnel was made under the

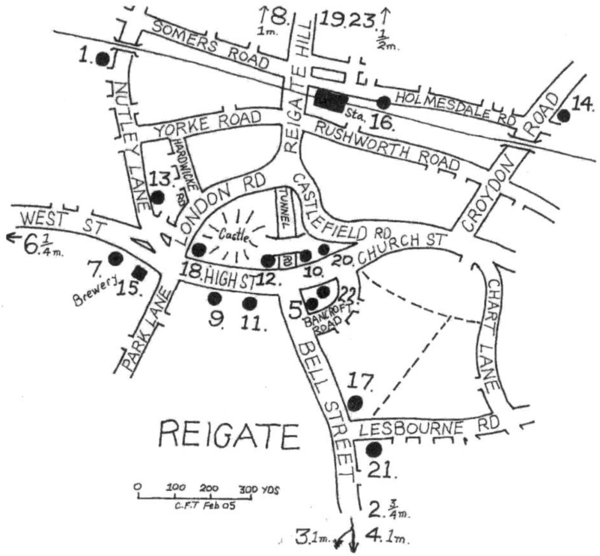

castle mound to improve the coaching route from London to Brighton in 1824. Dame Margot Fonteyn, prima ballerina of the Royal Ballet, was born on London Road. A statue stands opposite the site of the house, depicting her as a dancing water sprite, her favourite role. Many medieval tunnels and caves run under the centre of the town. A colony for inebriate women was founded at Duxhurst by Lady Somerset in 1896.

● Admiral Inn (Map 1)

109a Nutley Lane, RH2 9EF
OS: 249508
☎ (01737) 225300
12-11 (12-10:30 Sunday)
Fuller's London Pride
Greene King IPA

The "other" pub on Nutley Lane, this friendly local has recently changed hands and undergone a facelift. The outside has been repainted in beige, and this colour scheme has been followed through inside with a variety of creams and light browns giving a light and airy feel to the interior. A variety of film stills adorn the walls. The two rooms have been knocked back through into one room, as it would have been about thirty years ago. The bar still falls into two distinct areas. To the left is the lounge which has a large projection screen TV and a couple of comfy settees, as well as a few chairs and tables. The public "bar" to the right has less seating while all around the bar are a number of bar stools. Little of the nautical theme remains to link this pub to its name other than a circular window on each door into the bar with an etched ship's wheel. Although the lunches are simple pub fayre, take away authentic Thai dishes can be ordered a day in advance

for those able to plan ahead. No food is sold at weekends

◁ ☸ 🚌

Angel (Map 2)
1a Woodhatch Road,
Woodhatch RH2 7LJ
OS: 258488 (A217)
☎ (01737) 241800
No real ale
Very basic one roomed, keg only bar with pool table in a prominent position at the foot of Cockshot Hill. Dating from around 1700, it was acquired by the Thomas Neale brewery in 1843, eventually becoming part of the Allied Breweries empire. The old Ind Coope sign still hangs outside.

● **Barley Mow (Map 3)**
3 Eastnor Road, South Park RH2 8NE OS: 251489
☎ (01737) 242304
12-3, 5:30-11 (opens 11 on Saturday and(12-3, 7-10:30 Sunday)
Greene King IPA
Harveys Sussex Best Bitter
Shepherd Neame Spitfire

Small bar on the southern side of Reigate. Very much a locals' pub, but a warm welcome is extended to any new faces. Darts is played, and the silverware testifies to the fact that this is a community pub. Simply laid out with an L-shaped bar in the centre and seating to either side, this is a place to come and have a blether with the locals. Folk music played on Thursday nights.

☸

Batchelor's
6 London Road, RH2 9HY
OS: 250503 (A25)
Now a kebab shop, Bachelor's was previously called On the Rocks, which was very apt given its location. A small wine bar frontage gave no idea as to what was below. Going down several levels underground, bars were built into the caves underneath Reigate. Passages went off on different angles to provide a quite unique drinking experience. Loud music was the order of the day, but real ale was sold. It sadly closed around 1994 when the council deemed it an unsafe place to drink.

● **Beehive (Map 4)**
90 Doversgreen Road, Woodhatch RH2 8EG
OS: 257483 (A217)
☎ (01737) 246943
12-11 (12-10:30 Sunday)
Wells Bombardier
Young's Bitter
Guest Beer
A large, comfortable, but ultimately bland pub on the southern most outskirts of Reigate, the Beehive has five or six distinct drinking zones all served by the one central bar. There is plenty of seating throughout so finding a place to rest your legs should not be a problem. Food is the predominant driver of business, and is available every day from 12-9. The beer range tends to vary.

◁ ▶ 🚗 ☸ 🚭 ♿

● **Bell (Map 5)**
21 Bell Street, RH2 7AD
OS: 253402 (A217)
☎ (01737) 244438
11-11 (12-10:30 Sunday)
Greene King IPA, Abbot Ale
The Bell is reputedly one of the three oldest pubs in Reigate although little remains to indicate its age. It is another of the local pubs sold to Greene King by Allied Breweries (Friary Meux) in 1990. The tiny frontage opens into a

long, narrow, low ceiling pub that has a 60s, 70s and 80s music night on Friday evenings. There is a patio garden to the rear. The seat by the window is popular for those wishing to people watch.

◁ ❆ 🚌

Black Horse (Map 6)
93 West Street, RH2 9JZ
OS: 243505 (A25)
☎ (01737) 245694
Fuller's London Pride
Young's Bitter
Guest Beer
Formerly a cosy country pub of character, the Black Horse has been refurbished, the bar moved from the centre of the pub to one end, and the walls brightly painted. From the car park the route to the bar is past a wooden floored dining room. This leads to a number of drinking areas where there are several comfortable sofas along with more conventional tables and chairs. Having some slightly raised areas, parts of which are non-smoking, breaks these up. However, ramps allow all parts to be accessible to the disabled. Doors open out from the back onto a large garden. A number of wines (including two champagnes) are available by the glass from the large wine list. Food is available at all sessions, and there is an impressive cheeseboard with which to end your meal. Old photos on the walls show the pub as a Mellersh & Neale pub. Note that children under 14 are not allowed in the pub. The guest beer changes infrequently, and is from one of the major regional brewers such as Adnams or Wells. Sadly, although the intentions are good, ultimately the Black Horse is now a rather faceless gastro-pub.

● Blue Anchor (Map 7)
27 West Street, RH2 9BL
OS: 249503 (A25)
☎ (01737) 225106
11-11 (12-10:30 Sunday)
Fuller's London Pride
Wadworth 6X
During the week this pub does well out of the lunchtime trade, while in the evenings the age group gets younger and livelier. The origins of the pub are 17th century and there are some old beams and an open fireplace from this time. Today's pub has a spacious L-shaped bar with wooden floorboards and some comfortable seating. Possibly the biggest asset is the beer garden in summer, which is probably the best in Reigate. Overlooking the cricket ground with lots of bench seating it is the perfect way to while away the afternoon with a beer or two while tucking into food from the barbecue. Sunday lunches are roasts. No food is sold weekend evenings. A marquee is put up in the garden over the Christmas period that can accommodate an additional 150 people.

◁ ▶ ❆ 🚌

Bridge House Hotel (Map 8)
Reigate Hill, RH2 9RP
OS: 261522 (A217)
☎ (01737) 244821
No real ale
Situated at the top of Reigate Hill, this was once a coaching inn, but there is little, if anything, left to indicate this now. These days it is primarily a cocktail bar for diners in the adjacent restaurant. 39 letting rooms are available.

● **Bull's Head (Map 9)**
55 High Street, RH2 9AE
OS: 252502 (A25)
☎ (01737) 277171
11-11 (12-10:30 Sunday)
Fuller's London Pride
Greene King IPA
One of the oldest pubs in Reigate, the Bulls Head has been a pub since 1628 according to a plaque inside. The name derives from the town abattoir which used to be nearby. Inside, drinking takes place over two levels, with darts played in the higher part to the rear. It is another one of those pubs which do not rely on gimmicks to pull the customers in, just good service and a friendly atmosphere. No food is available Sunday lunchtime.
◁ ❄ 🚌

Café Rouge (Map 10)
1 Church Street, RH2 0AA
OS: 254503 (A25)
☎ (01737) 223700
No real ale
Well situated chain restaurant where the closest thing to real ale is the draught Hoegaarden which has sadly been pasteurised. There is a small raised bar area for those who just want a drink. Originally opened as Muswells, a chain of café bars owned by Allied Breweries, it became the Red River Café around 1994. It is open all day.

Cage (Map 11)
3 Cage Yard, High Street RH2 9AB OS: 253503
☎ (01737) 223222
No real ale
Small bar in a 17th century lock up adjacent to Morrisons supermarket. It was originally called Cobbles, and stands in what was originally the Mellersh & Neale brewery yard.

Holmesdale
Priory Road, OS: 251491
A street corner estate pub on the outskirts of South Park, this Friary Meux pub closed in the mid 1990s. The beer quality was considered good enough for it to be in three editions of the Good Beer Guide between 1979 and 1983.

● **Market Hotel (Map 12)**
2 High Street, RH2 9AY
OS: 253503 (A25)
☎ (01737) 240492
11-11 (11-12 Friday and Saturday, 12-10:30 Sunday)
Harveys Sussex Best Bitter
Young's Bitter
Guest Beers
The largest pub in Reigate has both downstairs and upstairs bars, although the upper bar is closed when it is quiet. This is about the only pub in Reigate where you have any chance of finding a truly interesting beer, although quality can be variable. Up to four guest beers are sold and these are often from microbreweries. The clientele varies according to the time of day with weekday lunchtimes dominated by office workers and with more of a mixture in the evenings. On Fridays and Saturdays the clientele is livelier and young-

er, but it's over 21s only. Dress restrictions apply – no dirty work clothes at any time, and no ripped jeans, trainers or caps at weekends. No food is sold Sunday.

◁ ❆ 🚭 🚌

● Nutley Hall (Map 13)

8 Nutley Lane, RH2 9HS
OS: 250504
☎ (01737) 241741
11-11 (12-10:30 Sunday)
Badger K&B Sussex, Best, Tanglefoot, seasonal beer

Long established, the Nutley Hall continues to be a genuine, friendly locals' pub. It is a small L-shaped bar, and unusually for this area, has a table football game. The pub hosts two cricket teams and are always on the lookout for new recruits. Many years ago, the upstairs rooms were served as a doss house; they now form part of the landlord's (hopefully renovated) accommodation. Although hard to find, it is behind the Upper West Street car park. As part of a traffic calming scheme, the road in front of the Nutley is being redesigned to include a "pocket garden". The pub is built over a number of caves and the cellar utilises these today. Food is only served weekday lunchtimes.

◁ 🚗 ❆ 🚌

● Panther Inn (Map 14)

50 Croydon Road, RH2 0NH
OS: 260507 (A242)
☎ (01737) 244545
12-11 (12-10:30 Sunday)
Greene King IPA, Abbot Ale

From the outside you cannot miss the Panther with its bright yellow exterior. Inside you will find a good, honest, welcoming street corner local with very laid-back staff. The clientele are mostly from the surrounding area and range from city types to plumbers - there are no social boundaries here. Despite its relatively small size, there are three separate drink-

ing areas, including one with a pool table, all served by the central bar. Sky Sports is available for those who want it, just ask the bar staff if the event you want is not showing. For the more cultured there is an art wall at the back end of the bar where every month or so a new local artist is exhibited, with the works available for sale on a commission free basis. The pub also hosts its own golf society and several darts teams. Outside is a patio garden. An over 21s policy is administered.

❆ 🚌

Pilgrim Brewery (Map 15)

West Street, RH2 9BL
OS: 247503
www.pilgrim.co.uk
☎ (01737) 222651
Pilgrim Surrey Bitter, Porter, Progress, seasonal beer

Surrey's oldest brewery is hidden in a yard off the main A25, although the entrance is marked by a hanging barrel sign. The brewery is sited in an old bakery, and has been here since 1985. Beer is only available for offsale and is available during working hours only. Polypins are available for advance orders only. Phone to check for the availability of beers.

● Prince Of Wales (Map 16)

2 Holmesdale Road, RH2 0BQ
OS: 255507
☎ (01737) 243112
12-11 (12-10:30 Sunday)
Shepherd Neame Master Brew Bitter, Best Bitter, Spitfire

Conveniently located beside Reigate train station, the Prince of Wales is an unassuming pub. In the 1800s the building was used to house railway workers. The garden used to be used as a loading area for cattle bought and sold at Reigate market, and until the 1990s, British Rail still used to own it. Today the garden has an aviary at one end. The pub is divided into three main drinking areas each served from the same U-shaped bar. On first inspection, aside from a large projector screen used for major sporting events, there is little ostentation. However go all the way round into the far back room and there are a couple of large Chesterfield sofas, plus a few high backed chairs in which to lounge about. There is also a proper fire for cold winter days. Otherwise this pub relies on the quality of its beer to draw custom. The beer garden backs onto the railway line. Lunchtime food is available Monday to Saturday, and on Sunday there are traditional roasts.

◁ 🚗 ❆ 🚌

● Priory (Map 17)

85 Bell Street, RH2 7AN
OS: 243677 (A217)
☎ (01737) 243677
11-11 (12-10:30 Sunday)
Courage Directors
Greene King IPA, Old Speckled Hen
Guest Beer

Formerly the Castle, the Priory reopened in June 2004 after a complete makeover. It now has a very contemporary feel with light colours, pale wood and some comfortable leather effect sofas as well as the more usual pub seating. It is air-conditioned in the summer months, and five flat panel TV screens plus a large projector screen for large events round off the modern look. Further entertainment comes in the shape of live music on Sundays, a quiz night on Monday evenings and a disco on Thursday evenings playing 80s and 90s music. The big selling point here is the early opening hours for breakfast – from 7am Monday to Friday, 9am Saturday and 10am Sunday. Food is then served all day until 8pm each day. Families are welcome before alcohol is served. A conservatory is a new addition to the rear of the pub, and outside there is a large terraced garden. The guest beer changes monthly and is from regional brewers. Note that the full range of beers may not always be available.

◁ ▶ ❆

Puccino's

65 High Street, RH2 9AE
OS: 252503 (A25)
☎ (01737) 249000
No real ale

Tiny café bar selling a limited ranege of alcoholic drinks, including bottled beer. It is a bright bar with round tables and a comfy settee at the back, with a small patio garden to the rear. It is very popular with families, particularly at weekends, and is open until 5pm (4:30 Sunday), with food available at all times.

Railway Hotel

Holmesdale Road OS: 254507 (A217)
As its name suggests, this Friary Meux pub was next to Reigate Station. Popular with pool players, it was demolished in the late 1980s and an office block was put on the site.

● Red Cross Inn (Map 18)

96 High Street, RH2 9AP
OS: 252503 (A25)
☎ (01737) 225352
11-11 (12-10:30 Sunday)
Fuller's London Pride
Wadworth 6X
Guest Beers

At the end of the High Street, the Red Cross is one of the older pubs

in Reigate. Thankfully now trading under its original name again after becoming the Tap & Spile in 1995, it is owned by the same company that owns the Blue Anchor down the road. With the original beams, bare floorboards, a large inglenook fireplace, leaded windows and the odd brick exposed wall, this place definitely feels like it has been around for a long time. Although one through room, there are two distinct drinking areas either side of the bar, which is opposite the main door. This area can get a bit crowded at peak times, but there is also a serving area around the corner on the right hand side of the bar. Live music on Thursdays. Two guest beers are available, changing every three months. Do not expect the full menu to be always available, but food is available each lunchtime and Monday to Thursday evening.

Reigate Manor Hotel (Map 19)

Reigate Hill, RH2 9PF
OS: 255516 (A217)
☎ (01737) 240125
No real ale

Hotel half way up Reigate Hill with small keg only bar. Opening hours depend on whether or not it is being used for a private function. Before his Second World War North Africa campaign, the building was used as the billet for Field Marshal Montgomery's officers.

Tickled Ivory (Map 20)

39-41 Church Street, RH2 0AD
OS: 255503 (A25)
☎ (01737) 221666
No real ale

A smart modern bar, with a late licence Thursday to Saturday, which features live music. A small split level bar at the front leads to a larger area to the rear. Food is served Monday to Friday lunchtime and it is closed on Sunday.

● Venture Inn (Map 21)

11 Lesbourne Road, RH2 7JP
OS: 257498
☎ (01737) 271576
11:30-3, 5-11 (11:30-11 Friday and Saturday;
12-10:30 Sunday)
Adnams Broadside
Fuller's London Pride
Harveys Sussex Best Bitter
Shepherd Neame Spitfire
Guest Beer

It is always a pleasure to find a pub which continues to maintain separate lounge and public bars rather than knocking them through into one large room. Both rooms are served by the one bar, with the hand pulls all being in the lounge, although beers are listed, and of course can be ordered, in the public bar. The guest beer changes every three weeks or so. This is a warm, female-friendly pub with no gaming machines. Sky Sports is available in the public bar though. A no smoking policy is exercised in the lounge bar for lunch while three smoke extractors are used in the public bar to keep the smoke at bay. In addition to the usual pub fayre at lunch, a selection of oriental dishes is available as well. Food is not available on Sunday. A sausage sandwich menu is also available every evening (except Sunday) between 6 and 8pm. In

tal dishes is available as well. Food is not available on Sunday. A sausage sandwich menu is also available every evening (except Sunday) between 6 and 8pm. In addition to the beers, there is a good choice of wine and malt whisky. An over 21s policy is maintained. The pub was originally called the Desert Rat.

◁ 🚭 (food serving times only)

White Hart (Map 22)
12 Church Street, RH2 0AN
OS: 254503 (A25)
☎ (01737) 246383
Fuller's London Pride
The White Hart is a fairly large one roomed bar with bare floorboards. It has a local band playing live every second Monday which can cause the "House Full" signs to go up. DJs play various genres of music on a Friday and Saturday night and a pool table can be found at the rear of the pub. For a while the pub was called the Faucet & Firkin, but has gone back to its original name. A more relaxed atmosphere is found at lunchtimes, with food being served Monday to Saturday.

● **Yew Tree (Map 23)**
99 Reigate Hill, RH2 9PJ
OS: 257517 (A217)
☎ (01737) 244944
12-11 (12-10:30 Sunday)
Fuller's London Pride
Greene King IPA
Shepherd Neame Spitfire
Young's Bitter
The Yew Tree is half way up Reigate Hill, next door to the Esso garage. Although there has been a pub on this site for 300 years, the current building dates back to 1938. With a mock-Tudor exterior, leaded glass windows and wood panelled walls, this is very much a traditional pub. The one bar serves two distinct drinking areas, separated by a large chimney breast in which there is installed a real fire. The pub is usually busy after work with people "working late" in the office. Keenly priced home made pub grub is served up for lunch in winter, and also for dinner in the spring and summer (no food Sunday evening).

◁ ▶ 🚗 ❆

REIGATE HEATH (B2)

The heath covers 130 acres of heath and woodland, and is a Site of Special Scientific Interest, and was once the haunt of highwaymen and smugglers. The post mill windmill on the Heath dates from 1765. It is unique in that it houses a chapel in its former roundhouse, having been converted in the late 19th century.

● **Skimmington Castle**
Bonny's Road, RH2 8RL
OS: 237497
www.skimmingtoncastle.com
☎ (01737) 243100
11-3, 5:30-11 (Opens 6 Saturday; 12-10:30 Sunday)
Adnams Bitter
Harveys Sussex Best Bitter
Wells Bombardier
Young's Special
The Skimmington Castle started life as a farm 400 years ago. It became a pub in 1825 but in recent years has been more akin to a restaurant than pub, especially at weekends, meaning that drinkers may find all the tables taken by diners. Good food is available each session. The pub has a great location though, and on a sunny day, the beer garden is a wonderful place to enjoy a few pints, with or without a meal. Inside there are a number of rooms, including a non smoking room down a few steep steps (where families are permitted), all served by the one bar. This is very much a cosy pub with lots of atmosphere. Low ceilings and a real fire only help to enhance this.

SALFORDS (C2)

Modern string of buildings along the A23. The Sal goes under the main road before joining the River Mole to the west.

General Napier
54 Brighton Road, RH1 5BZ
OS: 281464 (A23)
A main road local, the General Napier was a Friary Meux pub. It closed in 1997 and was later replaced by the Harvester, although the two places are unrelated apart from location.

Harvester
54 Brighton Road, RH1 5DA
OS: 281464 (A23)
☎ (01737) 773277
Bass
Typical Harvester pub restaurant, open all day, with the emphasis on food, which is served until 10pm every day and includes a kids' menu. There is a separate restaurant and both parts are split into different areas with partitions. The pub was built on the site of the old General Napier pub in 1998.

● **Mill House**
15 Brighton Road, RH1 5BT
OS: 282467 (A23)
☎ (01737) 767277
11-11 (12-10:30 Sunday)
Flowers Original
Fuller's London Pride
Marston's Pedigree
The pub is attached to a 48 room Premier Travel Inn. The name derives from the fact that it was built on the site of the first mill for Kelloggs in the country. Parts of the building date from the 18th century. This d was the miller's house, and remains of the old mill can be seen in the stream that runs alongside. The pub has several separate areas and is divided into a drinking area and a restaurant. The drinking area has an inglenook, some original beams and a few photos of the old mill on its walls. The pub is open all day, and opens for breakfast each morning from 7-10 (8-10 Sunday). Otherwise, food is served 12-2:30 and 5:30-9:30 Monday to Friday, 12-10 Saturday, and 12-9 Sunday. There are nappy-changing facilities in the disabled toilet.

SHERE (A2)

Shere is of Saxon origin and was mentioned in the Domesday Book. St James' church dates from 1190 and in the early 14th century a female hermit was walled up in a cell here. Many of the cottages date from the 16th, 17th and 18th centuries and there is a small 17th century prison.

● **Prince Of Wales**
Shere Lane, GU5 9HS
OS: 072476
☎ (01483) 202313
11-11 (12-10:30 Sunday)
Fuller's London Pride
Young's Bitter
Set in a prominent position just a short way above the centre of the village, this large pub has both public and lounge bars, the latter also serving as a restaurant with meals sold every lunchtime and evening except Sunday nights. There are five letting rooms, three double and two single, all en-suite. The pub interior is decorated with old agricultural implements. The

Prince of Wales used to be owned by the Reffell Brothers brewery of Gomshall which was bought by Young's of Wandsworth in 1926. It remained a Young's pub until they sold it in the 1990s.

Surrey Hills Brewery

Old Scotland Farm, Staple Lane, GU5 9TE OS: 063501
www.surreyhills.co.uk
☎ (01483) 212812
Surrey Hills Ranmore Ale, Shere Drop, seasonal beer

Sited in an old milking parlour, the brewery commenced commercial brewing in May 2005. It is attractively set in a rural area within the Surrey Hills. Beer is available for offsale only, in quantities from 4 to 72 pints. There will normally be someone at the brewery to sell you beer on Thursdays and Fridays from 12–2:45 and 3:45-5 and on Saturday from 10–12 noon, but phone first to check.

White Horse

Shere Lane, GU5 9HS OS: 073478
☎ (01483) 202518
Courage Best Bitter, Directors
Hogs Back TEA
Wells Bombardier

An historic building in the centre of this picturesque village, this pub has the accent on food. A haunt for smugglers in the 18th century, the pub was erected as a farmhouse in 1475. The interior, comprising several dining and drinking areas served from a single, small bar, is on several levels and is decorated with a variety of old artefacts. The pub is open all day and is on the Surrey Cycleway.

SIDLOW BRIDGE (C2)

Small scattering of houses around where the A217 crosses the river Mole. Emanuel church dates from 1861 and was designed by Henry Clutton, and features some fine stained glass windows, many designed by the eminent Victorian artist Henry Holiday.

● Three Horseshoes

Ironsbottom, RH2 8PT
OS: 249463
www.sidlow.com
☎ (01293) 862315
12-2:30, 5:30-11 (12-3 and 6:30-10:30 Sunday)
Fuller's London Pride, ESB
Harveys Sussex Best Bitter
Young's Bitter
Guest Beer

A cracking wee pub about ¾ of a mile off the A217 between Reigate & Hookwood, the Three Horseshoes is definitely worth a detour. Parts of it date back 300 years and it was originally a coaching inn on the old original London-Brighton Road. When entering, there is a small ante-room with just about enough room for a couple of small tables and a few chairs. The main bar itself is an L-shaped room. The area to the left of the entrance was once a forge, hence the name the Three Horseshoes. It still houses a real fireplace, which adds to the warmth of the place in the winter months. The area to the right, in front of the bar, is where the locals tend to congregate, and has oak beams and a timbered ceiling. It also contains an unusual trophy, about which, the less said the better. Through to the back of the bar is a recent extension, which houses a non smoking room, which is very much a welcome addition. Families are welcome until 9pm. Good quality, simple lunches are served every day between 12 and 2 (2:30 Sundays), and on Thursday to Monday evenings from 7-9. The management has changed following the sad demise of the previous landlord, but much to the relief of the locals, they have no intentions of making any drastic changes in the near future, although it is hoped that a separate restaurant will feature soon.

SMALLFIELD (C3)

Smallfield, now a large residential village, originated when the estate of Smallfield Place was given to John de Burstow in the 14th century. The moated manor was built around 1600 out of local sandstone and roofed with Horsham stone. It is one of the most important examples of domestic buildings of this time in the country.

● Plough

Plough Road, RH6 9HN
OS: 323431
☎ (01342) 842212
11-11 (12-10:30 Sunday)
Marston's Pedigree
Young's Special
Occasional **Guest Beer**

This large pub is set away from the village and is split into three areas. One of these houses a restaurant. At the back of this is a small area with sofas where non-smokers can drink. The main bar area has an inglenook, pool and darts, and there is another small area off it at the back. Home cooked food is available every day from 12-4 and 6-10 and there is a separate kids' menu. The fenced garden includes a children's play area with slides.

SMITHWOOD COMMON (A3)

Small rural hamlet.

Four Elms
Smithwood Common Road, GU6 8QP OS: 052409
A old rural pub on commonland away from the main road, it nevertheless won many trophies for cards and darts in the 1970s and 80s. It was a Watney pub, but was selling real ale shortly after that brewery rediscovered it in the early 1980s. It closed around 1997 and has since been converted into a house.

SOUTH GODSTONE (D2)

Main road village dating from Victorian times, it is the site of Godstone railway station. The countryside around contains a number of attractive farms and old houses.

● Fox & Hounds

Tilburstow Hill Road, RH9 8LY
OS: 354494
☎ (01342) 893474
12-3, 6-11 (12-3, 7-10:30 Sunday)
Greene King IPA, Abbot Ale
Guest Beer

A most attractive building, parts of which date back to 1368. It became a pub in 1601 and the first landlord was Thomas Hart, a tenant of Pendell Manor near Bletchingley. As well as brewing and selling its own beer, at one time it also served as a post office and blacksmith. There are several original beams throughout and a large inglenook in the no-smoking restaurant. The lower bar also benefits from a real fire. Look for the gaiter of a former pirate turned

smuggler, John Trenchman, who died in the cellar of the pub after being pursued by the King's revenue men. Legend has it that if this gaiter is removed, his ghost returns to haunt the pub. His earthly remains lie in Godstone churchyard. A former Westerham Brewery house until 1965, it passed to Ind Coope, later to become part of Allied Breweries until it was sold to Greene King in the late 90s. Today it is a friendly, family run establishment, with the daughter of the previous tenant now in charge. The pub has a deserved reputation for good food, which is sold in both the restaurant and bar, as well as for its excellent beer. No food is available Sunday evening. The bar area is low ceilinged and very cosy with high back settles. There is a pleasant garden at the rear. The guest beer is brewery supplied.

◁▶ ✗ ♞ 🚗 ❄ ⊘ 🚲

Railway Hotel
Eastbourne Road, RH9 8EZ
OS: 363483 (A22)
☎ (01342) 892104
Greene King IPA
Guest Beer
Convenient for Godstone station, this is a two bar locals' pub. Handpumps in the front bar only. There is a games room at the rear replete with pool table, dartboard and electronic machines. Railway prints and bits of memorabilia adorn the walls. The saloon was nearly demolished by a runaway lorry in the early 80s. A guest beer will be available in summer. Open all day.

Wonham House Hotel
Eastbourne Road, RH9 8EJ
OS: 364498 (A22)
This large hotel was set back off the main road, and sold a number of real ales, including those from fledgling microbreweries, and even appeared in the 1985 Good Beer Guide. Unfortunately changes led to it stopping real ale in the late 1980s and it closed around 1990. However, while open, it did a great service to real ale drinkers.

SOUTH HOLMWOOD (B2)

Part of the ancient Manor of Dorking, Holmwood Common was owned by King Harold before the Norman Conquest. In 1755 a toll road was built, linking Horsham with Dorking, but the area became notorious for highwaymen and smugglers. A granite memorial on the A24 at Mid Holmwood is a tribute to the millionaire Alfred Gwynne Vanderbilt, who was well known in the area through his passion for coaching. The local and county council purchased it from the Duke of Norfolk in 1956 and then donated it to the National Trust. A section of the Roman Stane Street has been preserved in Redlands Wood.

Holly & Laurel
Horsham Road, RH5 4NG
OS: 170452 (A24)
A large building on the main road, the Holly & Laurel was a Charrington's pub. In 1992 it became the Gourmet Pizza Company and stopped any pretence of being a pub. It was later sold to the free trade and in 1994 changed its name to Hollys, and sold a number of real ales. Today it is the Holly & Laurel Emporium and sells fireplaces amongst other items.

SOUTH NUTFIELD (C2)

South Nutfield is the location of Nutfield Station, and developed with the coming of the railway in the 19th century. Lytell Hall, a 19th century mansion which has housed the Brewing Industry Research Foundation, much used by national brewers, since 1948. To the south, Redhill Aerodrome was established in 1934 and was used by fighter aircraft in the Second World War. Today it is mostly used by helicopters and by flying clubs. Between 1942 and 1944 Polish and Canadian Squadrons used the Aerodrome and prior to D-Day over two hundred fighter aircraft were based here to support the invasion forces.

● Station Hotel

South Station Approach, The Avenue, RH1 5RY OS: 305492
11-11 (12-10:30 Sunday)
☎ (01737) 823223
Fuller's London Pride
Greene King Old Speckled Hen
Young's Bitter
Westons Old Rosie Cider, Herefordshire Country Perry

A much altered, large, late-Victorian establishment, built for Mellersh & Neale's Brewery, Reigate, to serve the community growing up around Nutfield railway station. It is just about possible to work out where the old partitions used to be within this big open plan bar. At one end is a big screen TV for Sky Sports, with darts and pool also available. An attractive tiled side-awning runs along one side of the building. There is a pleasant garden to the side, which is always popular in the summer months. A large children's play area is to found here. Quizzes are held on the last Thursday of each month and there is live music every Saturday night. The landlord is a very keen cider enthusiast, and these are sold by electric pump from a T-bar and are highly recommended. In the evening, food is only available on Tuesday and from Thursday to Saturday.

(Nutfield)

STAFFHURST WOOD (D2)

This hamlet is set within much woodland. The wood itself dates back to Saxon times when it was part of a royal hunting park and has been declared a Site of Special Scientific Interest. During the Second World War it was used as an ammunitions dump.

● Royal Oak

Caterfield Lane, RH8 0RR
OS: 407485
☎ (01883) 722207
11-3, 5-11 (11-11 Thursday to Saturday, 12-10:30 Sunday)
Adnams Bitter
Larkin's Traditional Ale
Westerham Black Eagle SPA
Guest Beer
Greene King Hen's Tooth in bottle
Worthington White Shield in bottle
Guest Cider

A rural pub whose regulars consist of a cross section of society, from farm workers to stockbrokers and landowners. A port club and a pie and ale club are available to regulars and both the ladies' and men's darts teams have recently won the award for being most social team in the local league. There is a very strong emphasis on the sourcing of both beer and food, with the beers being delivered by the breweries rather than third parties. The guest beer only changes infrequently and has recently been Greene King

IPA and Harveys Sussex Best Bitter. A number of good Belgian bottled beers are also sold, and the cider also varies, with Biddenden being a regular recently. The cider is served direct from a cask behind the bar. The pub is on a number of walkers' routes and both they and their dogs are welcome. Food is a strong presence, with as much as possible being bought from local farms, suppliers and shoots. The menu changes regularly, with the seasons being reflected, and fish is delivered daily. Food is served each lunchtime from 12-2 and evenings (except Sunday) from 6-9. Children's portions are available and the food is cooked to order, with all pies being homemade. Goods views over the surrounding countryside can be had from the garden.

STONEBRIDGE (B2)

Cluster of dwellings on the edge of Holmwood Common recently connected to North Holmwood by a new housing development.

Royal Oak

Chart Lane South, RH5 4DH
OS: 177478
☎ (01306) 885420
Greene King Abbot Ale
Shepherd Neame Spitfire
Guest Beer

Dating in parts from 1613, the Royal Oak overlooks open countryside. The small bar is split-level and has low ceilings. Darts is played in the lower part of this. On the wall are a number of framed Tooting Brewery invoices. A more modern addition to the walls is a flat screen TV, used mainly for televised sport. To the rear of the pub is a separate restaurant in a newer extension. This is open every lunchtime from 12-3, and Wednesday to Saturday evenings from 7-9:30. A daily specials board supplements the standard menu, and will include homemade curries and pies. Outside there is a play area for children and a patio garden. The guest beer changes monthly, and tends to be from a regional brewery. The pub is open all day.

STONELEIGH (B1)

On the Greater London border, Stoneleigh developed rapidly with the opening of a station in 1932. The area is now built-up suburbia, apart from the nearby Nonsuch Park.

● Stoneleigh Inn (Ewell Map 11)

The Broadway, KT17 2JA
OS: 221642
☎ (020) 8393 2745
11-11 (12-10:30 Sunday)
Adnams Bitter
Courage Best Bitter
Greene King IPA

This is a large pub that caters for all ages. It has a good community feel with quiz nights, mini-discos, ladies' nights, etc. Recently refurbished, the outside back garden is well used in the summer and there is also a front patio. Live sport on TV is a regular feature and there is a separate games room for pool, etc. The real fire is welcome on cold nights. The pub has an interesting mock Tudor upper level and roof. There is an upstairs function room that can be hired.

STROOD GREEN (B2)

Small mainly modern residential village, now incorporated as part of Brockham.

Spotted Cow
80 Middle Street, RH3 7HU
OS: 201482
This was the last pub ever built by Friary Meux. It was built on the site of an old 17th century Mellersh & Neale pub that required repair work, and this being 1960, it was decided that a modern pub would be better. The Spotted Cow was an ugly pub, with a very angular façade and a green roof. There were two bars, separated by a lobby, which had an off-sales window in it. The front of each bar had real cowhide on it, and behind the bar were fake barrel fronts adverting the delights of such beers as Friary Meux Treble Gold. The pub was bought by Greene King in 1990, and eventually became rather run down. It closed in the late 1990s as was demolished to make way for housing. A sad end to what had been a decent little local.

SUTTON ABINGER (A2)

This hamlet comprises a mixture of modern and timber-framed buildings. Fulvens Farm and Sutton Place Farm are two examples of the latter, dating from the 16th century and around 1700 respectively.

● Volunteer Inn
Water Lane, RH5 6PR
OS: 106459
☎ (01306) 730798

12-3, 6-11 (12-11 Saturday and 12-10:30 Sunday)
Badger K&B Bitter, Best, Tanglefoot, seasonal beers
The pub was formerly owned by Friary Meux, but taken over by Badger in 1998 and is set in a small hamlet in a grassy valley. The restaurant is separate from the bar and has a reputation for good food. Running along the front of the pub is a long and narrow bar which contains a double-sided fireplace, and is cosy in winter. The wide road outside marks the place where London Transport used to turn round the 412 bus round many years ago. The bus was kept on a farm in Holmbury St Mary overnight. The garden on the steep hillside is an excellent spot to eat and drink in the sun.

TADWORTH (B2)

Tadworth has been a settlement since pre-Saxon times, but is now part of the commuter belt. Tadworth Court, built in around 1700, now houses the Tadworth Children's Trust.

● Blue Anchor
Dorking Road, KT20 5SL
OS: 236557 (B2032)
☎ (01737) 819011
11-11 (12-10-30 Sunday)
Harveys Sussex Best Bitter
Greene King Old Speckled Hen
Guest Beer
An odd name for a pub located in landlocked Surrey, although at least there is such an item affixed to this 1930s former Charrington

pub's exterior. The inside has been subjected to a total reconstruction – lots of imported bric-a-brac, bare brick, rough-hewn wood and flagstone floor tiles, and all in typical Vintage Inn's style. Although effectively a single bar pub by having only one counter providing service, there are also separate dining and snug bar areas. This is a mostly food oriented establishment, with meals available throughout the day until 10 at night, and the pub is virtually no smoking throughout. The pub sign declares "Beer house, built in error 1843"- an enigma that sadly has eluded us. The guest beer tends to be from one of the larger independents.

◁▶ 🐴 🚗 ☸ ⊘ ♿

● Duke's Head

Dorking Road, KT20 5SL
OS: 237557 (B2032)
☎ (01737) 812173
11-11 (12-10:30 Sunday)
Adnams Bitter
Flowers Original
Young's Bitter, Special
An attractive red brick building with ground-floor shallow bow-fronted windows. Inside, little if any original features survive and the effect is open plan with different styles of seating areas with many dining tables. There are two real fires. The emphasis is very much on good food although the pub does hold an entertainments licence and there are cabaret evenings once a month. There is a designated no smoking area. The pub was acquired by the Reigate brewery of Mellersh & Neale from R&F Pagden of Epsom in 1931, and was rebuilt in 1932. It ended its brewery owned days under the Friary Meux badge of the Allied umbrella (some nice Friary signs remain) and is now a Punch leasehold. Food is served 11-3 Monday to Friday and 6-9 Monday to Wednesday (10 Thursday and Friday), Saturday 11-10 and Sunday 12-7.

◁▶ 🚗 ☸ ⊘

● Tumble Beacon

Dorking Road, KT20 5RX
OS: 239564 (B2032)
☎ (01737) 353529
11-11 (12-10:30 Sunday)
Fuller's London Pride
Shepherd Neame Master Brew Bitter
Occasional **Guest Beer**

A black and white Edwardian establishment set back from the main road on a small green, it has a most unusual wooden ceiling in the single L-shaped bar. Originally called the Bricklayer's Arms, it was renamed in 1972 to commemorate the Banstead Beacon that was constructed to warn of the arrival of the Spanish Armada. Very much a locals' pub with a big sports following (and big screen TV to match), but no less welcome to the passing visitor for all that. Pub games in the form of darts and shut the box are played. Happy hours operate Monday to Saturday between 5 and 7, and there is live music every Friday and some Saturdays. Lunchtime food is served weekdays between 12 and 2. This was originally a Mellersh & Neale house until their take over by Meux & Co in 1938, becoming Friary Meux in the late 1950s. The pub is now owned by Punch Taverns.

◁ 🐴 🚗 ☸

TANDRIDGE (D2)

The small church has fine timberwork that supports the tower and shingled spire by four huge corner posts and large cross-braces. The church dates from 1100 and was restored by the Victorian architect Sir George Scott who lived in the village. One of Surrey's largest yew trees is to be found in the churchyard.

● Barley Mow

Tandridge Lane, RH8 9NJ
OS: 372506
☎ (01883) 713770
11:30-3, 6-11 (11:30-11 Friday and Saturday,
12-10:30 Sunday)
Badger K&B Sussex, Best, Tanglefoot, seasonal beer
This comfortable family run village pub, built in the 1830s, has three separate areas. There is a boarded "public" area by the bar where darts can be played. This is linked by an arch into the carpeted front part, which is split into a "lounge" area and the restaurant. Families are welcome (there is a separate kids' menu), as are walkers and dogs (for which you can help yourself to dog biscuits from a jar on the bar). Tuesday night is quiz night. Food is available from 12-2 and 6-9 Monday to Saturday, and from 12-4 Sunday. Accommodation comprises two rooms.

TATSFIELD (D1)

The village is set high on the North Downs and overlooks Biggin Hill, with views over Surrey, Kent and Sussex, and the inhabitants were able to see London burning in 1666. The land was owned by Edward the Confessor before the Norman Conquest, and by the Bishop of Bayeux by the time of the Domesday Book. The small Norman church, the highest in the county, is 788 feet (240 metres) above sea level with good views to the south.

● Bakery

Westmore Green, TN16 0AG
S: 412568
www.thebakeryrestaurant.com
☎ (01959) 577605
12-3, 6-11 (closed all day Monday, open 12-4 Sunday)
Westerham – range varies
Basically a restaurant converted from an old 19th century turreted village store in 1978, further changes were required in 1983 when the premises were gutted by fire. Today's incarnation consists of a small front bar with stainless steel counter and a seating area. This leads through to a much larger room dedicated to dining use; both areas are finished in contemporary style. Of particular interest are the series of photographs depicting the building at various historic stages of its life. Although beer was being served by gravity straight from the cask at time of survey, a conventional handpump was being considered as a future option. The beer comes from the local Westerham Brewery, but which beer changes with the landlord's whim. There is a bar menu as well as an extensive and most impressive 3 course prix fixé menu. Closed Sunday evening and all day Monday. Food is available 12-2 Tuesday to Friday and 12-2:30 weekend lunchtimes and

7-9:30 Tuesday to Thursday and 7-10 Friday and Saturday evening.

◁▶✕♿🚗☸

Old Ship
Ship Hill, Westmore Green, TN16 2AG OS: 412568
☎ (01959) 577315
Greene King IPA
Young's Bitter
Successive remodelling has swept away almost every item of historical interest from this late Victorian pub, the sole remaining artefacts being a series of four inset coloured glass panels at ceiling height which may just have once formed part of the original bar-back of this former Charrington house. Sadly little character remains and the interior decoration is now predominantly pastel-shaded, together with some exposed brick in the right-hand restaurant/dining area. The carpet takes a bit of getting used to! The pub serves as the terminus of the 464 route which remains part of the "red" London Buses network. Whilst supping your pint, note the distinctive pitched-roofed wooden bus shelter opposite, one of a number surviving in the area, which were constructed and installed by London Transport in the late 1940s. The pub is open all day Saturday and Sunday.

TITSEY (D2)

Originally the estate village for Titsey Park, which was owned by the Greshams. In 1776 Sir John Gresham had the old church knocked down and rebuilt by the park gates. The foundations of a Roman villa were discovered in Titsey Park in 1864, and pottery, coins and a bronze mask were excavated. A 3rd century Romano-Celtic temple is situated nearby to the east of Titsey.

● **Botley Hill Farmhouse**
Limpsfield Road, Botley Hill, CR6 9QH OS: 395555 (B269)
www.botleyhill-farmhouse.co.uk
☎ (01959) 577154
11-11 (12-10:30 Sunday)
Greene King IPA, Abbot Ale, Old Speckled Hen
Shepherd Neame Spitfire, Bishops Finger
Westerham Black Eagle SPA
Set in an isolated and elevated position (850 feet, 259 metres) on the edge of Titsey Plantation, and on land owned by the Titsey Foundation, this white-rendered building was once a farmhouse dating from 1546. Local landowners, the Greshams, built the Royal Exchange in the City of London in 1571, and a grasshopper, which forms part of their family crest, can be found on the pub signage. It only entered licenced use comparatively recently (1994) having previously been tea-rooms since 1936. The inside is a cosy blend of low ceilings and doorways, two separate drinking areas, a restaurant, and a little nook and cranny all served by a longitudinal bar running the length of the rear which contains no less than nine handpumps. In the Grasshopper room there is an unusual fireplace with an engraved mantelpiece believed to Turkish in origin. Similar engravings can be found on the flagstones as well. Entertainment is a big theme here with a mix of cabaret, pop/rock and tribute bands all appearing in the pub's adjoining marquee. The pub is arguably the closest to the exclusive and "dry" village of Woldingham on the high ridge of the North Downs. Food is served 12-3 & 7-9:30 Monday to Friday

and 12-9:30 Saturday and Sunday. The Greenwich Meridian bisects the toilets!

WALLISWOOD (B3)

Small, pretty village near the Sussex border. Just to the north of the village, the Surrey Wildlife Trust owns the 37-acre Wallis Wood.

● Scarlett Arms

Walliswood Green Road,
RH5 5RD OS: 119382
☎ (01306) 627243
11:30-2:30, 5-11 (12-3, 6-10:30 Sunday)
Badger K&B Sussex, Best, seasonal beer

Named after Sir James Scarlett, the first Baron of Abinger, the pub was built as two cottages in 1620, becoming a pub in 1907. It is the epitome of the traditional country pub with a stone-flagged floor and oak beams. There is a recent extension found behind the impressive inglenook fireplace, creating four drinking areas in all. Food is served each lunchtime and evenings from Tuesday to Saturday.

WALTON-ON-THE-HILL (B2)

A Victorian village on the North Downs with strong horse racing connections and a well-known golf course which held the Ryder Cup in 1981. The church contains a Norman lead font, possibly the oldest in England. A Romano-British villa was excavated in 1948. This had been built in the 1st century. After being disused for fifty years it had been renovated and lived in until around 400AD. At the end of the 19th century local residents fought to retain common rights in the face of residential development and helped keep the open land on the edge of the village.

● Bell

Withybed Corner, KT20 7UJ
OS: 227557
☎ (01737) 812132
12-3, 5:30-11 (12-11 Saturday, and 12-10:30 Sunday)
Fuller's London Pride
Young's Bitter

This is a real gem which is hidden away off the road and a certain determination is required from the first time visitor to discover it! Turn off by the pond and keep turning right – it really is there! The pub is down bumpy tracks so don't rush. This ex-Charrington's (previously Page & Overton's) pub combines the far end of a short terrace of cottages together with a 1950s red brick-built extension into what presumably would have been the front garden. The cosy, low-ceilinged, welcoming interior still consists of separate parquet floored public and carpeted saloon bars; the former with a bar billiards table, the latter with an upright piano, and both furnished with genuine bric-a-brac, plus real fires. Darts is also played. The former Charrington's ownership is recalled by the leaded win-

dows and illuminated wooden bar back. The pub dates back to around 1854 and remained an Ale House without a spirits licence until c.1950. It is run today as a free house under the ownership of the small Croydon based pub chain, J.T Davies. Sandwiches and bar snacks are available at most times. Known locally as "The Rat", from days gone by when stable lads from nearby Epsom Downs used to frequent it.

🚗 ☸

Blue Ball
Deans Lane, KT20 7UE
OS: 228552
☎ (01737) 812168
Adnams Broadside
Courage Best Bitter
Fuller's London Pride
Young's Bitter
Guest Beer
Facing Walton Heath and overlooking the village pond, the pub is named after the centre of a racing winning post. The original 1880 building has gained a later ground floor extension along the length of its front. Inside, the bar sits to the right, neatly dividing the floor space up between a front bar, rear dining room and an in-between snug. Originally belonged to W F Hodgson's Kingston Brewery until its acquisition by Courage in 1943. Open all day, food is available every day from 12-9:45 (8:45 Sunday), and families are welcome until 7pm.

● **Chequers**
Chequers Lane, KT20 7SF
OS: 222548 (B2220)
☎ (01737) 812364
11-11 (12-10:30 Sunday)
Young's Bitter, Special, seasonal beer
Young's Golden Champion, Special London Ale in bottle
Parts of this pub date from 1815 and it once incorporated a brewhouse and bakery. Today the pub has been much altered and this

Young's outpost has an attractive red brick and half-timbered exterior which conceals a central servery adjoined by various interconnecting bars and seating areas, each with its own character and atmosphere. It was once the terminus of London General bus route 180 (later 80A) and there was a semi-circular bus pull-in where the front car park now is. A large garden hosts barbecues in the spring and summer months and food is served 12-3 and 6-10 weekdays and throughout the day at weekends (until 10 Saturday and 7 Sunday). Children are welcome until 7pm. Popular with sporting types, there is a golfing society and until recently the pub was frequented by a former footballing legend plus members of the press looking for a good scoop. Please remember this is a Young's house - they do not serve Best!

◁▶ 🐴 🚗 ☸ ♿

● **Fox & Hounds**
Walton Street, KT20 7RU
OS: 225553 (B2220)
12-11 (12-10:30 Sunday)
☎ (01737) 817744
Fuller's London Pride
Greene King IPA
This cream-painted building has seen various extensions over the years and now comprises a wood-panelled, parquet-floored, low-ceilinged pubby drinking area at the front, which leads through on the left to a rear dining area. The old Sussex flint-faced outbuilding at the rear is worth a second look. The pub is comfortable and furnished with a mix of contemporary

and old. New management has totally reversed the pub's declining fortunes and there is a pleasant and welcoming atmosphere throughout - enhanced in the winter months by two real fires. Real ale is a good seller here with London Pride outselling all other beers by 3:1. Food is served daily 12-3 (4 Sunday) and 6-9 Monday to Saturday and there is a quiz night every Thursday. There is a non-smoking area to the rear of the bar in this former Charrington house.

◁▶✕🚗❁🚭♿

WARLINGHAM (C1)

Although on the boundary of Greater London, Warlingham still has some attractive countryside around it. All Saints church is 13th century, and is thought to be where the Edward VI Authorised Prayer Book was first used. The first televised church service was held there on 24th September 1950. Sir Joseph Swan is buried in the churchyard. He invented the Carbon process in 1864, which allowed permanent photographic prints to be made, and also the electric light bulb. The almshouses and vicarage were built in 1663. In 1909 a gardener found the remains of a 1st century cinerary urn, complete with human remains. Tradition has it that a spring rises nearby when some change of great consequence in the State or Church is about to occur. Known as "Woe-waters" it rose before the plague in London in 1665, and the Glorious Revolution of 1688 which saw the overthrow of James II.

● Hare & Hounds

Limpsfield Road, CR6 9DZ
OS: 365583 (B269)
12-11 (12-10:30 Sunday)
☎ (01883) 623952
Fuller's London Pride
Tetley Bitter
Guest Beers

Large Edwardian pub set back from the main road with a small car park and outside drinking area. There are some attractive exterior architectural details and a newly painted, long rectangular signboard over the front entrance, depicting the pursuit of the hare. It has recently reopened after some major structural works which have altered the pub's interior considerably. Now open plan with a single bar along the back wall. Several photos of old Warlingham are dotted around the building. Real ale has made a very welcome return to this community pub which a previous management regime removed stating it was unviable. In addition to the regular beers, two guests are usually offered with at least one from a microbrewer. It sits next to a large Sainsbury's Superstore on which London Transport's Chelsham bus garage once stood. Although there is a wall mounted plasma screen television, the present landlord eschews the use of satellite broadcasts and will only allow it to be used for occasional major sporting fixtures and national events on terrestrial channels. Food is served Monday to Saturday from 12.00 - 7.00 and 12.00 - 3.00 on Sunday. Barbeques are held in the rear garden during the summer months. This was once a Charrington tied house and is now run as a free house operated by Sarumdale, a small pub operating company.

◁▶🚗❁🚭♿

● Horseshoe

Farleigh Road, CR6 9EG
OS: 357585
☎ (01883) 622009
11-11 (12-10:30 Sunday)
Courage Best Bitter, Directors

Occasional **Guest Beer**
Large roadhouse constructed by Mann, Crossman and Paulin in 1938, replacing the original Horseshoe which was built in 1847 on the site of an old beerhouse, the Blacksmiths Arms, itself dating from 1609. Now designated a Country Carvery, it is heavily food orientated with a separate restaurant off the main bar. Food is served each day from 12-3 and 6-9:30. A lunchtime singer entertains members of the Diamond Pensioners Club on the first Friday of each month. Children are al lowed in the restaurant, which is open from 12-9:30 on Saturday and Sunday. Outside is a patio garden.

◁▶✗🚗❄⊗♿

Olde Leather Bottle

2 The Green, CR6 9NA
OS: 355585 (B270)
☎ (01883) 627055
No real ale
Overlooking the village green, this large corner pub was originally a Nalder & Collyer (Croydon) house, later to become Ind Coope, then badged as Friary Meux, and finally Sedgwick's (whoever he may be). It has now descended into a loud young persons' venue where lager swilling and contemporary clothing are the norm. Open all day.

Wesleyan

432 Limpsfield Road, CR6 9LA
OS: 356585 (B269)
www.thewesleyan.com
☎ (01883) 626910
No real ale
A nine bedroomed hotel with restaurant and bar, sadly selling no real ale. Of brick and flint construction, it was built on the site of a former Wesleyan chapel, the present building dates from 1871 and was originally a private dwelling until 1982 when it was much extended and became a restaurant called Villa Sonia. Later additions came in 1991 when it also became a hotel. It was sold to a local family in 2003 and given its present name. Closed Sunday evening.

● White Lion

3 Farleigh Road, CR6 9EG
OS: 356585 (B269)
www.white-lion-warlingham.co.uk
☎ (01883) 629011
12-11 (12-10:30 Sunday)
Fuller's London Pride
Young's Bitter
Guest Beer
After much controversy surrounding alterations to one of Surrey's oldest pubs, the debate seems to have cooled off as things return to normal in this charming hostelry. A well orchestrated local protest succeeded in forcing Mitchells & Butler to considerably review and redraw their plans for the pub. Apart from the rather incongruous pub sign at the front there is little to detract from the most attractive façade of this ancient building - the oldest part being the middle section which is believed to date from 1467, when it was a farm house with attached cottages. It is flanked to the left by a pretty tile hung building and to the right by a rather out of character extension dating from around 1900, which replaced the original stable block. The interior is a warren of rooms ancient and modern. The nooks and crannies are a delight to explore - but do watch your head! All the new building work was concentrated at the rear and involved the construction of a kitchen and a new dining area. It has also improved access to the garden. The blend of old with con-

temporary does actually seem to work well together. The guest beer changes weekly and tends to be from one of the larger brewers.

WESTCOTT (B2)

A Victorian village with a triangular village green, on which stands a dovecote, thatched bus shelter and a stone-walled pound. Thomas Malthus, famous for his work "Principle of Population" on population control and expansion, was born here.

Cricketers

7 Guildford Road, RH4 3NW
OS: 139485 (A25)
☎ (01306) 883520
Greene King IPA, Abbot Ale
Guest Beer
Traditional locals' pub whose kitchen serves Thai food in the evenings, for eating in or taking away, from Wednesday till Sunday. Traditional roasts are served on Sunday lunchtimes. Part of the bar is laid for diners. The pub is open all day Saturdays and Sundays. Darts played. The guest beer tends to be from a large regional brewery.

● Crown Inn

Guildford Road, RH4 3QG
OS: 145486 (A25)
☎ (01306) 885414
11-3, 5-11 (11-11 Saturday, 12-10:30 Sunday)
Adnams Bitter, Broadside
Brains Rev James
Wychwood Hobgoblin
Guest Beer (summer)
Worthington White Shield in bottle
Addlestones Cloudy Cider
Traditional 19th century village pub with pool, darts and pinball and an open fire to one side, a front bar area with a wood burning stove and a section which is

mainly used for eating or watching the television. Walkers and dogs are welcome and you may occasionally find a spit roast pig on a summer Sunday or a barbecue when the rugby is on. The guest beer is likely to be from an independent brewery and the other beers may change occasionally. Food is served 12-2:30 and 5:30-9:30 but snacks may be available outside these hours. Live music some Wednesdays.

● Prince Of Wales

Guildford Road, RH4 3QE
OS: 165485 (A25)
☎ (01306) 889699
11-11 (12-10:30 Sunday)
Fuller's Chiswick Bitter, Discovery, London Pride, ESB
The landlord is proud of his beer in this main road village pub. A small entrance hall, which does have a table and chairs, leads to the main L-shaped wooden floored bar. This has loads of natural light, and has a dining area to the side. A wide variety of food is served, and an added attraction is take-away meals. This includes fish and chips, plus home-made pizzas, the latter only being sold from Tuesday to Saturday. Note the map on the wall showing the pubs of Sur-

rey in 1958. To the rear of the pub is a separate well used room containing a couple of pool tables and darts. This room is used for discos on Friday nights. Outside is a large and pleasant garden, which is below the level of the road.

◁▶ 🐴 🚗 ☸

WESTHUMBLE (B2)

The village is to be found off the A24 between Box Hill and Ranmore Common. The National Trust owns the ruins of a 12th century chapel. Fanny Burney lived in Westhumble between 1797 and 1801. Her house was named "Camilla" after her novel of the same name. Boxhill & Westhumble Station is now a listed building. This elaborate construction was built in 1867 for visitors for Polesden Lacey and Box Hill. This station was originally called Boxhill & Burford Bridge. The station signs now just call it Boxhill, although the fuller name appears on timetables and in station announcements.

Burford Bridge

Old London Road, RH5 6BX
OS: 172519
www.burfordbridgehotel.com
☎ (01306) 884561
No real ale
The bar in this historic hotel is open all day, but very sadly does not sell real ale. The hotel is in a beautiful setting at the foot of Box Hill. The upper area has a fire and is non-smoking. The building dates back in parts to the 16th century, and was originally founded as the Fox & Hounds in 1254. The current hotel dates in the main from 1801. Among the illustrious people who have visited it are Queen Victoria, Jane Austen, Wordsworth, John Keats, Robert Louis Stevenson and Lord Nelson. In fact it was here that Lord Nelson spent secret hours with his love Emma Hamilton before going to defeat Napoleon's fleet at the Battle of Trafalgar. The 16th century Tithe Barn is fitted out with beams from the ships of the Spanish Armada. Keats wrote part of Endymion while staying here.

● Stepping Stones

Westhumble Street, RH5 6BS
OS: 170517
☎ (01306) 889932
11-3, 5-11 (12-10:30 Sunday)
Fuller's London Pride
Greene King Abbot Ale, Old Speckled Hen
Ringwood Best Bitter
L shaped pub with a large restaurant area at the side. The area for drinkers, in front of the bar, is split into two, one carpeted and with comfy chairs and the other with bare boards. It is near both the Pilgrim's Way and the North Downs Way and walkers are welcome, as long as they leave their boots in the porch outside the entrance. It is also near the stepping stones over the River Mole at the bottom of Box Hill, hence the name. Denbies, England's largest vineyard, is less than a mile away and Polesden Lacey is a couple of miles past the station The recently refurbished pub now has a room at the back, which can be used as a function room or overflow for the pub, and is where the disabled toilets are. Good food plays an important part at the pub and this is available each session except Sunday evening.

◁▶ 🚗 ☸ 🚆 (Boxhill) 🚲

WHYTELEAFE (C1)

On the busy main A22. The suburban sprawl rises on either side and merges into Croydon, Caterham, and Warlingham.

● **Whyteleafe Tavern**
208 Godstone Road, CR3 0EE
OS: 339585 (A22)
☎ (01883) 626270
12-11 (12-10:30 Sunday)
Fuller's London Pride
Shepherd Neame Spitfire
This corner pub has one single horseshoe-shaped bar and is close to both Upper Warlingham and Whyteleafe stations. Fairly unremarkable in design, it is however, a focal point for the local community and caters for all tastes. Pool is played and there is a quiz on Tuesday night in this former Charrington house. A guest beer may be available in summer. No food is available Sunday.

WOODMANSTERNE (C1)

Village on Greater London boundary, which merges with Banstead. Constable often stayed with the old Surrey family of the Lamberts, some of whom were buried here 600 years ago. The Earl of Derby lived here in the 18th century in a mansion called The Oaks, which is the name of the fillies' classic run at nearby Epsom racecourse. It was demolished in 1960.

Woodman
Woodmansterne Street, SM7 3NL
OS: 276599 (B278)
☎ (01737) 371841
Fuller's London Pride
Shepherd Neame Spitfire
Worthington's Bitter
Guest Beer
An attractive solid-looking brick, flint and tile building with some late gothic flourishes in the form of a circular turret room with conical roof and weather vane. Amazingly there is still a proper public bar (with separate entrance) where darts is played, as well as a comfortable saloon, which also caters for diners throughout the day and evening. The village only got its pub in the early 1900s when it was built as an annexe to the local manor house. By utilising all its handpumps in both bars, the pub has hosted mini beer festivals during the summer months. Be warned: it is a long uphill walk from Woodmansterne station! Open all day.

WORCESTER PARK (B1)

The main part of the town is in Greater London. Henry VIII demolished the original village and built Nonsuch Palace in 1538, along with two deer parks. In 1606 the 4th Earl of Worcester was appointed as "Keeper of the Great Park" and this gave the area its name. Modern day Worcester Park is built on what was the Great Park, with the smaller Little Park becoming Nonsuch Park, which still survives today.

● **Gamecock**
Vale Road, KT4 7ED
OS: 219649
☎ (020) 8337 9442
11-11 (12-10:30 Sunday)
Courage Best Bitter
Wells Bombardier
Guest Beer
Suburban pub comprising three separate rooms, each with a bar. It is well used by locals of all ages with some good old fashioned conversation to be found in the main front bar. The right front bar is

more for TV sports, pool, darts, music and the younger set, whilst families tend to use the back room. The guest beer is from the Spirit list and changes weekly.

◁▶

Hogsmill Tavern

Worcester Park Road, KT4 7QE
OS: 212657 (B284)
☎ (020) 8337 5221
Greene King Old Speckled Hen
Wadworth 6X
Built in 1955, this is a Beefeater Inn where the bar is mainly frequented by youngsters, whilst the more mature, including families, makes use of the restaurant. There is a large garden at front and a children's play area. Open all day, with food available each lunchtime and evening, Monday to Saturday, and all day Sunday.

WOTTON (A2)

John Evelyn, the diarist, was born at Wotton House in 1620. He devoted much effort to planting gardens and woods and introduced the Scots pine and the larch to Surrey. He also encouraged hedge planting, and in particular yew hedges and topiary. St John the Evangelist church is Grade I listed, and is set down a small hill, and contains many references to the Evelyn family.

● Wotton Hatch

Guildford Road, RH5 6QQ
OS: 125475 (A25)
☎ (01306) 732931
12-11 (12-10:30 Sunday; opens at 11:30 Monday to Saturday in summer)
Bass
Fuller's London Pride
Guest Beer
This is a large roadside pub, set on the busy A25 Guildford to Dorking main road, and has a 300 year history. There are large well-appointed bar areas, including a conservatory providing a number of comfortable eating and drinking areas, all served from a single serving point. Outside, ample lawns form an excellent beer garden, with views over the North Downs. Formerly a Surrey Trust Company house, it later belonged to Fullers, who sold it to Bass in the 1990s.

◁▶

NOTES

East Pub

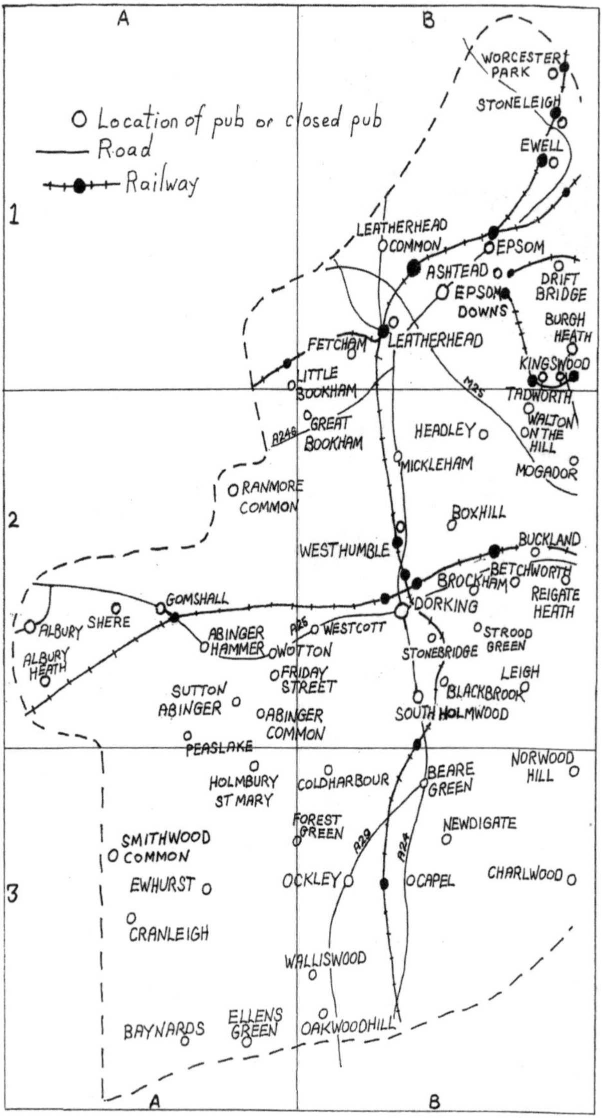
A
B
WORCESTER PARK
STONELEIGH
O Location of pub or closed pub
Road
Railway
EWELL
1
LEATHERHEAD COMMON
EPSOM
ASHTEAD
DRIFT BRIDGE
EPSOM DOWNS
BURGH HEATH
FETCHAM
LEATHERHEAD
KINGSWOOD
LITTLE BOOKHAM
M25
TADWORTH
GREAT BOOKHAM
A246
HEADLEY
WALTON ON THE HILL
MICKLEHAM
MOGADOR
RANMORE COMMON
BOXHILL
2
WESTHUMBLE
BUCKLAND
BETCHWORTH
BROCKHAM
REIGATE HEATH
GOMSHALL
DORKING
ALBURY
SHERE
ABINGER HAMMER
A25
WESTCOTT
STROOD GREEN
ALBURY HEATH
WOTTON
STONEBRIDGE
FRIDAY STREET
LEIGH
SUTTON ABINGER
BLACKBROOK
ABINGER COMMON
SOUTH HOLMWOOD
PEASLAKE
NORWOOD HILL
HOLMBURY ST MARY
COLDHARBOUR
BEARE GREEN
FOREST GREEN
NEWDIGATE
SMITHWOOD COMMON
A29
A24
3
EWHURST
OCKLEY
CAPEL
CHARLWOOD
CRANLEIGH
WALLISWOOD
BAYNARDS
ELLENS GREEN
OAKWOODHILL
A
B